PRAISE FOR CHRIS WALLACE'S *COUNTDOWN* SERIES

Countdown 1945: The Extraordinary Story of the Atomic Bomb and the 116 Days That Changed the World

"[A] superb, masterly book . . . *Countdown 1945* is filled with fascinating details. . . . On one hand, the book reads like a riveting novel as Wallace reveals the machinations and internal debates among the scientific community to devise a workable atomic bomb as quickly as possible. . . . But *Countdown 1945* is also a profound story of decision making at the highest levels—and of pathos."

—Jay Winik, *The New York Times Book Review*

"A compelling and highly readable account of one of the most fateful decisions in American history. Like John Hersey in his book *Hiroshima*, Wallace and Weiss humanize events too often reduced to technical or diplomatic arcana by telling their story through the lives of individuals. . . . The book moves along at a rapid clip, with colorful anecdotes enlivening the narrative."

—Gregg Herken, *The Washington Post*

"Vivid and engaging . . . Wallace has made a taut nonfiction thriller out of the dramatic days between Harry S. Truman's succession to the presidency, following Franklin D. Roosevelt's death on April 12, 1945, and the dropping of the first atomic bombs on Hiroshima and Nagasaki less than four months later. . . . This is a deeply absorbing reading experience about the fateful final months of a conflict that deserves to be known in detail to all Americans. It is what a popular history book should be: propulsively paced; well researched in primary sources; and written with sympathetic imagination, bringing people to life in their important moments. . . . The book is deservedly the nonfiction blockbuster of the season."

—James D. Hornfischer, *The Wall Street Journal*

"Propulsive, heart stopping, and impossible to put down . . . The tension in *Countdown 1945* is palpable. . . . Wallace and Weiss bring those 116 days of history to life in vivid color, crafting a story as unique as it is horrifying. Their writing is nothing short of phenomenal, a historical tapestry that reads like a carefully curated combination of Stephen King and Stephen Ambrose."

—**Steve Leonard, *Modern War Institute at West Point***

"Brisk, naturally propulsive . . . But *Countdown 1945* also reflects the rigor and fealty to facts that have distinguished Wallace."

—*Time*

"Everyone knows the outcome, yet Wallace manages to make this carefully researched account of the months before Hiroshima read like a tense thriller."

—**Bethanne Patrick, *The Washington Post***

"Gripping . . . *Countdown 1945* is such a good read, crammed with information, fleshed out with vivid anecdotes, and told in a narrative that never flags."

—*The Washington Times*

"There is no finer journalist in America today than Chris Wallace and no more dramatic story in American history than Truman's decision to drop the atomic bomb. *Countdown 1945* moves at a breakneck pace and even though you know the ending, you can't put it down. This is the most exciting book I've read all year."

—**Admiral William H. McRaven (U.S. Navy Retired), #1 *New York Times* bestselling author of *Make Your Bed* and *Sea Stories***

"As a reporter and a news anchor, Chris has been at the center of the biggest news stories of the last four decades. He's given perspective and insight when we've needed it most. Now, his same attention to detail fills the pages of *Countdown 1945*, the story of arguably the most consequential event in the U.S. since the Civil War. It's a stunning piece of work."

—**George Clooney**

"*Countdown 1945* goes beyond our history lessons. It tells moving, personal stories of Americans who played pivotal roles in one of our most important moments as a nation. From scientists at the top of their field, to heroic members of our military, to everyday Americans, it's an incredible story of how our country came together with a determined spirit to end a war and save countless lives."

—**Ambassador Nikki Haley,** *New York Times* **bestselling author of** *With All Due Respect: Defending America with Grit and Grace*

"*Countdown 1945* is a real-life thriller about one of the most important events of the twentieth century. Veteran journalist Chris Wallace takes readers behind the scenes and brings to life the compelling story of the 116 days leading up to Hiroshima. Written like a spy novel, this is a must-read history that will educate and keep you turning the pages. Not to be missed!"

—**Daniel Silva, #1** *New York Times* **bestselling author of** *The New Girl*

"Vivid, fast-paced, and wide-ranging, *Countdown 1945* is a fine telling of one of the twentieth century's most remarkable tales—how the United States designed, built, delivered, and detonated the first two atomic bombs over Japan."

—**Rick Atkinson, #1** *New York Times* **bestselling author of** *An Army at Dawn* **and** *The British Are Coming*

ALSO BY CHRIS WALLACE

Countdown 1945:
The Extraordinary Story of the Atomic Bomb and
the 116 Days That Changed the World

COUNTDOWN
BIN LADEN

THE UNTOLD STORY OF THE 247-DAY HUNT TO BRING THE MASTERMIND OF 9/11 TO JUSTICE

CHRIS WALLACE

WITH MITCH WEISS

AVID READER PRESS

NEW YORK   LONDON   TORONTO   SYDNEY   NEW DELHI

Avid Reader Press
An Imprint of Simon & Schuster, Inc.
1230 Avenue of the Americas
New York, NY 10020

First Avid Reader Press trade paperback edition May 2022

AVID READER PRESS and colophon are trademarks of Simon & Schuster, Inc.

For information about special discounts for bulk purchases,
please contact Simon & Schuster Special Sales at 1-866-506-1949
or business@simonandschuster.com.

The Simon & Schuster Speakers Bureau can bring authors to your live event. For
more information or to book an event contact the Simon & Schuster Speakers
Bureau at 1-866-248-3049 or visit our website at www.simonspeakers.com.

Interior design by Ruth Lee-Mui

Manufactured in the United States of America

1   3   5   7   9   10   8   6   4   2

Library of Congress Cataloging-in-Publication Data has been applied for.

ISBN 978-1-9821-7652-5
ISBN 978-1-9821-7653-2 (pbk)
ISBN 978-1-9821-7654-9 (ebook)

To William, Caroline, James, Sabine, Livi,
Jack, Teddy, and grandchildren still to come,
in the hope it will encourage you to read this book someday.

COUNTDOWN:
247 DAYS

August 27, 2010
Langley, Virginia

Leon Panetta was speechless. It was almost too perfect. A top Central Intelligence Agency operations officer had just told him about a "fortress," a three-story house at the end of a dead-end street in an upscale neighborhood in Abbottabad, Pakistan. Panetta fought back a wave of hope and excitement. He didn't want to share his optimism with anyone else in the room. Not a smile. Not a high five. Not yet.

As director of the CIA, one of the key parts of Panetta's job was protecting the United States from foreign terrorist attacks. That meant overseeing teams of operators, analysts, and agents working all over the world, many of them in dangerous hot spots in the Middle East, South Asia, and Africa. Every piece of information that crossed Panetta's desk had to be carefully vetted before he passed it on to his boss, President Barack Obama. But it was hard not to be enthusiastic about this tip. After all, this house might be the hideout for the world's most dangerous terrorist, a man who had all but dropped off the face of the earth: Osama bin Laden.

Panetta took a few deep breaths. As he worked to keep his emotions in check, he realized that so much had changed so quickly. Just a half hour earlier, he had been wrapping up a routine meeting. Every Monday, Wednesday, and Friday, some thirty intelligence analysts, experts, and case officers from the Counterterrorism Center would jam into a conference room down the hall from Panetta's office at CIA headquarters in Langley, Virginia.

Like clockwork, the sessions would start at 4:30 p.m. and last more than ninety minutes. During the meetings, the team would update Panetta about the latest issues in the Middle East, problems that could ultimately threaten the security of the United States and its allies. They'd routinely jump from topic to topic—and today's session had been no different. They discussed new developments in the war-torn nations of Iraq and Afghanistan. They talked about the dangerous role the notorious terrorist group Al Qaeda was still playing in both countries.

Maybe it was because it was late on a Friday afternoon in the waning days of summer, but this session seemed to drag on and on. So, when the meeting was over, the analysts, operators, and experts jumped up from their chairs and began filing out of the conference room. But as they grabbed their briefcases and papers, three men approached Panetta, Michael Morell, the CIA's deputy director, and Jeremy Bash, the spy agency's chief of staff.

"We need to see you alone," one of the men, Mike, the director of the Counterterrorism Center, said to them. That was a first.

Panetta could sense something was up from Mike's language and tone. If someone wanted to talk to Panetta or a deputy after a meeting, they'd casually ask, "Can we go small?" But Mike and two well-respected colleagues, Gary, the head of the Center's Pakistan-Afghanistan Department (PAD), and Sam, the agency's leading expert on Al Qaeda, were not feeling casual. Panetta could tell from the look on their faces. If *they* requested a private meeting, it had to be important.

"Why don't we go back to my office," Panetta said.

The group followed him out of the conference room and into the hallway. After a few steps, they reached one of the doors leading to the director's office. Panetta opened it, revealing a larger room with dark brown wood paneling and a wide window that stretched the length of the back wall, letting in natural light. Outside was a view of the Virginia woods below.

Panetta's desk was pushed up against a wall on one side of the room. Above it was a tattered American flag in a frame, hung there by his predecessor. The flag came from the World Trade Center. For Panetta, it served as a daily reminder of 9/11, its victims, and the hunt for bin Laden. On the opposite side of the room was a conference table, chairs, and a television mounted on the wall above. That was usually where Panetta held meetings with dignitaries and foreign guests. But this afternoon, it was where Panetta would hold the impromptu session with his colleagues.

Panetta sat at the head of the conference table, while Morell grabbed his usual chair at the other end. When everyone was seated, the three men wasted no time. They disclosed details about a courier they believed had close ties to Al Qaeda.

"We've found this guy named Abu Ahmed al-Kuwaiti," Mike said.

Panetta shrugged. He'd never heard of him. He looked over at Morell and Bash and could tell they hadn't either. So Mike, Gary, a case officer, and Sam, an analyst, took turns recounting the history of al-Kuwaiti—the new lead that had taken almost a decade to develop.

The trail went back to shortly after September 11, 2001—the day nineteen men hijacked four planes and carried out the worst terrorist attack in U.S. history. The terrorists flew two of the planes into the Twin Towers of the World Trade Center in New York City. A third plane hit the Pentagon just outside of Washington, D.C. A fourth crashed in a field in Shanksville, Pennsylvania. All told, almost 3,000 people were killed, including 2,606 when the Twin Towers collapsed.

The United States quickly traced the attacks to Al Qaeda, a terrorist group founded by Osama bin Laden, a sullen, bearded, rifle-toting Islamic revolutionary who had set up training camps in Afghanistan, a nation controlled by religious extremists known as the Taliban.

Hours after the towers collapsed, President George W. Bush promised

Osama bin Laden still photo from a propaganda video.

the nation in a televised address that America would take the fight to Al Qaeda. Less than a month later, a U.S.-led coalition launched Operation Enduring Freedom, a military offensive aimed at killing bin Laden, his terrorist followers, and dismantling the Taliban government, which had been supporting and protecting Al Qaeda for years.

With coalition forces on the ground, bin Laden and his allies fled to Tora Bora, a remote mountainous area in eastern Afghanistan near the Pakistan border. U.S. Special Forces thought he was trapped in a cave. After a five-day battle, they took Tora Bora in December 2001. But when the smoke cleared, bin Laden was gone. He had disappeared.

For nine years, Al Qaeda's leader remained an elusive figure, always just beyond the grasp of his pursuers. Was he in eastern Afghanistan? Maybe Pakistan, plotting new attacks? Or in Saudi Arabia, where he was born? No one knew for sure.

But then they got a lead from an unlikely source, Gary said.

Since the invasion of Afghanistan, the U.S. had been interrogating Al Qaeda prisoners at both the U.S. Navy prison at Guantánamo Bay, Cuba, and CIA secret prisons. Sometimes they'd use interrogation techniques that many critics called torture, such as waterboarding, to get information. Interrogators would often ask detainees about Al Qaeda members who served as couriers.

Gary said analysts believed bin Laden was too smart to let Al Qaeda senior commanders know where his hideout was. So if he wanted to get his messages out, somebody had to carry them—someone whom bin Laden would trust with his life.

During interrogations, one name kept coming up: Abu Ahmed al-Kuwaiti. Some detainees claimed he was an important courier with close ties to bin Laden. But others downplayed al-Kuwaiti's significance.

With Khalid Sheikh Mohammed, the architect of the 9/11 attacks, in-terrogators waterboarded him 183 times, making sure he was in a "compli-ant state," before asking him about al-Kuwaiti. He said, yes, he knew him, but denied al-Kuwaiti was a courier. And he said al-Kuwaiti had left Al Qaeda after 9/11.

But KSM didn't know the prison was bugged. So when he returned to his cell, interrogators heard him issue a warning to the other prison-ers: Don't mention "the courier." Another prominent Al Qaeda member said he didn't know al-Kuwaiti, then volunteered the name of a courier he said was working for bin Laden. Interrogators later concluded the name he had given them was fictitious. Gary said the misinformation only re-inforced their belief that al-Kuwaiti was important to the terrorist group. Otherwise, why would they be protecting him?

So, in Gary's view, if they could locate the man known as al-Kuwaiti, there was a chance he would lead them to bin Laden.

Gary looked at Panetta, Morell, and Bash. He could tell they were fol-lowing every word. He explained that after years of painstaking detective work, the CIA in 2007 discovered al-Kuwaiti's real name: Ibrahim Saeed Ahmed. He was a Pakistani man who was born in Kuwait and took on a nom de guerre when he joined Al Qaeda. Now, with al-Kuwaiti's real fam-ily name, CIA operatives were able to track down people close to him in Pakistan and beyond and intercept their telephone calls and emails. They looked for any bit of information, any clue that could lead them to al-Kuwaiti.

But Gary said every lead turned out to be a dead end—until June of 2010, just two months ago. That's when they intercepted a telephone conversation between al-Kuwaiti and another suspected terrorist under U.S. surveillance. From that call, the CIA was able to get al-Kuwaiti's mobile phone number, and trace the call to Peshawar, a major city in western Pakistan.

While they had his number and monitored his calls, they still didn't know where al-Kuwaiti lived. He was wily. He practiced strict operational security. After making a call from Peshawar, he'd turn off his cell phone and remove the battery so he couldn't be tracked.

They didn't think he lived in Peshawar. But if they could find him there, in a city of two million people, they could come up with a way to track him back to his home. And that's what happened.

In August, they followed his phone signal and spotted al-Kuwaiti driving a white Suzuki Jimny, a mini sport utility vehicle with a picture of a rhinoceros on the spare-tire cover. But instead of following directly behind him, they placed people at key positions along the roads leading out of Peshawar. They watched as he passed. And if he didn't drive by, they knew he had turned off and taken other roads. The next time, they'd place agents at locations along those side streets. It was a slow and tedious process, but it worked.

They eventually tracked him ninety-five miles east to Abbottabad, the home of a military academy known as Pakistan's West Point. With its lush scenery and proximity to the Himalayas, the city was a popular summer resort.

Afraid that al-Kuwaiti would see them, the agents didn't tail him to his house. But they continued to monitor his calls, and they soon discovered that he was secretive about every aspect of his life.

During one call between al-Kuwaiti and an old friend, another piece of the puzzle fell into place. The friend asked al-Kuwaiti a series of innocuous questions: Where did he live now? What's going on with his life? Al-Kuwaiti was vague. When his friend asked what he was doing for work, he reluctantly responded: "I'm with the same ones as before."

There was a pause, as if his friend already knew what al-Kuwaiti's words meant. He was still working for Al Qaeda.

"May Allah be with you," the friend responded.

At that point, Gary said their surveillance picked up pace. A few days later, agents tracked al-Kuwaiti to a dead-end street in an upscale neighborhood in Abbottabad. And then, there it was at the end of the street— a three-story house with twelve-foot-high concrete walls in the front, eighteen-foot-high walls in the back. The third-floor balcony was enclosed inside a seven-foot wall. The perimeter bristled with barbed wire. It was more than a house, Gary said. "It's a fortress."

Panetta's ears pricked up. After all these years, could this *really* be bin Laden's hideout? Was he really living in suburbia? The CIA director was stunned.

Panetta was a larger than life figure with big Italian emotions and gestures. When he thought something was funny, his laugh came straight from his gut. He liked to greet friends with big hugs. More important in the world of Washington, Panetta was a highly effective and shrewd bureaucrat who got things done. He was the ultimate D.C. insider, with friends on both sides of the aisle. Over the years, Panetta had been an influential congressman, President Bill Clinton's chief of staff, and now President Obama's CIA director. He was never tainted by scandal. And the sometimes fiery director was never at a loss for words, either—especially four-letter ones. But now he didn't know what to say. This was totally unexpected.

While Panetta thought about the possibilities, Gary reached into a folder and pulled out satellite images of the compound. He handed copies to Panetta and the others. As they stared at the pictures, the officers told them what else they knew.

CIA satellite image of compound, Abbottabad, Pakistan.

Al-Kuwaiti lived in the compound, which was much larger than any of the surrounding homes. It was so large, secluded, and secure, they believed al-Kuwaiti was sheltering a high-value target—but they didn't know for sure. There was no way to see inside the house from the ground or from above. The windows were made of an opaque material.

Of all the things in the surveillance photos, Panetta's eyes kept coming back to the balcony on the third floor, which was shielded by a privacy wall. The whole purpose of a balcony is to stand outside and soak in the view. That was especially true in Abbottabad, which was called the City of Pines because of all the trees.

Who puts a privacy wall around a balcony? Panetta asked. But he already knew the answer. So did Morell, his chief deputy, who purposely sat at the other end of the conference table from Panetta at most meetings so he could inconspicuously watch the staff's reaction to the director's comments. By now, the information made the hair on the back of Morell's neck stand up. No one stated the obvious—the name was never mentioned. But they were all thinking the same thing: The wall was erected to protect someone very important. Maybe, someone like bin Laden.

Panetta didn't want to get too far ahead of himself. Yes, it was a compound, but so what? It didn't prove bin Laden lived there. It could be another high-value terrorist or a crime lord. Who knows? They needed proof. This compound was in Pakistan, a sovereign nation. They couldn't just knock on the door. No, they had to be sure before they could do anything.

And there was something else. Just two months earlier, Panetta had been pressed on ABC News about bin Laden. What was the United States doing to find him? Panetta said that the last time the CIA had "precise information" on bin Laden was "the early 2000s."

"He is, as is obvious, in very deep hiding. He's in the tribal areas of Pakistan. The terrain is probably the most difficult in the world," Panetta said. "If we keep that pressure on, we think ultimately we can flush him out."

If bin Laden was in the Abbottabad fortress, the CIA had been wrong all along, he thought. He wasn't going to focus on the negative. They had this new lead, the best in a long time. And as much as he wanted to alert President Obama, he knew he couldn't tell him yet. They had to dig deeper, look closer.

"We need to know more—a lot more," Panetta said. "It requires deeper investigation. I want every possible operational avenue explored to get inside the compound."

But Panetta knew that would be easier said than done.

COUNTDOWN:

236 DAYS

September 7, 2010

Virginia Beach, Virginia

Robert O'Neill checked off the last item on his list. He had finished with his power of attorney, updating his will and life insurance. There were a few weeks to go before his deployment to Afghanistan, but he knew it was never too early to take care of business.

O'Neill was a details guy. He was that way about everything in his life. If he did things the right way and worked hard, he could handle any situation.

So far, it had worked. He was thirty-three years old, a fifteen-year member of the U.S. Navy's Sea, Air and Land Forces, an old man in the elite unit. Sure, he wasn't as young as the fresh-faced "Meats" who'd just completed intense SEAL training, but that didn't matter. He still kept up. Besides, he didn't look his age. He was a badass.

O'Neill was six feet tall, two hundred pounds, with the barrel chest and thick arms and legs characteristic of most SEALs, but his blue eyes and reddish-blond hair gave him a baby-faced charm. He was outgoing, funny, charismatic, a natural-born leader.

He was going to need it all on his next deployment. He was headed to Afghanistan again, this time as a team leader. He'd probably spend most of his time at a base in Jalalabad, monitoring missions instead of hunting bad guys in the middle of the night. After years of life-threatening operations, maybe that wasn't such a bad thing. But O'Neill knew he'd miss the action.

He leaned back in his chair and sighed. It was late. His wife and little girls were asleep in the next room. He had reached a point in his life where saying goodbye to them had become routine. Hell, this was his seventh deployment in five years. When he enlisted back in 1995, he had never heard of bin Laden, or Al Qaeda. Afghanistan? Wasn't that where Sylvester Stallone fought the bad guys in *Rambo III*?

O'Neill considered himself a simple kid from Butte, Montana, a mining town in the shadow of the Rocky Mountains. His parents divorced when Rob was six. The four children lived with their mom and enjoyed an idyllic childhood, playing outdoors with neighborhood friends. They acted out scenes from 1980s action movies, ambushing one another with toy guns, leaping off rooftops like ninja warriors chasing the bad guys.

His father, Tom, lived nearby and spent as much time as he could with his children. The elementary school had an outside basketball hoop, and Rob spent hours there, shooting jump shots and free throws. His father encouraged his interest in the game. During basketball season, Tom picked up his son after school and took him to a sports club in downtown Butte, where he taught him to dribble, shoot, and pass. They did layup drills and played pickup games with other members. They always ended their on-court session with a free-throw contest.

No one could leave the gym until they hit a certain number of foul shots in a row. First it was 20 in a row. That was easy. Then they'd work their way up, until Rob set his record of 105 free throws in a row. After practice, father and son went out for steaks. Young Rob eventually won a spot on his high school basketball team.

Like many Montana dads, Tom O'Neill also took his boy hunting for deer and elk in the steep mountains surrounding Butte. On a hunting trip in 1994, just after Rob's eighteenth birthday, his father introduced him to Jim, a Navy SEAL home on leave.

Rob was impressed by Jim's quiet confidence. A friend that week had dropped Jim off in the mountains, and he'd spent three days out there, tracking deer and elk for the upcoming hunting season. He'd found a great spot, a "honey hole," he said. Did Rob want to see the lookout?

The next morning, they drove in the pre-dawn dark up into the mountains and parked in a secluded area well off the road. "We'll have to walk in from here," Jim said. "It's about a mile, uphill. You up for that?" Rob didn't hesitate.

It was a sheer climb through heavy brush. Rob had to push hard to keep up. His lungs burned, but he wasn't going to stop.

When they reached the peak, they spotted about forty elk. They didn't shoot any. Rob tried not to wheeze.

"That was a helluva climb," Jim said. "You ought to think about joining the SEALs, O'Neill."

Rob smiled, flattered. But he wasn't ready to join the military. Not yet.

When Rob graduated high school, he enrolled at Montana Technological University. After a couple of semesters, he realized he wanted something more. He took Jim's advice and enlisted in the U.S. Navy. He wanted to become a SEAL. But before he could even qualify for a tryout with the Navy's special operators, he had to learn something. How to swim. Up until that point in his life, there had been no need to. He'd spent most of his time on land. It wasn't like he lived by an ocean or a big lake.

He signed a deferred enrollment, which gave him six months to get into top physical shape before he reported to boot camp. Every morning, he'd swim laps at the community college pool. He struggled until he ran into a high school friend who'd won a swimming scholarship to the University of Notre Dame. The friend took O'Neill under his wing and showed him basic swimming techniques.

O'Neill quickly got into a routine. He'd swim, then strap on his joggers and run rings around Butte. At home, he practiced on a pull-up bar in a doorway. He'd crank up Guns N' Roses' *Use Your Illusion* to motivate himself, and he'd pull himself up, over and over. He felt himself getting stronger. His dad was proud of him, and his mother supported his decision.

The entire family gathered at Butte's Bert Mooney Airport on a cold January night in 1996 to see him off on his boot-camp adventure. But O'Neill wondered if he could survive the SEAL training. He was a bundle of nerves by the time he arrived at Recruit Training Command Great Lakes in Chicago.

He knew all the steps he'd have to take to make it into and then graduate from the Basic Underwater Demolition/SEAL training, or BUD/S. First, O'Neill had to pass a punishing physical screening just to qualify. He was one of only a handful of recruits in his class who aced the screening. Then, O'Neill moved on to the twenty-six-week SEAL tryout. Nothing could have prepared him for the physical and mental hell that followed. The weeks passed in a blur of running, swimming, calisthenics, obstacle courses, classroom training, and high-decibel harangues from the instructors anytime he missed a beat.

There were times when he was so beaten down and tired that he felt like giving up. But something inside told him to go on, that quitting was out of the question. Not even Hell Week—a punishing 120 hours of nonstop chaos, when instructors pushed the recruits to the brink, twenty hours a day, no sleep. Instructors barked orders: push-ups in the sand; run; crawl through the dunes on your belly; jump headlong, fully clothed, into the surf. It went on and on and on. O'Neill was delirious, cold, wet, exhausted, always hurting.

But again, he made it. At the end of 1996, O'Neill graduated BUD/S as a special warfare operator. He joined SEAL Team 2 in Virginia Beach. He passed his final exams, pinned his gold Trident insignia on his lapel, and was deployed to Kosovo.

SEALs hadn't seen any real action since the invasion of Panama in 1989. But that would change soon. O'Neill's team was stationed in Germany. Early one afternoon, he was sitting in a GI bar, the television was tuned to CNN. There he watched as a plane crashed into one of the World Trade Center towers in New York. The room fell silent, stunned as another

Rob O'Neill.

plane hit the other tower. "Osama bin Laden," someone said. "This is Al Qaeda. We're under attack."

O'Neill felt his life shift in a moment—terrorism on American soil. He was itching to get into the fight. He prayed for the chance to find and bring bin Laden to justice. It would be years before he joined the battle. But he took steps along the way to ensure that when he did, he'd be in the thick of the action.

After Germany, O'Neill was deployed to the Mediterranean. No action there, but he applied for the United States Naval Special Warfare Development Group (DEVGRU)—better known as SEAL Team 6. They were the best of the best, the guys who went on the toughest and most dangerous missions.

When O'Neill returned to Virginia in 2004, he was invited to try out for the Green Team, the nine-month selection and training course that was the pipeline for SEAL Team 6. He knew if he could make it through the training, he'd be drafted by one of the team's six squadrons.

All the candidates were seasoned SEALs. The instructors knew they could handle the physical aspect. So part of the training focused on whether they were "psychologically fit"—able to function at high levels under the harshest conditions. They wanted to know if you had what it takes to handle yourself, alone, trapped behind enemy lines, being chased by gun-toting insurgents. O'Neill also learned intricate and dangerous skydiving techniques, and trained for close-quarters battles, how to enter buildings occupied by armed and hostile enemies, often complicated by the presence of unarmed civilians. O'Neill thrived. After nine months, he made it. He was headed for Iraq, or maybe Afghanistan.

While O'Neill waited in Virginia for his orders, his younger sister Kelley called him up for counsel. She had just escaped a bad relationship and wanted to start over someplace far from Butte. O'Neill took a few days off, flew to Montana, fixed his sister's car, and thirty-six hours later they were back in Virginia Beach.

Kelley moved into her brother's spare room and found work at a local sports bar. When her brother stopped in at the pub to say hello, he spotted a cute blonde waitress named Amber. They were married a year and a half later, just before he was sent to Afghanistan in April 2005. It was O'Neill's first deployment to a war zone, but it wouldn't be his last. The United States was fighting wars in two nations, running short on troops, so as soon as O'Neill finished one tour of duty, he was assigned to another.

During multiple deployments, SEAL Team 6 was in the middle of the action. Over time, O'Neill went out on hundreds of missions, striking at the heart of suspected Al Qaeda terrorist positions. He learned to fight in the shadows, using his night-vision goggles to hunt the bad guys. O'Neill discovered that combat wasn't as bad as he'd feared. He was able to keep his shit together and make critical decisions in the middle of firefights.

And that served him well in early June 2008, when he led a small team on a dangerous mission in a remote mountainous area near the Pakistan border. Intelligence reports showed that insurgents were crossing into Afghanistan and hitting targets near Asadabad, a flyspeck on the valley floor.

The fighters were led by Zabit Jalil, a Taliban leader who had orchestrated a deadly ambush on a SEAL recon team in June 2005.

O'Neill carefully planned the mission: Helos would carry him, three other SEALs, and forty Afghan soldiers at night to an area at the base of a mountain. Then before dawn they'd hike to the top, where they'd have a clear view of the border. O'Neill hoped the insurgents would see them and attack. Once they did, his team would call in artillery and air support to take out the enemy.

But things didn't go as planned. As soon as the sun came up, O'Neill could see activity near a makeshift checkpoint on the Pakistani side of the border, about a half mile from his position. As the morning went on, he glimpsed truckloads of men approaching the checkpoint. O'Neill shook his head in disbelief. He realized they were in the middle of an Al Qaeda and Taliban supply line. Then, without warning, hundreds of hostile troops attacked. O'Neill quickly discovered the insurgents were right on top of his squad. How close? He didn't know the exact distance. But they were so close he could hear them shouting, *"Allahu Akbar"*—"God is great."

Enemy rounds kicked up the dirt in front of him. At one point, he thought he was going to die. But O'Neill stayed calm and called in air strikes. When the bombs dropped, the insurgents fled back to the checkpoint. O'Neill knew they probably thought they were safe since they were inside Pakistan. But O'Neill was relentless. He ordered U.S. bombers to hit the area. When they did, everything around the checkpoint was destroyed.

The firing stopped, then two helicopters swooped in and extracted O'Neill's team. He'd later find out that Jalil had been seriously wounded. It was the worst combat O'Neill had faced. He tried to push it out of his mind, but it was hard to forget.

When he returned to the United States, he was awarded the Silver Star. He flew his parents in for the ceremony. It was a proud moment. When he joined the navy, his mother worried about him being killed or wounded. He'd comfort her by saying, "Mom, stop worrying. I'm here to do something special."

But at the ceremony, when she heard details of the mission, she was more worried than ever about his safety. He was in more danger than she could imagine. She was frantic about her son. So, to calm her down, he promised to stay out of harm's way. "I'll never get another Silver Star again. That's the last time," he whispered.

But tonight, in his living room, O'Neill knew it might be difficult to stay out of trouble. Almost a decade after a U.S.-led coalition invaded the country, Afghanistan was still a mess. The Taliban was resurgent in the south, and Al Qaeda fighters continued to cross into Afghanistan from safe havens in Pakistan. It was unlikely O'Neill would be in the field during his deployment, but he couldn't rule it out, either. No, not when SEALs were still hunting high-value targets. O'Neill sighed. He wished he hadn't made that promise to his mother.

COUNTDOWN:

233 DAYS

September 10, 2010
Washington, D.C.

President Obama waited for Panetta to arrive in the Oval Office. The CIA director had requested a meeting, saying he had an important new development in the search for Osama bin Laden. Obama wondered what Panetta wanted to share. Even with the best intelligence in the world—the most sophisticated tracking equipment—Obama knew the trail for bin Laden had gone cold.

Seven members of the president's national security team, including deputy national security advisor Tom Donilon and White House counterterrorism chief John Brennan, waited with the president for the briefing in the newly redecorated Oval Office. Paperhangers had just finished putting up light beige striped wallpaper. Along with a pair of new caramel-colored couches with black and brown throw pillows, it gave the room more of an informal feel than it had had with Obama's predecessor.

With portraits of presidents Abraham Lincoln and George Washington on the walls, the Oval Office was a comfortable place for Obama to hold detailed meetings with top advisors, to read, or to think about important issues. And bin Laden was one subject that was never far from the president's mind—especially now, one day before the ninth anniversary of 9/11.

At a news conference earlier in the day in the East Room, Obama had wanted to focus on economic issues. Rows of newspaper and television reporters were ready as the president moved to a lectern with the presidential seal. Before taking questions, Obama said he wanted to "talk a little bit about our continuing efforts to dig ourselves out of this recession and to grow our economy."

But as soon as he finished, the first questions were about bin Laden. A journalist reminded Obama that he had promised to "run a smarter war on terror" than Bush. "But you still haven't captured him, and you don't seem to know where he is," the reporter said.

Obama tried to deflect the question, saying killing bin Laden "wouldn't solve all our problems." But he said it did remain "a high priority of this administration."

"We have the best minds, the best intelligence officers, the best special forces, who are thinking about this day and night. And they will continue to think about it day and night as long as I'm president," Obama said.

What the president didn't disclose was that he had been pushing Panetta for more than a year to find bin Laden. The public didn't know that bringing the terrorist leader to justice was one of Obama's top priorities. For many, that would seem to run counter to his public image. So many people believed that Obama was a dove. He wasn't. The misperception could be traced to a speech Obama made years earlier at an antiwar rally.

After the United States drove the Taliban and Al Qaeda from power in Afghanistan, President Bush began making the case for invading Iraq. But Obama, then a state senator from Illinois, decided to speak out. At an October 2002 protest in Chicago's Federal Plaza, he made his position clear. "I don't oppose all wars. . . . What I am opposed to is a dumb war." He said the Iraq conflict was being pushed by "political hacks" to distract the nation from major problems. The text of the speech was circulated on the internet, where he came to the attention of Democratic Party strategists.

But people who believed that Obama was some kind of reflexive antiwar activist weren't paying attention. During the 2008 presidential campaign, he had staked out a hard-line foreign policy position. In the

Democratic presidential primaries, Obama said he'd be willing to attack inside Pakistan—with or without approval from the Pakistani government—to kill bin Laden and other top Al Qaeda leaders. His main rival for the Democratic nomination, Hillary Rodham Clinton, labeled Obama naïve. After Obama landed his party's nomination, the Clinton attack line was picked up by Republican presidential candidate John McCain.

But Obama didn't back down. During a debate with McCain, Obama vowed once again to take out bin Laden if he ever appeared in America's crosshairs, no matter where he was—Afghanistan, Pakistan, or Timbuktu.

"If we have Osama bin Laden in our sights and the Pakistani government is unable or unwilling" to do it, the United States would, Obama promised. But he wasn't finished. No, Obama wanted to make it clear to the American people what he'd do: "We will kill bin Laden; we will crush Al Qaeda. That has to be our highest national security priority."

That statement seemed to be more aligned with a military hawk than a candidate who had been running as an ambassador of hope and optimism. So, when Obama was elected, some wondered if he'd really follow through with his campaign promise to get bin Laden. His top advisors didn't have to wait long for an answer.

After Obama's inauguration in January 2009, he quickly discovered that no one had a clue where bin Laden was hiding. Yes, the intelligence community was still pursuing every lead it could find. But to Obama, it seemed that capturing bin Laden was no longer their top priority. So the new president wanted to give his team a push. After a national security briefing on May 26, 2009, Obama asked four officials to meet with him: Panetta, Donilon, Rahm Emanuel (his White House chief of staff), and Michael Leiter (director of the U.S. National Counterterrorism Center). They followed the president up a flight of stairs from the Situation Room in the West Wing basement to the Oval Office.

Obama said he'd be quick. He'd been thinking about bin Laden, and now that he'd settled into the presidency, he wanted the intelligence community to reprioritize. It was time to root out the elusive terrorist.

"I want bin Laden to come to the front of the line. This has to be a top priority. I want regular reports on this. Starting in thirty days," Obama said.

Obama knew there was no way the United States—even with its overwhelming military force—could truly defeat Al Qaeda as long as bin Laden was alive. He remained the terror group's spiritual leader, a godlike figure. Just when everyone thought he must be dead, there he was in a new video, with a camouflage jacket over his flowing white robe, clutching his trusty AK-47 and spewing anti-American messages from behind a bushy salt-and-pepper beard. With every video he released, every time he thumbed his nose at America, he gained more followers.

To follow up, Obama sent a memo to Panetta, giving the CIA director thirty days to come up with a detailed plan to locate and target bin Laden. And Panetta started meeting with his bin Laden team at 4:30 every Tuesday afternoon, pressing for new leads. At the end of every national security meeting, Obama turned to him and asked, "Are we any closer?" But so far, Panetta never had anything new to report.

President Barack Obama in the Oval Office with White House Chief of Staff Bill Daley and Director for Counterterrorism for the National Security Council Audrey Tomason.

Now that would change. Panetta walked into the Oval Office with Morell, Mike, Gary, and Sam. They sat down on the couches and greeted the others in the room. The CIA director was prepared. He had spent the last few days reviewing every relevant intelligence report and satellite photo. He'd discussed the information with his key people until they all were dreaming about that fortress at night.

Panetta told the president and members of his national security team they had tracked someone "who used to be—and could still be—one of bin Laden's couriers" to a house in Abbottabad, Pakistan. "If that's the case, we're hopeful that he can lead us to bin Laden." Gary and Sam handed out satellite images of the compound to everyone in the room.

As Obama stared at the images, Gary and Sam walked the commander in chief through the history of the lead, much the same way they'd done a few weeks earlier in Panetta's office. In the days leading up to this meeting, Gary and Sam had worked a total of fifteen hours writing and rehearsing what they'd say, getting their language just right and highlighting the key points. They had delivered their briefing for Panetta, then gone back to their offices to edit their presentation and practice again. They had been told they had seven minutes to tell Obama what they'd found.

So, on script, they recounted the CIA's interest in couriers, how they believed early on that they might be one way to track down bin Laden. They described the compound and then went over some new intelligence they had discovered more recently. They explained that the courier, his brother, and their families lived in the fortress. The brothers were tall, fair-skinned, and bearded. They looked like everyone else in the neighborhood. No one knew what the brothers did for a living. And the families almost never left the compound. Not to attend the local religious school. Not to visit a doctor. There were no signs of internet access or telephone lines running to the compound.

The compound was segmented so it was difficult to move from one part of the property to another. It was a challenge even to get into the place. You had to open one gate to drive in, then get out of the car, close the gate behind you and open a second gate to drive into the main part of the compound. Even though the brothers had no apparent means of support, they'd managed to buy this million-dollar property. Surveillance showed one brother was always at the fortress. If one left, the other always stayed behind. The people inside didn't put their trash out for collection like everyone else in the neighborhood. Instead, they burned it on-site, in a wide yard where goats were pastured. Through telephone intercepts, the intelligence team discovered that the brothers' wives were lying to their extended families about where they lived.

Something was going on there. After laying out everything they knew, the CIA briefers said there was a possibility the brothers could be harboring bin Laden.

Panetta jumped in, "Mr. President, it's very preliminary. But we think this is the best lead we've had since Tora Bora," he said.

Silence. No one in the room wanted to show what they were really thinking. Tony Blinken, Vice President Joe Biden's national security advisor, was skeptical. Yes, it wouldn't have been brought to the president's attention if there wasn't something there. But they'd had so many false leads over the years, it was hard to take this too seriously. Donilon was impressed. Panetta and his team were "quite careful" about what they knew and what they didn't know. Maybe there was something to this.

Obama, as usual, showed no emotion. He was calm and collected, and clearly interested, but there were too many "maybes," he said. Couldn't the brothers be protecting a powerful criminal? Maybe a different high-ranking Al Qaeda figure?

Obama's poker face didn't bother Morell. He'd worked with the president long enough to know he didn't bark orders or blurt out his thoughts. He usually deliberated at length before making any decision. But that day, sitting behind his desk, Obama surprised Morell. The president was very direct and clear.

"Number one, Leon, Michael, find out what the hell is going on inside the compound," Obama said. "And number two: don't tell anybody else.

This is known only by us. Don't tell the secretary of state. Don't tell the secretary of defense. Don't tell the chairman of the Joint Chiefs. . . . This is just us for now."

The president got it, Morell thought to himself. He knew there was enough there to move forward. They had to get more information and get it back to him quickly. Morell knew that would be difficult. He just didn't know how difficult and dangerous it would prove to be.

COUNTDOWN:

232 DAYS

September 11, 2010

Somewhere in the Adirondack Mountains

The leaves crunched under Jessica Ferenczy's feet as she trekked along the grassy path to the river. She could see the water glistening in the distance, through the trunks of the oaks and maples. Another quarter mile and she'd be there, at their special spot.

Ferenczy was tired. After she'd finished her evening shift, she'd headed back to the 115th Police Precinct in the New York City borough of Queens. She'd quickly changed into civilian clothes, jumped into her Jeep Cherokee, and by midnight, she was headed north on the New York State Thruway. Three hours later, she let herself into her little cabin in the Adirondack Mountains. It was the early hours of the morning. She tried to sleep, but she couldn't relax.

She made coffee. She sat quietly in the kitchen, jotting down her thoughts in a spiral-bound notebook. At dawn, the birds began to sing outside. Jessica stopped writing and stared out the window. A bright pastel sunup painted the sky. When the early mist burned away, she picked up her paper and a pen and headed out to the river.

She walked with thoughts worn smooth by nine years of repetition. This place was hers, the cabin and seventy acres of trees and wilderness and riverbank. This was supposed to be *their* place. Jerome should be here with her. They should be together. But Jerome Dominguez, the love of her life, was gone forever. She would never see him again.

Ferenczy reached the river's edge and sat down in a sturdy wooden lawn chair by the fire pit. She pulled her mobile phone from her pocket and shut it off. No interruptions. This was her time.

It would be sunny and warm today, much like it was on the morning of September 11, 2001. She leaned back and shut her eyes and let herself feel how broken she still was.

She could still see his handsome face. Dominguez was a buff Spanish-American with a magnetic smile and personality. For two years, he was part of the NYPD's Emergency Service Unit, an elite squad that responded to all kinds of crises. Before that, he was an NYPD Highway Patrol officer. He was a saver of lives. Over his fifteen-year career, Dominguez had stopped suicides, rescued hostages, and extricated people trapped in wrecked cars.

He was a real-life Batman. He kept tools in his car, just in case he needed to help stalled drivers or assist at an accident scene. He was also a member of the New York Air National Guard's 105th Security Squadron.

Dominguez was never off duty. In 1999, on his way to an air force base in Texas for a Guard training session, he saw a school bus overturn on a rural road. He stopped at the scene and quickly took charge, pulling a dozen kids to safety just before the bus burst into flames. The rescue was written up in local newspapers. A TV station did a segment for the evening news, but Dominguez was reluctant to take any credit. He said he'd only done what was needed, nothing more.

When he worked at the NYPD Highway Patrol, he usually arrived to emergency calls on his Harley-Davidson Road King. He was dashing. Six feet tall, 205 pounds, with brown hair in a high-and-tight military shave, brown eyes with hazel around the edges, a barrel chest, and thick muscular arms. But it was his smile, with a little dimple on his left cheek, that was so disarming.

Ferenczy smiled in her chair.

Jerome was outgoing, sweet, a gentle guy who could charm anyone, especially women. His black leather jacket completed the picture. . . . He looked like he'd stepped off the pages of an entertainment magazine.

That leather jacket! He was wearing it the night they met, December 19, 1998. Back then, she was a police officer in the 30th Precinct in Harlem, a predominantly black neighborhood in upper Manhattan. She had volunteered to help with the precinct's annual community Christmas party.

They'd arranged to treat the kids to visits with officers from special NYPD units. The mounted patrol was bringing a horse, and a bomb squad guy was showing off an explosives-sniffing dog and a little robot that disabled suspicious devices. They'd finish up with the Highway Patrol motorcycle cop and his Harley chopper.

When the special units showed up in the parking lot, Ferenczy's job was to escort the kids outside to snap Polaroids of them with the officers. But the night was bitterly cold, with temperatures in the teens, and a windchill that made it feel like single digits.

Ferenczy shuffled the kids back and forth from the precinct's muster room to the parking lot, getting colder with each passing minute. It got so bad they decided to send home the animals and take pictures inside with the robot, so no one would get frostbite.

While Ferenczy was loading more film into her camera, someone said they heard a motorcycle pulling into the parking lot. That poor biker cop! They'd forgotten to call him off.

Thinking she'd only be in the parking lot for a minute, she ran outside in just a T-shirt and jeans, leaving jacket, hat, and gloves inside. She stepped out into an Arctic blast.

"Holy shit," she muttered, her breath emerging like a cloud. She'd have to make this quick.

She saw the taillight of a police motorcycle. The guy's back was turned to her. Ferenczy was so cold she ran up behind the policeman and snuggled against him for warmth. She still hadn't seen his face . . . he could have been anybody! As her face grazed his left shoulder, she noticed something wonderful. He smelled perfect: a mixture of soap, motorcycle exhaust, and campfire smoke.

She didn't know why, but she blurted out, "Hmmm . . . Is this my Christmas present?"

"Yes, I am," he responded. He never missed a beat.

From that moment on, they never spent a day apart.

They came from different worlds.

Ferenczy's father, Arpad, grew up in rural Hungary during World War II and emigrated to the United States in 1956. He ended up in New York City, got married, had two daughters, and settled on Long Island, New York. His marriage didn't last long.

Ferenczy had a special bond with her father. He taught her how to fish and work with tools. He took her on road trips, sleeping in tents in state parks. Jessica was self-sufficient, independent, and dependable.

She didn't know what she wanted to do after high school. She drifted from job to job, and finally decided to take the NYPD entrance exam. Why not? Being a cop meant good money and benefits. She was twenty-five when she graduated from the police academy in 1993.

While she'd had some boyfriends, she didn't consider herself a "girly"

Jessica Ferenczy and Jerome Dominguez.

kind of woman. Ferenczy adapted to the masculine culture around her. She worked out and had muscular shoulders and arms. She shaved the sides of her blonde hair into a mohawk.

Meanwhile, Dominguez came from a distinguished family. His father, Jeronimo, was a doctor, a devout Roman Catholic with a successful medical practice. The family lived in the Pelham Bay Park section of the Bronx, in a waterfront home that was once a fishing retreat for legendary New York City Mayor Fiorello La Guardia.

Dominguez and his brother, Frank, had a wonderful childhood. They always had friends in their house, playing war games and swimming, jumping from their porch into the water of Long Island Sound. And one day, young Jerome saved his brother's life.

Frank suddenly fell into a seizure, and Jerome recognized that his brother was in trouble. He bolted upstairs and told his mother, who called an ambulance. From that moment on, Jerome knew what he wanted to do for a living: help people in trouble.

After graduating high school, he entered the police academy. He graduated in 1985, and two years later, enlisted in the Air Force National Guard.

For a long time, Dominguez struggled with his weight, once ballooning to almost three hundred pounds. He realized he had to change his lifestyle or he'd face serious health issues. One day he began running, and he didn't stop. He hit the gym and started training with weights. When he showed up at Ferenczy's precinct that night, he was a hunk. When the pair came in from the cold, Jessica's friends noticed the goofy look on her face. She was smitten with the motorcycle cop.

After the Christmas party ended and everyone went home, Dominguez called Ferenczy on the phone. They talked for hours. Jessica had to work the next day, a Sunday, but Jerome knew she was off the following day. He called her on Monday morning.

"Can I come over for breakfast?" he asked.

"Come on over," she said.

She hung up and rushed around her tiny apartment in Lindenhurst,

Suffolk County, trying to straighten up. She left the door unlocked so Dominguez could just walk in when he arrived.

Ferenczy was washing dishes when he showed up. Their eyes met. She had an odd feeling, like he was supposed to be there. Like he had walked through that door a hundred times before.

Dominguez dropped his keys on the kitchen counter, walked to her, put both hands on her face, and kissed her. Ferenczy let go of the dishes. It wasn't like the kiss was super-exciting or lusty. It wasn't like she had been hit by lightning. No, it was more like she had been kissing this man her whole life. It was a perfect fit.

It was like that for just about everything in their relationship. They even joked about it.

"I'm going to find you sooner in our next life," she'd say.

He felt the same way. Dominguez said they'd been together in a past life, but somehow got separated. And every time they found each other, something happened to tear them apart. Until now.

They moved in together and subsequently bought a house on Long Island. Dominguez wanted to get married in a big church ceremony at Saint Patrick's Cathedral in Manhattan, but he had been married years before. The relationship ended in divorce. In order to marry in a Catholic church, he had to have his first marriage annulled—which he promised to do.

Meanwhile, Dominguez introduced Ferenczy to his parents and brother, and they treated her like family. When they had started dating, she took him to her favorite campground, a secluded place north of New York City where she'd sleep under the stars. He loved the outdoors, and soon that became their spot, their getaway, a place where they could talk and laugh under the stars, a place where they could discuss their future.

Dominguez said he wanted to retire after twenty years on the force and set up a training center for police officers and military personnel. It would have to be well outside the city, deep in the mountains, he said. Ferenczy loved the idea. They started to save money.

On July 6, 1999, her birthday, the couple headed to their state park.

They walked into the woods and found a convenient rock on the riverbank. Under the moonlight, they made their vows. They promised to love and honor each other, and to look out for each other's parents. They exchanged rings. An official ceremony would come later, but for all intents and purposes, they were married.

When they returned to the city, they told everyone about their ceremony. They continued their journey together. They saved, enjoyed family and friends, laughed, made love, bought their first house. Everything seemed perfect. They complemented each other's strengths and shortfalls. He liked to spend money; she was the saver, the one who paid the bills on time. He lived life to the fullest, riding motorcycles, scuba diving—"go big or go home," he'd say. She was more grounded. "You have to think things out first, and plan for the future," she'd say.

They planned a camping trip for the weekend of September 7, 2001. Just before they left the house, Dominguez went to check the mail. The letter had arrived at last: The diocese had granted the annulment. Thrilled, he hugged Ferenczy and called his parents. They'd tie the knot officially on December 19, 2001—the third anniversary of their frigid meeting in the precinct parking lot.

They spent the weekend at their favorite campsite, worked on the guest list for their wedding. Saturday and Sunday passed in a haze of swimming, drinking, and suntanning.

Ferenczy spent the following day testifying in a lower Manhattan courtroom, and was called to return the following day. Dominguez said he'd drive her to the precinct, where she could catch a ride to court with another officer. Ferenczy dressed like a professional that day, in a suit, heels, makeup, and earrings. When they arrived at the police station, she leaned over to give Dominguez a kiss goodbye. But he wasn't having any of that. He held her face with his hands—just like he'd done the first morning they were together—and kissed her long and passionately.

The other officers in the lot rolled their eyes and cheered. "Get a room!" they said. It was all in jest. They were the perfect couple.

After arriving at the courthouse Ferenczy learned she had some time to kill. As she headed for a local deli for some breakfast, she called Dominguez.

"You want to meet me to get something to eat?" she asked him.

Dominguez said yes. He said he and his partner were nearby. "I'll be there soon," he said. They talked a little bit longer, then the phone cut out.

Ferenczy noticed a cop up the street was looking up at a building about ten blocks down. "Oh shit," she mumbled. It was an airliner, flying way too low, headed straight toward the cluster of skyscrapers on the southern tip of Manhattan. The airplane slammed straight into the North Tower— Tower One—of the World Trade Center. Smoke and flames belched outward, debris rained down to the ground.

Ferenczy stood in stunned silence, then opened her phone. There was no signal. At that moment, a million people were doing exactly what she was doing, calling out to their beloveds.

She started to panic. Dominguez was headed in her direction. He probably knew what just happened. Hell, he probably saw it, too. He's going in there to rescue people, she thought.

Despite her heels and formal clothes, Ferenczy took off running toward the World Trade Center. She passed the courthouse and saw cops dropping their folders with paperwork and other important items on the front steps, turning, and running toward the danger.

Three blocks down, Ferenczy stopped to call Dominguez. She got a signal, but it just kept on ringing. "Come on, pick up!" she said. Then a second plane hit the South Tower. Ferenczy called her police partner, woke him up. "Get your clothes on and head downtown!" she shouted into the phone. She started running again, into the chaos.

Then, just as Ferenczy was ready to run into Tower One, a police lieutenant grabbed her by the arm. "Get back and help secure the courthouse," he shouted. "Move the prisoners from the cells. No one knows if the city is under attack. We have to get them out of there."

Under orders, Ferenczy turned back.

The lieutenant saved her life.

Dominguez went to the World Trade Center immediately after the first airplane struck. He was last seen around the twentieth floor of Tower One. His voice was heard on radio dispatches, warning other police not to enter the building because it was unstable.

When the buildings collapsed, Ferenczy knew he was gone. She felt it in her soul.

The rest of the day, and the next few months, passed in a blur. She used up her sick leave and vacation time, but she just couldn't handle the pain.

A year later, she returned to work at the precinct. The first day, though, she had a panic attack when she and her partner headed into lower Manhattan. She had to stop the car and throw up outside the cruiser.

After so many years of sweet and easy life, her world turned dark and difficult. She and Dominguez had been engaged, they'd lived together and bought a home together, but they were not married, so she had to fight to receive his benefits. She and a group of other survivors battled then Mayor Rudy Giuliani to increase funding for the Twin Towers Fund to help victims' families.

A year after 9/11, Ferenczy was in Saint Patrick's Cathedral—not to marry Jerome Dominguez, but to lay him to rest. His parents insisted on the funeral service even though his body was never recovered.

Ferenczy hated bin Laden. And the funeral only reminded her of everything she'd lost. It reminded her of everything others had lost that horrible day—husbands, wives, brothers, sisters, children, friends. She wanted America to bring bin Laden to justice. Go after him, follow every lead, just like a relentless police detective on a murder case.

But sitting inside Saint Patrick's, she couldn't dwell on that. She eventually received an insurance benefit and used part of it to buy the Adirondacks property. Life went on, years passed. She still had good friends on the force. But not a day went by where she didn't mourn for her lost love.

She turned to writing to help ease her pain. Every September 11, December 19 (their anniversary), and April 25 (Dominguez's birthday), she wrote an online tribute on the "Legacy" web page that carried his obituary.

So today—the ninth anniversary of the day she lost Jerome—on the quiet riverbank, she opened her notebook. She felt responsible for keeping his memory alive, but it seemed like she'd already said everything that needed saying. She wasn't sure what to compose for his Legacy page. Then it all came flooding back, that first night, the stunning cold.

Today I always try to think about the day we met, rather than the day you kissed me for the last time. I think about the crisp coldness of the air when I first saw you, the sound of the children's laughter at the Christmas party going on inside. The smell of your leather jacket when you got off the bike. The warmth of your hand when you first held mine. Touching you that first time was . . . coming home.

I was startled by the clarity of my thoughts, the certainty of my recognition of you. Though we had never met, I knew you. I tried to be funny, cover my surprise with a joke. So I breathed in the scent of you and said "Is this my Christmas present?" and without turning your head—or looking at me, you replied "Yes, I am" and you pulled me tighter to you.

Some hours later, I told my partner that I had just met my husband.

I love you now, as I loved you then . . . still after all this time, after all that has come to pass, all that has gone since

I love you still, Beloved Boy.

I miss you Husband.

Until we are together again My Love.

Always Your Wife,
Jessie

She smiled. God, how she wished he was there with her. She wanted to talk to him so badly. She'd have to make a decision soon, whether to keep working or retire early. She loved being a cop, but her heart just wasn't in it anymore. She wanted time to build the cabins, to develop this land, to turn it into a place to honor his memory. She'd need more money to make that happen.

But that was a decision for another day.

COUNTDOWN:
205 DAYS

October 8, 2010
Langley, Virginia

Michael Morell was always busy. The deputy director of the world's largest intelligence agency was forever on the phone, answering emails, or poring over reports. But since Gary and Sam had told the president about the compound in Abbottabad, the volume of work—and the pressure—had picked up exponentially. It was almost more than one man could juggle.

After all these years of dead ends, they were getting close. Morell could feel it. The hunt for bin Laden was nothing new for him. He'd already been tracking the terrorist for five years before the September 11 attacks.

Morell didn't draw attention to himself. Unlike Panetta, four-letter words didn't roll off his tongue. He was quiet and reflective, medium height and thin, with short brown hair parted carefully on the side. His suits and button-down shirts were always neatly pressed, his ties conservative, his glasses oblong and owlish. He could've passed for a literature professor at an Ivy League school.

In his early fifties, Morell had decades of experience in the CIA. He was the consummate insider, with the meticulous mind of an analyst. Morell was passionate about his work. He knew everything there was to know about Osama bin Laden. He respected the twisted genius behind his well-timed attacks and fierce ideology. But he despised bin Laden's offhand

Deputy CIA Director Michael Morell with Leon Panetta.

dismissal of the deaths of thousands of innocent people. Morell knew that more would die unless the aging terrorist was caught.

He had spent the weeks since the White House meeting with his case officers and analysts, stringing together as much new information as possible about the compound. They had ramped up intercepts of telephone calls, asked for more satellite photos, set more people on the ground in Abbottabad to discreetly collect information. Their efforts were starting to pay dividends.

They knew now that a third family lived in the "fortress," and none of them ever left the premises. The neighbors didn't know there was another family living there. One way the CIA discovered it was by studying those satellite images, and looking at the amount of laundry on the clothesline. And there was another nugget: The brothers owned the house—at least on paper—but the invisible family lived on the top two floors, the best quarters.

The new information didn't prove bin Laden was there. But if he was, he had been hiding in plain sight. That challenged the CIA's working hypothesis, the presumption that had guided them for years.

The CIA analyst's job was to pull together all the evidence and expertise on a given topic and provide an answer to a question a policymaker had asked or should ask. An analyst typically developed a working hypothesis based on intercepts, human intelligence operations, photographs and videos, and other streams of information. That hypothesis then drove further collection of information.

With bin Laden, the questions were: How would he hide? Where? What security would he employ?

For years, everyone assumed he was holed up in the tribal areas in western Pakistan, probably in a cave or a remote area, separated from his family and surrounded by well-armed guards. There was a good chance that his health was failing, and perhaps that he was hooked up to a makeshift kidney dialysis machine.

He would never live in a compound with families. He wouldn't live in a place with military helicopters flying overhead. He'd have set up layers of defenses around his booby-trapped lair, posted guards, and created tunnels or other elaborate escape routes.

The new lead ran counter to that entire narrative. It suggested that bin Laden was living in a villa in the suburbs with his wives, kids, and two families of retainers. He was residing in a sleepy, picturesque city in the shadow of the Himalaya Mountains. Named for James Abbott, a British officer and administrator, the city was a tourist hub with a military academy and medical school. The streets were filled with cadets, medical students, and retirees who enjoyed the temperate weather and the nature trails leading to the mountains. If bin Laden was living *here*, then the CIA had been wrong about almost everything, for an awfully long time.

Morell shook his head. His gut told him that bin Laden was in the compound, but he needed more proof, and more time. He couldn't move too fast. If bin Laden suspected anything, he would slip away like a viper.

That's why Morell was in his office so late, peering at paperwork. He'd learned early on that you had to keep pushing until you got it right.

Morell grew up in Cuyahoga Falls, Ohio, a blue-collar community outside Cleveland. His father, Joseph, worked at a Chrysler plant, while his mother, Irene, stayed at home.

His father was a perfectionist. He kept an elaborate carpentry shop, and tried to pass along the skill to his son. When young Morell presented his dad with his first birdhouse project, his father inspected it with a critical eye. "It's not good enough," he said.

When the boy protested, his father took a hammer and smashed the birdhouse to pieces. "Start over again," he said.

The second time, when he finished, it was a "near perfect birdhouse."

That lesson stayed with Morell. When you do something, you do it right. No shortcuts. After high school graduation, Morell attended the University of Akron and majored in economics. He thought he'd go on to graduate school, earn a PhD, and teach economics. But one of his professors suggested he send a résumé to the CIA.

"They hire economists there," he said.

Morell shrugged. Really? he thought. An economist could be a spy?

"Economics is one of the few academic disciplines that teaches critical thinking," the professor said. "That's the top skill needed to be a successful intelligence analyst."

Morell wasn't sold on the idea. He didn't know much about the CIA, or what an economist would do there. He had never traveled overseas, or learned a foreign language, or even followed world events on the news. He would be a fish out of water.

Still, he sent in his résumé. And to his surprise, he was invited for a visit. When Morell arrived, he was introduced to "a group of amazing, talented people who were dedicated to an important mission."

The year was 1980. U.S. embassy employees in Iran had been taken hostage. It seemed that was the lead story every night on the evening news.

The Soviet military was in Afghanistan, trying to keep the pro-Moscow regime in power.

When the recruiter asked if Morell wanted a job, he said he wasn't sure, that he hoped to go to graduate school. The recruiter sealed the deal by agreeing that was a good idea.

"Come to work here. Do a good job. We'll eventually send you to graduate school on our dime," the man said.

That's all Morell needed to hear. He joined the CIA in 1980. He earned $15,000 a year as an intelligence analyst, and the agency sent him to Georgetown University, where he got his master's degree in economics.

From the beginning, Morell was sharp and focused. He worked his way up in the agency, specializing in East Asian economics. It was a far cry from spy movies, but for Morell, it was satisfying work that had an impact on the world.

By 1998, he was well respected in the agency. He married and started a family. When Mary Beth was in the hospital giving birth to their third child, the phone rang in the delivery room. It was for Morell.

It was good news: The CIA's new director, George Tenet, wanted Morell to be his executive assistant. Morell was stunned. "That's interesting," Morell said. "But I'm a little busy right now." He didn't let it show, but inside, he was thrilled. This would be a career-altering promotion.

When Morell returned to work a few days after his son's birth, Tenet called him into his office. The CIA chief congratulated him, opened a box, and handed Morell a cigar from his private stash.

Tenet became Morell's mentor. The son of Greek immigrants, Tenet had a way of making everyone around him feel comfortable—from the analysts to the janitors. He was known to burst into song, belting out Aretha Franklin's "Respect" and other soul hits. It wasn't unusual to see him dribble a basketball in the CIA hallways.

It helped ease the mood in a high-pressure workplace. Morell needed that. His job was incredibly stressful. He had to review every piece of information headed for Tenet's desk and make a quick decision whether the director needed to see it immediately or if it could wait. It was a balancing act. If he passed along too many things, the director could get overwhelmed. If he kept something critical from Tenet, it could be disastrous.

In his new job, it became clear to Morell that the threat of international terrorism had become the dominant issue, one that Tenet said kept him up at night. This was a change for Morell. He'd had little involvement in the agency's counterterrorism efforts before. Morell soon got to know all the bad guys in the terrorist world.

He learned about Osama bin Laden and Al Qaeda—the name is Arabic for "the base." Their roots dated back to 1979, when the Soviet Union invaded Afghanistan to prop up that nation's Communist government.

In the wake of the invasion, Muslim insurgents, known as the mujahideen, rallied to fight a jihad, or holy war, against the Soviets. One of their supporters was bin Laden, the seventeenth child of a Saudi Arabian construction magnate. At first, bin Laden provided the mujahideen with money, weapons, and fighters. But he decided he wasn't going to sit on the sidelines. So he traveled to Afghanistan and fought alongside the insurgents in the rough mountainous terrain.

When the Soviets were driven from Afghanistan a decade later, most of the nation was taken over by Islamic extremists known as the Taliban. Their leaders allowed bin Laden to set up training camps for Al Qaeda. Meanwhile, bin Laden worked tirelessly to unite disparate militant groups, from Egypt to the Philippines, under the banner of Al Qaeda and his ideal of a borderless brotherhood of radical Islam.

While bin Laden waged jihad all over the world, the United States was his primary target. In the years before 9/11, Al Qaeda conducted a series of high-profile terrorist attacks against America. They included the August 7, 1998, bombings of two U.S. embassies—one in Tanzania, the other in Kenya—that killed more than two hundred people.

Morell was in Tenet's office two days after the attacks, when the CIA chief briefed President Bill Clinton and a cadre of security officials that an international terrorist named bin Laden was responsible.

Preparing for that presidential phone call had been nerve-wracking for Morell. He'd lost patience with the analysts assembling "talking points" for the call.

"What the hell are they doing down there?" he'd said.

"Calm down," Tenet told him. "They're doing the best they can."

In a crisis situation, everyone works hard and there's no need to push, Tenet told him. That's counterproductive.

Once they were certain bin Laden was behind the attacks, Clinton ordered missile strikes against Al Qaeda training camps in Afghanistan and a chemical weapons plant in Sudan.

The embassy bombings changed the atmosphere at the agency.

Before then, the CIA had been prohibited from using lethal force against the terrorist leader. Now, with White House approval, a memorandum of notification (MON) was drafted, which allowed the CIA, using its Afghan surrogates, to kill bin Laden during an operation if it was deemed "unfeasible" to capture him. It essentially allowed the CIA to execute Osama bin Laden.

After the 2000 presidential election—and the controversial victory of George W. Bush—Morell's telephone rang again, this time with a job offer from the White House. Morell was tapped to become the new president's daily briefer. He would still work for the CIA. But every morning, he'd go to the White House to tell Bush about the day's most pressing national security issues, and share the briefing in paper form with the president's closest advisors.

It was an important job. He had to make sure the commander in chief understood the key points in the President's Daily Brief (PDB), which was written by intelligence analysts. But Morell was free to tell the president about information outside the report. If the president had any questions, Morell tried to answer them.

As he contemplated the new role, Morell sought advice from Jami Miscik, a CIA official who had just spent a few days briefing Bush at the governor's mansion in Texas.

"You will really need to be prepared every day," she said. "He will fire questions at you at a rapid pace, and he expects you to be able to answer most of them. He will test you to see how much you know, and he will test you to see if you are willing to say you don't know when you've reached the limits of your knowledge."

She paused for a moment. "He doesn't want you guessing or speculating if you don't know. In short, get ready for a challenging assignment."

Morell accepted the job. But as he was leaving his office that day, he began having second thoughts. Was he up to the challenge? What would an early morning assignment do to his home life? He hadn't told his wife yet.

That night, he explained to Mary Beth what the job entailed. It was a major promotion. He would begin work in the middle of the night, but he would be home by noon.

She encouraged him to take it. At the time, they had three children at home; the oldest was seven. The new hours meant he could help around the house, pick up the kids at school, and oversee their homework.

Morell threw himself into the job. He found Bush engaging and down to earth. Bush, in turn, challenged Morell. He briefed the president once about comments made by a Middle Eastern leader to the CIA chief of station in that country. "This is interesting," Bush told Morell, "but what I really want to know is not what he's saying about me to the CIA, but what he is saying behind my back to Saddam Hussein."

From the time Bush took office, the CIA was flashing warning lights about bin Laden. He was planning a high-profile attack, but Morell knew some members of the administration—and the Pentagon—were skeptical about the warnings.

Tenet didn't back down. He kept pushing the administration to take the threats seriously. Morell was there when a member of Secretary of Defense Donald Rumsfeld's staff told Tenet the CIA was being fooled. The Pentagon was sure that Al Qaeda was conducting a misinformation campaign to get America to waste resources.

Tenet angrily turned to the official. "I want you to look in my eyes," he said. "I want you to hear what I have to say. This is not deception. This is the real deal." In early August 2001, Morell asked terrorism analysts to write a PDB titled "Bin Laden Determined to Strike in US."

On August 6, while the president was on vacation at his Texas ranch, Morell sat with him in his living room and explained why he had the analysts write it. There was still no specific information to suggest these attacks were aimed at "the homeland." But everyone knew bin Laden would like "nothing more than to bring the fight here to our shores."

A month later, the attack arrived, as the CIA had predicted.

Morell was in Florida with the president, who was rolling out a new education policy. There was nothing in the intelligence report that morning regarding terrorist threats. After the briefing, Morell accompanied Bush to an elementary school in Sarasota, where the president was scheduled to read a storybook and pose for photos.

Just as they pulled up to the school, Ari Fleischer's phone rang. Bush's press secretary answered, and then turned to Morell. "Michael, do you know anything about a plane hitting the World Trade Center?"

"No," Morell said, "but I'll find out. Ari, I sure hope this is an accident and not terrorism."

"I sure hope so, too," Fleischer said.

When the second airliner hit the other tower, they had their answer. Bush was reading a book to sixteen second graders in a small classroom when Andy Card, his chief of staff, approached the president. "A second plane has hit the World Trade Center," Card whispered in Bush's ear. "America is under attack."

The president finished. He and his staff raced back to Air Force One. When the plane was airborne, they watched the televisions in horror as people started jumping from the top floors of the buildings in New York City. The towers then collapsed and disappeared in the smoke. The president and his staff were stunned. Word came that another plane had crashed into the Pentagon. Morell's mind fastened on his family, on the ground in Fairfax County, Virginia. It was all happening so fast.

White House Chief of Staff Andy Card with President George W. Bush.

Card walked into the staff section of the plane.

"Michael, the president wants to see you," Card said.

Morell nodded. He walked into Bush's office on the 747. The president looked Morell in the eye. "Michael, who did this?" he asked.

Morell took a deep breath. He hadn't seen any intelligence, he said. What he was about to say was his personal view, not agency policy.

"I would bet my children's future the trail will lead to the doorstep of Osama bin Laden and Al Qaeda," he said.

And it had. Now, after all this time, after all the dead ends and frustration, they might be close to finally bringing the mass killer to justice.

Outside his CIA office was darkness. Morell would miss dinner again.

His children were older now. They didn't seem to notice his absences so much. How many late nights had he spent at the office? And when he was at home, how many phone calls had stolen away time that really belonged to them? How much of that time at home was spent with his mind still at work?

The phone rang. Please, Morell thought, let this be something worthwhile.

COUNTDOWN:
198 DAYS

October 15, 2010

Somewhere in eastern Afghanistan

His Navy SEAL team was going in soon, and Will Chesney was already feeling the excitement. He picked up a currycomb and gave Cairo a brisk brushing, smoothing the glossy black fur all over the dog's muscular body. A high-value target was hiding in a compound dug into the side of a mountain in eastern Afghanistan. They'd fly in as close as possible without tipping off the enemy, then fast-rope down from the helicopter and sneak on foot to the site. It was dangerous as hell, but every one of their missions was. This one was especially nerve-wracking, because Cairo, his seventy-pound part Belgian Malinois, part German shepherd canine partner, was going in for the first time in more than a year. Chesney hoped Cairo still had what it took to be a SEAL. Could he remain cool under fire, having been almost killed in action the last time?

Chesney knew he had to stay focused on right here, right now, but the past kept replaying itself in his mind.

It was night, July 29, 2009. Chesney's team was out to overrun a possible improvised explosive device manufacturing operation. Two helos took them to the destination, and as the choppers approached, four men fled the building. Chesney's team chased them by air, and watched the scene unfolding below.

The men split into twos, jumped onto small motorcycles, and raced away from the building. At first, the motorcycles were in the open, but then they disappeared into a cluster of trees. The helicopters landed and the SEALs chased the heavily armed insurgents on foot. Chesney knew this was risky, but they had no other option. They couldn't let them get away.

Cairo quickly picked up the insurgents' scent. Chesney unhooked his leash and let him go.

The canine easily cleared a four-foot-high stone wall and disappeared into the trees. Shots were fired. Panicked, Chesney called for Cairo to come back. There was no response. Chesney moved toward the trees, toward the gunfire.

"Cairo! Come on, buddy!"

Chesney scanned the field, wall, and trees with state-of-the-art night-vision goggles. About a hundred feet away, a figure emerged. Chesney shouted loud enough to be heard over the gunfire.

"Cairo!"

The dog lurched toward Chesney, then collapsed. Chesney ran to him. Cairo had been shot in the chest and front leg. He was bleeding out, struggling to breathe. His eyes closed.

"Hang in there, boy," Chesney whispered.

The call went over the radio. "FWIA!"—friendly wounded in action. The team made no distinction between human and canine. Cairo was a SEAL like all the rest of them. A combat medic rushed over and pushed piles and piles of gauze into the bullet hole as the dog's blood kept gushing. When the medevac landed, Cairo and Chesney were loaded onto the helicopter.

There were no veterinarians at the base, but a team of combat surgeons and nurses performed emergency surgery on Cairo. Chesney did not leave the dog's side.

He later learned that Cairo had struggled to make it to Chesney's sightline; gravely wounded and unable to jump that tall stone wall, Cairo had to walk his way around it.

That first night, Chesney stretched out on the chilly tile floor in Cairo's room, his arm gently slung across the dog's back. In the morning, Cairo woke Chesney with a lick.

"Hey buddy," Chesney said. "Welcome back."

Recovery took a while. Cairo was shipped back to the United States for physical rehabilitation. He'd make a full recovery, the doctors said, and as far as Chesney could tell, there were no psychological ramifications related to his injuries. But the only way they'd know for sure was to take the dog back into combat.

Chesney smiled to himself. It was crazy, being so attached to a dog. He didn't set out to become a dog handler back when he'd enlisted in the navy, but like so many things in his life, it just happened to work out that way.

Chesney grew up in a trailer park in southeastern Texas, near the Louisiana state line. He was a bit of a loner, "a self-sufficient kid." He worked hard for everything he had. Chesney wasn't the best athlete. He wasn't

Will Chesney and Cairo.

blessed "with great intellect," but he knew he was more resilient than the other teenagers around him. He could get his "ass kicked and come back for more." He could go to a shitty job every day and not complain about it.

Just before he graduated high school in June 2002, Chesney enlisted in the navy. He didn't want to go to college. He didn't want "just to be a sailor." He wanted to do something special; he wanted to *be* something special. He wanted to be a Navy SEAL.

His father encouraged him to go for it. Chesney's mother wasn't so thrilled. She read the newspapers and watched the TV news. There was a war on. Kids in the military were coming home in coffins.

In June 2002, America and its allies had defeated the Taliban and bin Laden was on the run. But it was just a matter of time before the United States invaded Iraq. And then what? The United States would be involved in two wars, and she wasn't ready to sacrifice her only child.

Chesney understood her concerns, but he was an adult, and this was his decision. He spent the summer working out, getting in shape for the challenge to come. In boot camp, he passed the physical prescreening for the SEALs. Then six months later, on November 21, 2003, he graduated from BUD/S. He was assigned to SEAL Team 4 and sent to Iraq. Chesney quickly learned that SEALs spend more time training than they do on deployment.

During a break in urban-warfare training in 2006, he saw a demonstration on how "working dogs" were being incorporated into special operations. He was taken by a magnificent dog, a Belgian Malinois—black and tan like a German Shepherd, but smaller, leaner, and more muscular.

Thirty members of Chesney's unit watched in awe. The handler told them about the dog's incredible sense of smell—it could detect explosives better than any technology out there. Dogs could sniff out roadside bombs before they had a chance to blow up. They could detect an otherwise-invisible IED hidden near the perimeter of a mountain base. The dog's keen senses and killer instinct could be used to discover and chase down fleeing insurgents in a manner "that was at once brutal and efficient."

On cue the dog attacked one of the handlers, who wore a protective "bite suit." Chesney was fascinated with how the dog's eyes fixed on the target, how it shifted its weight, and bounced lightly on its paws, eager to run, waiting for the command.

Chesney realized the dog was a weapon, and an impressive one, at that. The young SEAL had no experience with dogs and had never had much interest in animals.

A few months later, Chesney was deployed to Iraq for the second time. It was during one of the nation's deadliest periods, and he lost a good friend in the fighting. Now, more than ever, he wanted to join a SEAL team that went on the most dangerous missions, the ones "that had the highest chance of providing lasting change." He wanted to join SEAL Team 6.

And when he returned to Virginia Beach, Virginia, in May 2007, he got his chance. He persevered through nine months of high-pressure training and was selected for the elite unit.

Team members were encouraged to specialize in particular skills. Chesney remembered the dogs, and soon learned they were being integrated into SEAL teams. The dogs and the soldiers were getting accustomed to working around each other—dogs padded past while the SEALs did shooting drills, tested munitions, shouted, ran, and slept. The canines had to be well conditioned to the sounds of battle and the sudden motions of men at war.

Chesney's team was deployed to Kandahar, Afghanistan, in the summer of 2008. Two dogs—Falco and Balto—went with them. Chesney was amazed at how well the creatures kept pace. When the group had to jump out of a helicopter and fast-rope fifty feet to the ground, the handlers hooked the dogs onto their drop lines and took them along. The dogs were fierce, loyal, and brave. Chesney began to think of Falco and Balto as members of the squadron. He started spending more time with the dogs.

He learned that Falco's primary handler was giving up the responsibility at the end of his deployment, so Chesney asked if he could take over the dog's care when he left. The guy liked the idea, but tragedy intervened on their next mission—Falco jumped on an insurgent, and another bad guy shot and killed the dog.

Once back at the base, the SEALs held a memorial service. They recounted stories of what a great friend and soldier Falco was. They laughed and cried and shared a cake in his honor.

When Chesney returned to the United States, he followed through with his plan of becoming a dog handler. Here was a chance to do something different, as well as important. He had spent many hours with Falco and Balto, so he was familiar with military dogs. He met Cairo in 2008, and the two of them spent seven weeks of intensive training in California. Cairo became Chesney's roommate, partner, and best friend. For Chesney, it was an awesome responsibility. Cairo was not only a hard worker, but he was as friendly, fun, and affectionate a dog as anyone could ever hope to find.

Chesney and Cairo deployed to Afghanistan in June 2009. On their first mission they had to cross a courtyard with a few dozen sheep penned inside. They had trained for just about everything, but never farm animals. As the sheep began to bleat, Cairo stopped, fascinated. Chesney reached down and picked up the dog. The last thing they needed was Cairo being distracted by "an all-you-can-eat lamb buffet."

But Chesney underestimated Cairo. The dog stayed cool as they walked through the rest of the compound and interviewed the people who lived there.

On the following missions, Cairo was a total pro. He raced into buildings, chased down targets, and never missed a trick. When Cairo bit someone, the damage was extraordinary. Once he almost severed an insurgent's arm.

Then, on the July mission to find the bomb-builders, the dog was shot down. He was flown home for additional treatment, while Chesney continued his deployment. When he got back to the United States in October 2009, Chesney visited the rehabilitation center in Texas. The doctors said Cairo had made a full recovery, and there was no reason he couldn't return to active duty. Chesney was worried about the creature's health but was more concerned about his spirit. Would he still be the same dog? How would he act in combat? Would he rush into the dark with the same zeal?

When Cairo arrived back in Virginia Beach, Chesney met him at the kennel. It was a joyful reunion, with Cairo dancing, yipping, and finally leaping into his arms.

"Hey, buddy, how you been?" Chesney said and laughed. "It's OK, Cairo. Dad's back. Everything's going to be all right."

And now, here they were together in Jalalabad, ready for their first post-injury mission. The two of them walked to the flight line and climbed aboard the chopper with the others. The Chinook took off and headed to their target. Cairo was calm, but Chesney felt a little nervous.

Within a half hour, they were there. Chesney clipped himself and Cairo to the drop rope, and with the rest of the team, they fast-roped out of the chopper to the ground. As soon as Chesney hit the surface, he knew there was trouble. They had to scale an extraordinarily steep hillside, a sheer forty-five-degree angle, rocky and uneven.

Then Chesney discovered a bigger problem. The helicopter was about to leave, and he couldn't unhook the carabiner—a metal loop with a spring gate—that attached him and Cairo to the rope. The rotors roared, he twisted and pulled. . . . Man and dog were about to be yanked into the sky. He shouted and swore, terrified and angry at the same time, hoping to God the helicopter crew had noticed by now as he grabbed and pulled and twisted the carabiner.

No one is going to believe this, he thought.

He was exhausted, but he kept trying. Finally, Chesney was able to release the catch. The Chinook peeled off into the night.

Chesney dropped to his knees, panting. His arms and legs burned from wrestling with the helicopter. But Cairo wasn't going to let him rest. He nudged Chesney with his head—his way of saying, "Let's go."

All Chesney could do was laugh. "What are you looking at?" he asked.

With that, Chesney knew he could focus on the mission. Cairo was back.

COUNTDOWN:
192 DAYS

October 21, 2010
Langley, Virginia

Sitting alone at his desk, Leon Panetta watched the sun dip behind the trees outside his window. Another day and still no answers. He didn't want to feel frustrated, but he couldn't help it. It was that damn fortress in Abbottabad. He couldn't stop thinking about it. He needed to know everything about the compound and the people inside. So he pushed his analysts to work harder, drill deeper. Every day, he'd ask them if they had anything new.

And he kept putting the same question to two of his closest aides, Morell and Bash. It was clear that somebody had gone to extraordinary lengths to secure his privacy. Panetta knew the compound was larger and more valuable than any home in the area. "Who's inside?" he'd ask. Morell and Bash would shrug. They didn't know. Not yet.

With his golden retriever, Bravo, by his side, Panetta realized the compound was consuming his life. It was another late night after another long day filled with calls and meetings. How long would it last? He didn't know. There were a lot of things he hadn't known about the job when he told the president he'd take it.

Panetta had been running a public policy school he created in California when Obama called. The president said he needed someone with Panetta's credentials to lead the spy agency. So Panetta moved to Washington while his wife Sylvia stayed behind to run the school in Monterey. Meanwhile, he took Bravo with him to D.C. to keep him company. Most days, his dog would sit faithfully by Panetta's desk, greeting visitors.

President Harry Truman once said, "If you want a friend in Washington, get a dog." And so it was with Bravo. He went everywhere with Panetta, even to top-secret meetings. And Panetta was glad Bravo was there. When it got too stressful, he'd play with his dog or take him for a walk. And when he did, Panetta would be reminded of all the "humanity in the world."

Panetta wasn't used to this kind of frustration. He had succeeded in just about everything he tackled, and he wasn't going to fail now. If it meant working longer, working harder, he'd do it. That drive came from his parents, devout Italian immigrants who instilled a sense of hard work and public service in their children. When it was time for college, Panetta joined the Reserve Officers' Training Corps (ROTC) to help pay his tuition at Santa Clara University. After college, he went on to law school.

Shortly after graduation, a friend set him up with Sylvia, a "dark-haired

CIA Director Leon Panetta with Chief of Staff Jeremy Bash.

beauty" from a neighboring college. They were married in 1962, and in a year's time Leon had a wife, a son, a law degree—and a draft notice.

Panetta was sent to the U.S. Army Intelligence Center of Excellence, where he learned to step up and manage security in moments of crisis. As a lawyer, he also represented servicemen in courts-martial.

He mustered out of the military in 1966 and had to decide what to do with his life. Panetta was intrigued by Washington, inspired by a charismatic young Catholic politician who was the first member of their religion to be elected president: John F. Kennedy.

But Panetta had no political connections, so he took an unconventional step. He wrote a letter to Joseph Califano Jr., an attorney in President Lyndon Johnson's administration. Panetta appealed to Califano as one ambitious young Italian to another. To his surprise, Califano answered. He said he'd introduce Panetta to people in Washington.

As the young man made the rounds, going from one congressional office to another looking for work, he landed a staff job with Tom Kuchel, a Republican senator from California. Panetta's career took off.

In 1977, Panetta was elected to the U.S. House of Representatives as a Democrat from California. He served until 1993, when he was appointed director of the Office of Management and Budget under new President Bill Clinton. A year later, with his administration in disarray, Clinton tapped Panetta as his White House chief of staff.

Over the years, Panetta earned a reputation for hard work, competence, and honesty. In the wake of 9/11, the CIA's reputation—and the intelligence community as a whole—had taken a hit. How could bin Laden have taken them so by surprise? It got even worse when no one could find "weapons of mass destruction" in Iraq—the main reason President Bush cited for toppling Saddam Hussein.

Panetta wasn't tainted by the wars in Iraq or Afghanistan. He had a strong reputation for his managerial skills, his bipartisan standing, and the foreign policy and budget experience he gained under Bill Clinton.

Obama believed that Panetta was the right person at the right time to lead the CIA. And a few months into his presidency, he gave Panetta new marching orders—to make the hunt for Osama bin Laden a top priority. But now, just like his predecessors, he was bogged down in the search for the leader of Al Qaeda. The scrubby borderlands of Pakistan were a long, long way from the silk ties and marble corridors of Washington, D.C.

Panetta thought he'd caught a break one day in late 2009. His agents had arranged to meet with a Jordanian doctor who claimed a connection to Al Qaeda's second in command, Ayman al-Zawahiri.

Humam al-Balawi had been detained by Jordanian authorities for posting opinion pieces on the internet that encouraged jihad—the violent struggle against the enemies of Islam. After his release, the doctor approached a highly respected Jordanian intelligence officer. Al-Balawi said he'd had a change of heart and wanted to infiltrate Al Qaeda, a mission he said would help him redeem his family name. So, in the summer of 2009, with his handler's help, al-Balawi disappeared in Pakistan. When he returned a few months later, he said he had met al-Zawahiri—and knew details about the terrorist leader that were consistent with his personal and medical history.

The development was such a big deal that Panetta briefed Obama. If he got that close to al-Zawahiri so quickly, maybe the doctor could eventually lead them to bin Laden. Panetta wanted his analysts to talk to al-Balawi to find out more, including how he was able to infiltrate the terrorist group.

So they set up a big meeting at a CIA facility inside Forward Operating Base Chapman in the Khost Province of Afghanistan. Al-Balawi and his Jordanian handler came in a car with an Afghan driver. As they approached FOB Chapman, the vehicle was waved through several checkpoints until the driver reached a building where more than a dozen people were waiting outside for the important visitor. CIA station chief Jennifer Matthews, who had worked with Gary, was among those who greeted the informant. But moments after al-Balawi stepped out of the vehicle, he did the unthinkable. He detonated a suicide vest, killing Matthews, four CIA employees, two CIA security contractors as well as himself, his Jordanian handler, and the driver. Six other CIA officers were wounded.

It was the most lethal attack against the CIA in more than a quarter century. It haunted Panetta. He tried to put it down as "another disappointment." But he recognized it as a major intelligence failure. And he was forced to confront the possibility they might "never find that son of a bitch."

He met with the families of the seven dead officers at Dover Air Force Base in Delaware when their bodies were returned to the United States. He attended the funerals, and was moved by the resolve of the stricken families. They knew no details of the CIA officers' mission. They only knew what Panetta told them at Dover: They were working to prevent another 9/11 and bring Al Qaeda senior leadership to justice. Each of them relayed the same message to Panetta: Don't give up. Keep going. Make this death mean something.

The route to the cemetery at one Massachusetts funeral was lined with people holding American flags and signs that said: "Thank you for your service."

Panetta leaned over and whispered to another CIA officer, "We're silent warriors. We don't say much. We don't say a lot about what we do. But here are ordinary Americans lining the streets to pay tribute to a CIA officer. We're doing the right thing for the country."

It was critical to keep searching for that bastard.

Panetta went back to Washington and pulled every file related to the bin Laden hunt. Years' worth of tactical notes, videos, CIA organizational charts. He asked questions: Who was responsible for what part of the search? What were they doing today? How did all the pieces fit together? Panetta came to the stark conclusion: The CIA had to change its ways.

From his experience, Panetta knew an organization's structure and reporting chain had to reflect its priorities. Finding bin Laden was the president's and Panetta's top objective, but Panetta wasn't receiving regular updates, and more important, there was no single person inside the CIA to turn to for information and operational updates. Panetta had a limited view of the bin Laden effort and only sporadic contact with the individuals who were chasing the Al Qaeda leader.

After the Khost tragedy, he called a meeting of the agency's top officers in the director's conference room at CIA headquarters. When everyone was seated, Panetta got right to the point.

"Who here is in charge of finding Osama bin Laden?" And just like Panetta had thought, everybody raised his hand.

Panetta sighed. Four decades in management had taught him one lesson: "If everyone is in charge, nobody is." There was no senior official solely devoted to the mission, no person accountable to Panetta who woke up every morning and went to bed every night working on the hunt for bin Laden. He knew it had to end right there.

After some internal discussions, he put Gary and Sam in charge of the mission. Gary was a career case officer who had served in the field. He had been running the Counterterrorism Center's PAD for years. To keep pressure on the team, and to signal that this effort was a top priority, Panetta assigned Gary to brief him every Tuesday afternoon, even if he had nothing new to report. As the months dragged on, Gary grew to dread Tuesdays.

Sam was an analyst who was Gary's deputy. They both oversaw counterterrorism missions along the Afghan-Pakistan border. Soon, the bin Laden hunt consumed their lives.

And now maybe all of their hard work would finally pay dividends. Hell, it had led them to that fortress, right? Panetta just needed a little patience and a little luck. They were all trying hard. He had faith it would all come together. He took a deep breath, then reached for Bravo's leash.

Maybe a good walk with his dog would help Panetta unwind before he called it a day.

Leon Panetta with Bravo.

COUNTDOWN:
182 DAYS

October 31, 2010
Cleveland, Ohio

On the last day of a four-state campaign tour, President Obama knew he faced an uphill battle. He was trying to prevent a Democratic Party meltdown. Midterm elections were only a few days away, and they had become a referendum on his presidency. The polls didn't look good. Neither did the crowds at his rallies. The Wolstein Center at Cleveland State University held fourteen thousand people. But tonight, only eight thousand people were showing up to hear Obama. Not a good sign.

Times were tough. Obama's term had started out so full of promise, but slowly things had turned south. The optimism of his "Yes We Can" 2008 campaign had been ground down by economic recession. After two years on the job, the stress had turned his hair gray. He joked about it at campaign rallies, but it wasn't really a laughing matter.

Many voters had become disillusioned with Obama. And it led in part to the rise of a new conservative movement: the Tea Party. While members of the anti-Washington group endorsed traditional conservative causes—lower taxes and reduction of the national debt—some also embraced extreme conspiracy theories. They spread vicious rumors about Obama. They said he was a radical Muslim, an African carpetbagger born in Kenya—a bizarre claim pushed by Donald Trump, the New York City real estate magnate and star of *The Apprentice*, a glitzy reality TV show.

If that wasn't enough, U.S. troops were still bogged down in Iraq and Afghanistan, despite Obama's campaign promise to end the wars. In fact, Obama had dramatically ramped up the American presence in Afghanistan from thirty thousand troops to more than one hundred thousand.

Maybe the compound in Abbottabad would provide the good news Obama needed just now.

After the meeting with Panetta and the CIA analysts back in September, Obama had tempered his expectations. What was the likelihood that bin Laden was really in Abbottabad? It didn't seem plausible. But the outcome—whether bin Laden was captured, killed, or escaped—could determine whether he'd get another four years in the White House. How ironic would it be if the man responsible for bringing bin Laden to justice was a president that most Americans believed was a dove? If that happened, it wouldn't be the first time Obama had confounded his critics.

After two years on the job, Americans were still getting to know the president. For many, it was a miracle Obama had gotten this far. They liked to point to his election as a sign of just how far the United States had come since the Civil War.

Obama's father was black, a Kenyan scholarship student at the University of Hawaii. His mother was white, from Kansas. Their marriage didn't last long, but their son, Barack Obama II, was born in 1961.

He was raised by his grandparents in Hawaii and graduated from Columbia University with a degree in political science. Obama moved in 1985 to Chicago, where he worked on the South Side as a community organizer for low-income residents. Three years later, he entered Harvard Law School. He returned to Chicago to practice civil rights law. He taught constitutional law part-time at the University of Chicago Law School, first as a lecturer and then as a professor.

Obama was restless. If he wanted to make a real impact, he'd have to get involved in politics. He was elected to the Illinois State Senate in 1996.

In 2004, Obama ran for the U.S. Senate. That summer, he was invited to deliver the keynote speech in support of John Kerry at the Democratic

National Convention in Boston. Obama impressed the crowd—and the nation—with his youthful eloquence. His star was on the rise. His U.S. Senate bid in Illinois earned him 70 percent of the vote. He used that to catapult his run for the White House.

The 2008 Democratic primary saw him locked in a tight battle with former first lady and then senator from New York Hillary Rodham Clinton. He defeated her, then picked Delaware Senator Joe Biden to be his running mate. Together, they defeated Republican lion John McCain.

It hadn't been easy.

He was a black man with a funny name. Some on the right liked to focus on his middle name—Hussein—as if to say, "See, he's not really American." But Obama combined charisma, his big smile and baritone voice, his keen intellect, and a message of hope to overcome the doubters. He campaigned on an ambitious agenda of financial reform and reinventing health care and education.

The night he won the election, a tidal wave of goodwill swept through large parts of the nation.

Maybe he'd been too optimistic. The goodwill couldn't last. He had inherited a global recession caused by the reckless behavior, deregulation, and bad loans by the big banks and insurance companies. The banking and housing collapse had plunged the United States into its worst financial crisis since the Great Depression.

After only nine months on the job, President Obama was awarded the 2009 Nobel Peace Prize for his "extraordinary efforts to strengthen international diplomacy and cooperation between people." Some questioned why this young politician was given a Peace Prize when the United States was still fighting two wars. What had Obama done to deserve it? The president himself said he was surprised and "deeply humbled."

At the awards ceremony in Stockholm, Sweden, Obama sounded more like a hawk than a peacenik as he outlined his position on war. While he praised peacemakers of the past, like Martin Luther King Jr. and Mahatma Gandhi, he said sometimes wars were just. He was no pacifist.

"I know there is nothing weak—nothing passive, nothing naïve—in the creed and lives of Gandhi and King. But as a head of state sworn to protect and defend my nation, I cannot be guided by their examples alone. I face the world as it is, and cannot stand idle in the face of threats to the American people. For make no mistake: evil does exist in the world.

"A non-violent movement could not have halted Hitler's armies. Negotiations cannot convince Al Qaeda's leaders to lay down their arms. To say that force is sometimes necessary is not a call to cynicism—it is a recognition of history; the imperfections of man and the limits of reason."

During the 2008 presidential campaign, Obama had said the United States would kill bin Laden, given the chance. Once in office, Obama authorized more deadly drone strikes against high-value targets than President Bush ever did. He also put pressure on Panetta to find bin Laden.

Most of his antiterrorist actions happened in secret. If the public had known, it might have gone a long way to changing the narrative that Obama was too weak and cerebral to act. Maybe the narrative would change if the United States captured or killed bin Laden on the president's watch. But Obama didn't have time to think about that now. No, it was time to focus on his prepared speech. Maybe there was a chance he could still change a few voters' minds before they headed to the polls.

COUNTDOWN:
181 DAYS

November 1, 2010

Northern Virginia

Gary rolled out of bed at 5:30 a.m. and padded to the kitchen. He filled a bowl with Raisin Nut Bran, splashed on some milk, and filled a glass with orange juice. He stared out the window as he ate, trying to look beyond his grizzled reflection into the dark backyard.

Another early morning, another long day full of meetings and reports, telephone calls and emails. Abbottabad.

He put the dishes in the sink and went to get dressed. His wife and kids would be stirring soon, getting ready for school and work. Gary hadn't seen much of them recently. He was working longer hours, and that meant his wife was shouldering more of the household responsibilities. She hadn't said much, but the tension was there.

On his way out, Gary looked across the kitchen at the bowl and spoon standing in the sink, the milk container still out on the counter. He stepped back to the sink, grabbed the sponge, and cleaned up after himself.

He'd have to pick up some slack at home, even if his daily work happened to be the intelligence community's top priority. Gary had been tracking bin Laden and his terrorist network for years. He still could not prove that bin Laden was in the compound, but he knew anyway. He just had to work harder, and soon a break would come along.

His relentless work ethic had gotten him to this point—had guided him even when it looked like his career at the CIA was over. Gary was one of the leaders on a team in Baghdad that had warned Secretary of Defense Donald Rumsfeld in 2004 that insurgents were behind an increase in violence in Iraq. Rumsfeld dreaded another Vietnam-like quagmire, with U.S. troops bogged down for years by an invisible enemy. He refused to listen to the agency. There was no insurgency in Iraq, Rumsfeld insisted, and the analysts who contradicted him paid the price. Gary, the team's second-in-charge, was busted down to a desk job back at CIA headquarters in Langley. His brilliant career was "dropped in the shredder."

Now, years later, Gary could smile about it. He'd been sent to what he thought was a career-ending job, but like the mythical phoenix, he had risen from the ashes. He was now the team leader in the hunt for bin Laden. Funny how things worked out.

He headed to his car for his predawn commute to CIA headquarters. With a deep knowledge of the Middle East, Gary was the head of the Counterterrorism Center's Pakistan-Afghanistan Department. First thing this morning: a talk with Sam, his deputy, the agency's leading expert on Al Qaeda. In reality, Sam and Gary were equals in this mission. They both were passionate and driven, consumed by the little pieces that helped complete the mosaic.

Gary was the elder, a weather-beaten veteran in his midforties. He was six-foot-four, two hundred pounds. He was a little quiet, an observer, but when challenged, he would "make his points." Sam was a fresh-faced younger man in his early forties, with light hair and a bright future.

The CIA was a hell of a career choice. The agency was responsible for providing national security intelligence to U.S. policymakers, and collecting information used to stop overseas threats. At the direction of the president, they also conducted missions and engaged in covert activities to help keep the nation safe from terrorist attacks. The work was high-pressure and usually thankless. Mistakes could be fatal.

The CIA was born after the Japanese surprise attack on Pearl Harbor on December 7, 1941. President Franklin D. Roosevelt created the Office of Strategic Services to coordinate intelligence activities and analyze strategic information during World War II.

After the war, President Harry S Truman recognized the need for a centralized intelligence agency. The Cold War was cranking up, and the United States needed good intelligence to counter threats from the Soviet Union and China. In 1947, Truman signed legislation that created the Central Intelligence Agency. Sixty-three years later, the agency had twenty-one thousand employees and a $15 billion annual budget.

Gary could feel the history every time he walked into CIA headquarters—several buildings on a 260-acre campus in Northern Virginia, a few miles west of Washington, D.C. Even at this early hour, the Counterterrorism Center's PAD was up and running, with about half its staff of several hundred hard at work.

His office was underground in the main building. It looked like any corporate space with cubicles and drop ceilings. His office had a long slit window that ran across the top of one wall, letting in artificial light from the common area on the other side. You could spend hours there and never know whether it was day or night.

The boss settled in, read the overnight reports from agents all over the world, and scanned his emails. His office was down the hall from Sam's, and his deputy poked his head in to say hello once he'd read the morning's "top material."

Gary and Sam had what they called "a battle rhythm." They'd check in to ensure they were on the same page, then Sam would head back to his office. He had responsibilities within Gary's department, but he also had higher-level analytical work and managed other people and missions.

Gary was a "repeat offender," a guy who stayed long-term on particular projects. Most CIA assignments lasted two years, and those who wanted to advance in the agency moved on to other areas. But Gary wasn't looking to jump around. He had a good, secure position as part of the war on Al Qaeda, a mission where institutional knowledge was vital. He and Sam were in this for the long haul, organizing the strategic and tactical war on Al

Qaeda leadership. They were keen on getting bin Laden, but until recently the bulk of their work had focused on his lieutenants. Lower-level leadership was more tactical, and drove the daily, weekly, and monthly cycle of attacks in the Middle East.

The CIA prosecuted an invisible war against Al Qaeda, on several fronts. While they handled different aspects of that war, Gary and Sam needed each other. They worked together to get the information. Teamwork was key. All intel was shared. With the CIA relying heavily on covert action—lethal drone strikes, Special Forces raids—the right intel meant they could hit any target in any part of the world at any time.

Things had changed profoundly since the time when Gary was bounced from Iraq. When he'd returned to headquarters in 2004, he thought his career was over. He got "a real unpleasant set of reviews and evaluations," but Gary dusted himself off and moved forward.

When he watched 9/11 unfold on television, Gary promised himself he would not leave the CIA until Al Qaeda was defeated, until the United States had "completely decapitated its leadership." He wanted to make sure they were never able to launch another attack against the United States. Gary toiled in relative obscurity, tracking down leads as he tried to fulfill his promise. And then, in 2009, after Obama was inaugurated, Osama bin Laden became a top priority again. Gary's work situation suddenly improved.

When he met Panetta, he felt energized. The new director was a savvy leader who wanted to meet regularly with everyone. Panetta wasn't a spook. He hadn't had experience with the CIA before he was appointed by Obama. But Panetta understood how the Washington bureaucracy worked—what he could do and how he could do it. He was well connected and well liked. If Gary's people came up with the leads, Panetta could make things happen.

Then, when the puzzle pieces joined up and the courier led them to the compound in Abbottabad, Gary and Sam knew it was time to tell Panetta the news. They didn't exaggerate the importance of the lead. If anyone was skeptical about the compound, Gary was. But it was also "painfully clear that this lead might be significant."

And Panetta got it. Gary knew just where the director would go with the information. "Get ready," Panetta told them. After they briefed Obama, the president told them to step it up, to find out who lived in the compound.

Now Gary was working even harder and pushing others in his department to do the same, and it was becoming a bigger deal. Forget about any semblance of family life. Up and out at 5:30 a.m., and home and asleep after 9 p.m. He spent part of his weekends catching up with his work. And now, with Panetta's constant pressure, the pace was picking up even more. How long could he and the others keep this up? He didn't know. He only knew they were too close to worry about that now.

COUNTDOWN:
179 DAYS

November 3, 2010

Abbottabad, Pakistan

Dr. Shakil Afridi watched the wiry little man close the door behind him and walk calmly out the front gate. The man was a CIA agent. Right here in the clinic.

Unlike many Pakistanis, Dr. Afridi believed the United States was an ally, doing the right things to help his country through a dark, violent period. Now the Americans wanted to make him wealthy, very fast. And all he had to do was the right thing. He'd be paid thousands just for setting up a hepatitis vaccination program in Abbottabad.

Afridi had run several such programs in the past. It wouldn't be hard. And it was a handsome offer. What the CIA was asking, among all the hundreds of other shots he'd administer, was try to vaccinate the people living in one particular house in the city. The agent said he'd give him details once the doctor decided to come on board.

Afridi sat quietly and calmed his mind.

This was not a simple decision. Working with a foreign agency like the CIA could spell trouble. If Pakistan's notorious Inter-Services Intelligence (ISI) found out, his life would be in jeopardy. There were plenty of risks, and a long list of unanswered questions. He'd told the agent he needed some time to think about it.

Afridi had a lot to lose. He'd worked hard to become a doctor. A well-respected surgeon, he had just arrived in Abbottabad. The agency had chosen him because of his reputation, the man had said. Charity workers had told the CIA how Afridi had been helping the poor for several years, treating many who had no access to health care.

The doctor was no fool. He knew they were buttering him up, that there had to be more to all this. An entire vaccination clinic program, just to reach the people in one house? Who were they? This was all too sketchy. But it had to be very important, to go to all this trouble.

It would have to be completely secret. He couldn't tell his wife, brother, no one. His wife was a teacher. They had three young children. What would happen to them if the government found out? The doctor had worked so hard to lift himself out of poverty, to become a professional. Was this opportunity worth risking it all?

Afridi was from a tribal area of Khyber, a part of Pakistan near the

Dr. Shakil Afridi.

Afghanistan border notorious for centuries as a smuggling route. During the Soviet invasion of Afghanistan, the mujahideen had set up a forward operating base in the region. Khyber was also the heroin capital of Pakistan. The mujahideen operated labs to refine the opium poppies that grew in Afghan fields. They used the drug profits to fund their wars.

After 9/11, when the United States invaded Afghanistan, many Taliban and Al Qaeda fighters moved to Khyber. Miles of landscape had been scarred from years of U.S. military drone attacks as well as Pakistani anti-insurgent operations.

Afridi grew up amid the suffering and destruction of war. He decided to become a doctor like those who patched up the bloodied fighters in his street. Very few people from his poor rural area got an education, let alone went to medical school.

But Afridi beat the odds. With endless support from his family, he graduated from Khyber Medical College in 1990 with a specialization in general surgery. His practice grew, and eventually he was appointed chief surgeon at Jamrud Hospital. It was there he joined in vaccination programs sponsored by foreign charities that hoped to cure polio in Pakistan.

The campaigns made a genuine difference in the Khyber Agency district. Aid packages from NGOs like Save the Children continued to arrive at his clinic. It was no surprise the network of foreign spies kept an eye on the people involved in multinational aid programs.

Afridi didn't know it, but he was part of an elaborate plan to identify Osama bin Laden. The CIA hoped that a vaccination drive in Abbottabad could somehow get Afridi or another health professional inside the compound, where they could obtain DNA from the people who lived there. The agency had DNA from bin Laden's sister, who had died in a Boston hospital earlier in 2010. If DNA samples from inside the compound matched bin Laden's sister—case closed. Their target was in the house. Then they could start planning their next step.

They didn't tell that to Afridi. They only said they'd pay him to set up a vaccination program. CIA operators had to make sure they could trust him first.

Working inside Pakistan was treacherous business. Pakistani leaders had been insisting for years that bin Laden had died during his escape from Afghanistan. If he wasn't dead, he was probably hiding in the mountains in eastern Afghanistan. When it came to terrorism, Pakistan cooperated with the United States, and the government received billions in American aid in exchange. Pakistan was a vital U.S. supply route to the front in Afghanistan. But it was no secret that factions within the Pakistani military and its dreaded intelligence service maintained ties with the Taliban, maybe even Al Qaeda. That rubbed Afridi the wrong way. He'd seen the pain the Taliban and Al Qaeda had caused his people.

Something else niggled at Afridi's mind. The agent had mentioned a house in Abbottabad. Why did they want to target someone in particular? Why did they have to go undercover? What were they trying to accomplish?

His head was spinning. Were they looking for someone in the military? The prestigious Pakistan Military Academy was there in the city. Only a thousand students were admitted to the school each year, the best and the brightest.

But Abbottabad was more than a military town. It was a summer resort for the elite, with sparkling air, miles of forest, and the Himalaya Mountains as a backdrop. It wasn't a cheap place to live. Whoever was in that house had to have money. That made Afridi even more nervous.

He sighed and stood. He shut off the lights, locked up, and headed for his car. He'd have to make a decision soon. He wanted to sleep on it.

COUNTDOWN:
177 DAYS

November 5, 2010
Langley, Virginia

Leon Panetta was furious. The people around the table tried not to flinch as he barked. For almost two months, Panetta had been encouraging, cajoling, pushing his analysts to work harder and smarter, to come up with new ideas to somehow identify the people living behind the compound's walls. The agency had plenty of work all around the world, but Panetta was focused like a laser on this one objective.

"We're the CIA, for God's sake! The world's top intelligence agency. Hollywood makes spy thrillers about us." He hammered at the tabletop. "But now we can't figure out who's inside a house a half mile from the Pakistani Military Academy?"

Property records? Deliverymen? Doctors? This wasn't some isolated spot. The compound stood in a busy city of two hundred thousand people. There were stores and marketplaces everywhere, perfect spots to collect information. People loved to talk about their neighbors.

"Dig deeper, people!" he growled.

Panetta was usually charming and diplomatic, especially when he was glad-handing politicians on Capitol Hill. He rarely lost his temper. But when he did, he said exactly what was on his mind—and the counter-terrorism experts today were getting both barrels.

"This is the top priority of the CIA," he said. "Don't worry about budgets. Just figure out who this guy is."

The meeting had started out calmly enough. Panetta had entered the room feeling optimistic, expecting a few new bits of intelligence from the group. Ever since the president was informed about the "fortress," a small team of CIA analysts and field operatives had been working endlessly. Agents snooped quietly around the city. They staked out the street long enough to develop a roster of who went in and out of the house, their habits, where they bought flour and olive oil and lightbulbs. They analyzed surveillance and satellite photos. They knew that al-Kuwaiti lived inside the guesthouse, and his brother Abrar lived in the main house, along with their families.

The scrutiny yielded up a significant discovery: the third family—including a man, a woman, and a teenage boy—lived upstairs in the main building. Almost every day, the man emerged from the house and strolled the courtyard for an hour or two. He walked back and forth, day after day,

Compound in Abbottabad, Pakistan.

moving around the compound like an inmate in a prison yard. The analysts dubbed him "The Pacer."

But the satellite imagery could never provide a clear view of the man's face, so he couldn't be identified. Panetta suggested sending in a "human spy," or moving in closer with electronic devices. The operators said that was impossible, unsafe, unworkable. The last thing they needed was to blow their cover.

As time passed, The Pacer started driving Panetta crazy. Was that bin Laden, walking up and down? A decoy? Was this another setup?

Over the following weeks, they examined every angle, high and low. Osama bin Laden was at least six-foot-four. At a distance, The Pacer seemed to have the gait of a tall man. Panetta had brought in expert satellite-image analysts to nail down The Pacer's height. But that was a bust. The test results determined the man was somewhere "between 5-foot-8 and 6-foot-8."

Panetta asked Gary to find a way to get a camera close to the compound: "Do whatever the hell you have to do." But Gary said it was too risky.

He suggested sending in a team at night to plant cameras in the trees overhanging a section of the yard where The Pacer exercised. Panetta knew it was risky, but how else were they going to get a look at the man's face?

"You know, I've seen movies where the CIA can do this," Panetta said.

But Gary reminded him this wasn't a Hollywood blockbuster. Their cameras didn't have enough battery life to make it feasible. Besides, the trees were deciduous, meaning the leaves would fall off in the winter, exposing the cameras. (Apparently, someone in the compound thought the trees were a security risk, too. A newer satellite image showed they had been cut down.)

"Can we tap into the sewage pipes leading from the compound and do DNA testing on the outflow?" Panetta asked.

That was quickly ruled out. Panetta continued for weeks positing every kind of idea. And Gary, the practical, detail-oriented veteran who headed up the team, almost always delivered the disappointing "why nots." It seemed to the chief he expended more energy shooting down ideas than finding ways to make them work.

Gary had tried every trick possible without jeopardizing his people on the ground. This wasn't his first surveillance. He had been around for a while. Gary had seen his share of "tough, tough spots."

He had served several overseas stints. As head of the Counterterrorism Center's PAD, he knew the Islamic world as well as anyone. He and Sam had pushed their team ceaselessly for more and better information. They had done everything they could think of, Gary told Panetta that morning.

The boss hit the ceiling. "Have you people used all the tools in the toolbox?" he said, looking right at Gary.

Gary was quiet, frustrated in part by Panetta's "inability" to understand that intel work didn't follow timelines. He knew that Panetta was new, so he hadn't seen the whole movie. He hadn't seen the pace with which a case moves. In Gary's mind, Panetta didn't have a good feel for the luck factor and how that turns a surveillance around. And Gary knew one other thing: Panetta wasn't a passive guy. No, he had ideas and spit them out: "Why don't you try this?" "Why don't you try that?" But when Gary explained why they wouldn't work, Panetta would get angry and run hot. Gary knew Panetta viewed the analysts and case officers as "static and inflexible," not ready to embrace his ideas, and not aggressive enough in generating their own.

Gary was reading his boss right. While Panetta respected Gary, he thought perhaps he was burning out. Gary was an operator, a collector of information. He seemed more oriented to tactics than strategy.

Panetta had seen more of Sam since he took over the agency—they'd consulted on the drone program and a few other issues. In Panetta's mind, Sam was the officer who put the whole picture together. Maybe it was time for a change.

For now, Panetta could see his anger wasn't getting him anywhere. Before adjourning the session, he told the team they'd better bring ten new ideas to the next meeting—or else.

The team left the room in silence.

When they were gone, Panetta turned to Morell and Jeremy Bash and expressed his frustration.

"I don't think Gary is up to this," Panetta said. "Is it time to replace him? I think he's grown discouraged."

Bash knew that was a bad idea. Gary and his team had worked their asses off, and were feeling just as frustrated as Panetta.

Bash urged Panetta to wait, to give him time to sound out Gary. He'd let the rest of the group know that their jobs were on the line.

And that's what Bash did. He gathered all the dispirited agents together and told them that new ideas were all they had to come up with, nothing more. Just dismissing Panetta or other CIA leaders' ideas as "impractical" was not enough.

"Suggest anything—no matter how outlandish," he said. "Get your thinking going. You have to reassure Panetta that you're not out of gas." Take the ideas and trace out how they might work. Write it all down, he said.

"This is like math class. You need to show your work," he said.

Panetta had demanded ten ideas. Bash pressed them to come up with twenty-five.

"Don't worry about whether you can do it. Don't worry about whether it's a good idea. Just put it on a piece of paper," Bash said.

Bash didn't care what they came up with. He had to motivate them. They were stuck right now, but he knew they could do it. They were elite agents, the best of the best. He'd seen how hard they had worked just to get this far.

Brainstorming for motivation is Team-Building 101, but Bash was willing to use whatever tools came to hand. He, like Panetta, was new to the spy world. He was an attorney, a Harvard Law graduate who'd always been interested in national security issues. He'd been a security advisor to Al Gore's presidential campaign in 2000. Later, he was a member of Gore's legal effort during the thirty-six-day ballot recount in Florida.

The team reconvened a week later. Panetta sat down at the head of the conference table as Gary, Sam, and the others filed quietly in.

The agents didn't have ten ideas, or twenty-five. No, they had thirty-eight. They had come up with thirty-eight ways to try to get information about the compound and, more important, The Pacer. They even put together what they called the "Chart of 38."

Panetta smiled as they rattled down the list. Some ideas were outrageous, like throwing a stink bomb into the compound and taking photos when the occupants fled, or putting listening devices in groceries that were delivered to the compound. Maybe use a sound system to blast a deep, booming voice—a James Earl Jones type—that would proclaim: "This is the voice of Allah. I command you to leave the house!"

Yes, some of the ideas were crazy. Panetta didn't know if they would lead to new information. But so what? Wild ideas were better than no ideas at all.

And during that session, something else happened. Panetta could feel energy surging back into the group. In the end, that's what he wanted more than anything else. That, and Osama bin Laden—dead or alive.

COUNTDOWN:
138 DAYS

December 14, 2010
Washington, D.C.

President Obama headed to the Situation Room. Panetta was going to update the president and his White House national security team on the compound in Pakistan. Obama hadn't heard anything new since the September meeting, but he knew they wouldn't have asked for this session if they didn't have something to tell him.

The president had other things on his mind. He was packed to leave later in the day for two weeks of vacation in Hawaii. He was calling it a vacation, but Obama, like his predecessors, couldn't just turn off his cell phone and disappear. For the commander in chief there were no getaways. He'd still get his daily briefings and make and receive important calls. He just wouldn't be doing it at the White House. Maybe, if he was lucky, he could spend some time on the beach with his wife and daughters.

But before he could head to Hawaii, Obama had to attend the bin Laden briefing. He understood that even in hiding, bin Laden remained Al Qaeda's most effective recruiter. With every video, he radicalized more disaffected men and women around the world. The national security experts—and Obama's daily briefs—warned that the terrorist group was more dangerous now than it had been in years. Every day seemed to bring another terrorist bombing or plot.

Eliminating bin Laden was key to reshaping America's counterterrorism strategy. Obama believed the United States had lost its focus. Instead of concentrating on bin Laden and the others who had planned the 9/11 attacks, the United States opted into a "War on Terror" that did little to curb terrorist violence. Obama believed that taking out bin Laden was a way to remind the world that terrorism was not a monumental force, and terrorists were nothing more than "a band of deluded, vicious killers—criminals who could be captured, tried, imprisoned or killed."

Obama knew the Middle East was a tinderbox in part due to America's foreign policy mistakes. The U.S. had invaded Iraq under a failed premise promoted by intelligence officials. They'd warned that Saddam Hussein was offering a safe haven to Al Qaeda terrorists. Worse, they believed Iraq was storing weapons of mass destruction. Neither one turned out to be true.

The Iraq invasion alienated much of the Muslim world and destabilized the entire region. Iraq and Iran had been enemies for decades. They'd fought a bloody war in the 1980s. With Hussein gone, Iran's power and influence spread unchecked across the Middle East. And now, from all U.S. intelligence reports, Iran was moving ahead with a nuclear program. Obama and other world leaders worried that Iran might try to develop nuclear weapons. If that happened, the balance of power in the Middle East would change forever.

Obama didn't know what to expect from Panetta. After the last meeting, the president saw they didn't have enough information to show the terrorist was there. Anyone could be living inside that compound—an Al Qaeda leader, a criminal, or maybe some powerful family's mad granny. It was unlikely that bin Laden would be living in such a heavily populated area. That would be too risky.

Panetta's team was a late addition to this pre-vacation meeting. When the president convened his full team of White House and Cabinet advisors, it was called the National Security Council. But he still wanted to keep top officials like Secretary of State Clinton and Defense Secretary Robert Gates out of the loop on the latest bin Laden intel to prevent any

President Barack Obama with (from left to right): CIA Deputy Director Michael
Morell, CIA Director Leon Panetta, and advisors Tom Donilon and John Brennan,
in the Situation Room.

leaks. The sessions were held in the Situation Room, a place where the
nation's most carefully guarded secrets were discussed on a regular basis.

The Situation Room wasn't one office. No, it was really a suite of
rooms shrouded in secrecy. Housed in the basement of the West Wing,
the main area—called the John F. Kennedy Conference Room—could
hold a couple of dozen people. The room was dominated by a long brown
boardroom table—its top usually covered with legal pads and pens. Cell
phones or personal electronic devices had to be placed in a small box or
locker outside the room. Flat-screen television monitors dotted the drab
beige walls.

Only those with top-level security clearance were allowed inside, making it the perfect place for Panetta to share the latest intelligence from Abbottabad. With the Secret Service in place, the president entered the main
room, which was filled with people in dark suits: Panetta, Morell, Bash,
Sam, and Mike.

Panetta said he wanted to update the president on their surveillance of the compound, then turned it over to Mike. Obama listened carefully as the head of the CIA's Counterterrorism Center unreeled the latest facts.

The courier al-Kuwaiti had purchased the property under an assumed name. The compound itself was unusually spacious, much larger than the neighboring homes, and was even more secure than they'd thought. The occupants had gone to great lengths to conceal their identities. The ages of the children appeared to match those of bin Laden's known children. And the third family, like the others in the compound, never left the premises.

Sam stepped up and took over the briefing.

"There is a man," he said. "We call him The Pacer." Using aerial surveillance, they had observed this man who never left the compound. He would regularly walk in circles around the perimeter of a small garden in the courtyard before going back inside the main house. The surveillance couldn't provide them with a clear image of the man's face or height, or anything that could help them positively identify The Pacer. But that didn't dampen Sam's enthusiasm.

"We think he could be bin Laden," Sam said.

Then he showed Obama a video of The Pacer. The president could see that it was impossible to identify the person—at least from this surveillance tape. Obama showed no emotion. He soaked up the information, then asked the question on everyone's mind. "What else can we do to confirm The Pacer's identity?"

They had been working feverishly to do just that, Sam said. Any unusual movement in or near the compound was immediately noted, he explained, and they worried about arousing suspicion. If there was a hint they were being watched, The Pacer might flee in the middle of the night.

Obama looked at Sam. "What's your judgment?"

He hesitated. Anything he said would be speculation, but he had helped put this intricate puzzle together. He might not have the proof, but he knew what his gut was telling him.

"There's a good chance he's our man," he said.

Panetta agreed. He said that "it is the CIA's judgment" that al-Kuwaiti was harboring bin Laden. It was a big bureaucratic step forward. But Panetta quickly added that the agency had only "medium confidence" in the assessment, which was still based on circumstantial evidence. They still had no proof that he was in the compound.

Obama had heard enough. He knew they had enough information to at least begin developing options for a possible attack on the compound. So, in the Situation Room that day, the president turned to Panetta and said that in addition to urging the CIA director's team to continue working to identify The Pacer, he wanted Panetta to start thinking about Concepts of Operation (CONOPs)—how the United States should go after bin Laden if the president decided to act.

Obama was clear about something else: He didn't want the military involved in the planning. Not yet. Secrecy was of utmost importance. Once again Obama stressed that he only wanted a handful of people to know. If information leaked out, whatever opportunity they had to get bin Laden would be gone, and all their labor would have been wasted.

Top floor of Abbottabad compound.

The president was certain of one thing. If The Pacer really was bin Laden, they could not involve the Pakistanis. True, they had worked closely with Pakistan on some counterterrorism operations, and yes, this was deep inside Pakistani territory. But some people in the Pakistani military showed signs of ties to the Taliban, and maybe Al Qaeda. They couldn't risk someone tipping off bin Laden.

The Pakistanis would be incensed if the U.S launched an attack on Pakistani soil. Who could say how they might retaliate? But if The Pacer was bin Laden, Obama knew he might have to take that risk. Right now, it was too early to make any decisions. They needed more information—and fast.

COUNTDOWN:
133 DAYS

December 19, 2010

New York City

The alarm went off. Jessica Ferenczy lifted her head from her pillow. It was Sunday morning. No work today, but she had a little road trip planned. She jumped out of bed and started getting ready.

From upstairs came the bustle and scent of breakfast. Bacon, eggs, and a wailing child. Larry and the kids would probably ask her to join them. At one time she'd have dug in, but this time she'd politely decline. She'd tell them she needed to hit the road.

Ferenczy was getting used to living alongside a noisy young family. Larry, her supervisor, and his wife had invited her to move in a few months previous—an act of mercy. Jessica had been dealing with emotional issues at work and increasing isolation at home, but here at Larry's house, she was becoming part of the family. Ferenczy did her part, too. There were three children in the house—two toddlers and a teenage boy. When she was off-duty, she helped care for the two younger children. And you can't be depressed when you're around babies, she thought.

Ferenczy grabbed some pens and a notebook and stuffed them in her bag, snatched her jacket, and bounded up the stairs. She said goodbye to the family and hurried out of the house. When she started her car, she realized she shouldn't have skipped breakfast. On her way to the main road,

Ferenczy stopped at a 7-Eleven and grabbed an egg sandwich and coffee to go. That would have to hold her for a while.

She was driving to Montauk, a village at the furthermost tip of Long Island. During the summer, the beaches there were crowded, but no one would be around today, not with this cold wind blowing off the Atlantic. That was OK.

This was one of her special remembrance days. She planned to park the car atop the cliffs at Montauk Point State Park and sit overlooking the Atlantic Ocean. There she would enjoy the view, listen to the wind, and write.

This was their anniversary. Twelve years earlier, on December 19, Jerome Dominguez had pulled his motorcycle into the parking lot of her precinct in Manhattan and stolen her heart.

Montauk Point held special memories for her.

Dominguez loved motorcycles. He was a member of the NYPD's motorcycle unit before he transferred to the elite Emergency Service Unit. Ferenczy had never ridden on a motorcycle until she met him.

After they moved in together, he tried to teach her to drive one. She was reluctant at first, but after he bought her a new Harley-Davidson Sportster, she had to learn.

They practiced in parking lots and the streets in West Islip, Long Island, where they lived at the time. When he felt she had the hang of it, he gave her a test.

"You get onto the highway and I'll follow you in the car," Dominguez said.

"Am I ready?"

"You're ready," he said. "Just four exits up the highway."

She nodded. "I got it."

Ferenczy inserted the key in the ignition, put her hands on the grips, and rolled onto the street. She jumped onto Montauk Highway. She slowed at the fourth exit, but changed her mind. The bike felt good, the weather was perfect, and Jerome was right there on the road with her. She could almost feel him grinning. She kept going and going. At one point he pulled alongside.

"You're doing great," he shouted. "Keep going!"

So she did, for another eighty miles, until she ran out of road at the eastern tip of Long Island.

When she finally braked to a stop in the shadow of the Montauk Point Lighthouse, Dominguez leapt from his car to celebrate. They high-fived, then hugged. He was so proud of her. "That's my baby," Dominguez told everyone around them. "She rode all the way here."

They walked then, along the cliffs overlooking the ocean. They sat and watched the waves crash. They walked to the gates of Camp Hero, a World War II base with a radar tower. Jerome read the sign out front and tried to make a joke. "Hey, they named the park after me," he said. Jessica smiled. They kissed and laughed.

It was a beautiful day, in a time of her life that was filled with wonderful days. Jessica hadn't had many of those since Jerome died.

After 9/11, her job only got rougher. She transferred from Manhattan to Queens. She kept her nose down, worked hard, and kept everything inside. By 2010, she had seventeen years on the police force. People around her thought she was a badass. But inside, she was breaking down.

Then one night, she screwed up.

She and several other police officers were chasing a suspect who was fleeing from a burglary. She followed the man into a backyard. She looked inside a car parked in the driveway. When she didn't see anyone, she kept going. But an officer who was trailing her by six feet also glanced into the car, and there was the suspect, hiding inside.

"He's in the car!" the police officer shouted.

Shit. She had just practically looked the perp in the eye and didn't see him!

The officers arrested the man, but Ferenczy was consumed with guilt. She played the scenario over and over in her head. She should have spotted him. What if he had pulled a gun on another officer? She should have opened the car door.

Back at the station, Larry, her supervisor, called her into his office for a talking-to. He was pissed off. Ferenczy was a good cop, he said, but she was taking too many chances. Now she was putting other officers at risk.

He knew about Dominguez. He knew things hadn't gone well for her since he died. She lost the home they'd bought on Long Island. Her stepmother had just died, and she was trying to take care of her elderly father. She lived alone in a tiny apartment, and had stopped hanging out with her colleagues.

"You're in a rut," Larry said. "You need a change. We have room at our house. Why don't you move in with my family for a while?"

Ferenczy knew she needed help. She agreed.

And so far, things were working out. She didn't know how long she would stay, but she was in no hurry to leave. She'd started attending a counseling program, and recently had learned about a special police program for officers dealing with depression. She clearly wasn't functioning on a high level, on or off the job, but she felt some hope stirring, anyway.

Restless after the long drive, she buttoned her coat, grabbed her bag, and stepped from the car. The wind whipped off the ocean. Jessica walked to the cliffs and along the seafront. She'd forgotten her gloves, and by the time she got back to the car her hands were stiff with cold. She turned on the car, turned up the heater, and warmed her fingers in the defroster blast.

Then she pulled out her paper, uncapped a pen, and started to write:

Baby, Baby
Happy Anniversary My Love. Today is the day we met, and you changed my life forever. You gave me such a gift to make me feel so loved and appreciated. All the things I thought were my faults, were all your favorite things about me. To have been truly loved is so precious to me, and even now when I cannot hold you in my arms, I can still see your smiles and feel your kisses on my face while I sleep. Not many people

can say with such certainty that they Really love and have been loved in return.

True Love is Death's Sole Defeat. We will never be apart, as I hold you here inside me, in my heart forever. Until my days here are over and my time has slipped away, I will hold you to me until we are together again. I love you now, as I always have, as I did before we met.

Beloved Boy, Happy Anniversary Husband. I love you. I miss you so much. Until we are together again.

Jessie

It was bittersweet. He wasn't physically here in Montauk, but she felt his presence. Thinking of Jerome didn't make her cry now. It made her smile.

COUNTDOWN:

121 DAYS

December 31, 2010

Monterey, California

Leon Panetta was ready. He had put on his dark suit and polished black belt, fastened the buttons on his white shirt, and slipped on his black dress shoes. His face was shaved smooth and his hair was neatly trimmed. Perfect. Panetta was excited about this dinner party, where he and Sylvia would welcome the New Year with old friends.

It would be his last night out before heading back to Washington. Panetta had spent nearly two weeks of the holiday time at home in Monterey, California, recharging from the endless pressure and secrecy of the bin Laden operation. After his last briefing with the president, Panetta was optimistic. That day, when he returned from the briefing, he huddled with his team. Panetta reiterated what his analysts already knew: The CIA's top priority—maybe the most important case in the spy agency's history—was finding out who lived behind the compound's walls. Panetta knew he'd be facing more stress, more long hours, when he returned to work.

He was seventy-two years old. Most of his friends and colleagues had retired long ago and were enjoying life, but Panetta seemed to be working harder than ever. And that was OK. His father had instilled in him a strong work ethic. This job wasn't going to kill him. Much of his work involved reading and motivating people. But when it got too stressful, Panetta would try to find time to jump in the pool and swim laps. As a former member of Congress, he could still use the House gym.

Needless to say, Panetta was thankful for this California getaway. When he'd arrived at his childhood house deep in the Carmel Valley, he started feeling refreshed. Accompanied by Bravo, Panetta filled his days with pruning and hauling brush in the orchard. He cut firewood and trimmed the walnut trees. It was invigorating, going home, knowing where every light switch and squeaky floorboard was, caring for the trees his family had tended since 1946. The mailbox at the end of the long driveway still had "C Panetta"—for his father, Carmelo—painted in bright red letters. He'd grown up on this land, and he and his wife had raised their three sons here. His six grandchildren came to liven up the place at Christmas. The pace was a lot slower in California than in Washington, and Panetta loved that.

After leaving the Clinton administration, Panetta had thought he was done with Washington. So he and Sylvia created the Panetta Institute for Public Policy at the California State University in Monterey. He wanted to train young people in the honorable profession of public service. That's what he was doing when President Obama called.

Obama said he needed someone with integrity to run the CIA, to restore its tarnished reputation.

Panetta said he'd take the job, even though it meant less time at the institute. He left behind the long, quiet days and evenings with family and friends, and morning hours in the orchard. Sylvia didn't move to Washington with him. Panetta tried to fly home as often as he could, at least once a month. But the separation was difficult.

In Washington, Panetta rented an attic apartment from an old friend. It had one bedroom, a small living and dining area, and a bathroom. It was near Lincoln Park. Every day the man who ran the world's biggest spy agency would walk Bravo in the park before returning to his digs. His apartment in the attic was good enough. He didn't spend much time there anyway. Just about every morning, at 6:30, Panetta would jump in his car with Bravo. They wouldn't return until late at night. The CIA was able to put special equipment in the apartment so he could make classified calls.

In Monterey, Panetta was himself. He kept a low profile and blended right in with everyone else in town, picking up milk at the grocery store or sitting in the back row during Mass at the Carmel Mission. Panetta was a devout Catholic, educated by Jesuit brothers, immersed in a gospel of justice and compassion for the poor. He had instilled that in his sons. Two became attorneys, and one a cardiologist. One had served a deployment in Afghanistan with the Navy Reserve.

As much as Panetta wanted to, he couldn't shut out the world entirely. There were still moments when his mind drifted back to his office, the conference room, or the courtyard of the fortress in Abbottabad.

He was balancing a lot of competing interests. He had to keep Congress in the loop. At their meeting in September, Obama had sworn everyone to secrecy, forbidding anyone to mention the compound. But the bin Laden operation was costing a lot of money, and CIA funding was granted by Congress. Panetta needed to go to Capitol Hill for a "reprogramming" of funds to continue the stakeout. Just before the holiday, Panetta, without Obama's knowledge, had briefed key congressional leaders about the operation. He promised to keep them updated and asked the leaders not to leak the information.

It was a risky move, but Panetta didn't have a choice. During his confirmation hearing, he had given Congress his word that he'd keep them informed of CIA operations. He knew congressional leaders were entitled by law to know. Still, he knew Obama couldn't find out he'd told them, and neither could anyone else on the bin Laden team. And now the November midterm election had put Republicans in charge of Congress, raising the stakes even higher.

When Panetta got back to Washington, he'd have to tell a small but new group of senators and congressmen why he needed extra funding. People with political agendas, people who might not feel obliged to keep a secret. Republicans had already started fighting Obama over every piece of legislation. Would one of them scuttle months of work to score some political points?

And before he left for Monterey, Panetta did one other thing without the president's permission. He briefed the leadership of the Department of Defense. His trusted aide Morell, accompanied him when he met in private with Defense Secretary Gates; Admiral Michael Mullen, the chairman of the Joint Chiefs of Staff; Marine Corps General James "Hoss" Cartwright, the vice chairman of the Joint Chiefs; and Michael Vickers, the undersecretary of defense for intelligence.

Panetta told them that CIA analysts believed they had found bin Laden. The purpose of the meeting was simple: Even though the president didn't want to "read in" the military, Panetta wanted to give them a heads-up. At some point, he knew they might need the Pentagon's help with the mission, and he didn't want the DoD blindsided. Plus, it would be good to have early buy-in, especially from Gates. He knew Gates might have reservations about a possible attack on the compound because of his experience in a failed operation back in 1980 to rescue American hostages being held by Iran. At the time, Gates was an executive assistant to the CIA director and had been involved in the planning. And the defense secretary had never forgotten the disaster.

Panetta didn't want to think about all that now. Tonight, he wanted to relax at The Sardine Factory, a venerable seafood and steak house on Monterey's Cannery Row. It was a local institution, with occasional celebrity sightings and movie shoots. Clint Eastwood had filmed several scenes there for his 1971 movie *Play Misty for Me.*

The owner, Ted Balestreri, had been Panetta's friend for forty years, and had recently teased him during a round of golf: "You can't even find your golf ball. How are you going to find bin Laden?"

When the Panettas arrived, they walked down a flight of stairs and joined a table of some fifteen couples in the wine cellar. Leon felt at ease. He talked and drank and hugged friends and laughed—a laugh so big his face would crinkle up. With classical music playing in the background,

Balestreri made sure everyone had far more than enough to eat. It was an endless meal, with waiters bringing out tray after tray of food. It was exactly what Panetta needed.

After a few glasses of wine, Balestreri began bragging about the restaurant's cellar, and a rare jewel that had fallen into his hands: a bottle of 1870 Château Lafite Rothschild.

Balestreri's friends quizzed him on what occasion might make him uncork the $10,000 bottle. "I'm not going to open it up," he said. But Balestreri turned to Panetta. "When Leon catches Osama bin Laden, then we'll open that bottle."

Sylvia glanced at her husband and saw "a certain glint in his eye."

"You're on," Panetta said.

There was no more talk of bin Laden that night. The group welcomed 2011 in the accustomed way. On the ride home, Panetta smiled to himself. If everything worked out, he'd not only get rid of the world's most wanted terrorist. He'd get to sample a really fine wine.

COUNTDOWN:

120 DAYS

January 1, 2011
Jalalabad, Afghanistan

Robert O'Neill jumped out of bed, pulled on a pair of shorts and a T-shirt. He slipped his feet into flip-flops and headed to the Operations Center. It was the first morning of a new year, and O'Neill realized he was dressed for a campground resort, not a military base in the middle of an Afghanistan war zone.

So much had changed with this deployment. No more bullets whistling past his ears, no more jumping out of strike-force helicopters into the dark. O'Neill was still a Navy SEAL, but now he was management. He worked behind the battle lines, directing operations from the base in Jalalabad and keeping the top brass informed about where "high-value targets" might be.

There wasn't much demand for spit-polished collar brass and salutes these days. O'Neill had let his beard grow, seeing as it was winter. It came in red.

Things were a little slower than usual. Fighting usually slackened in midwinter as opposing sides dug in to establish gains already made, or made plans to retake losses. This winter was no exception. Coalition troops were solidifying positions in former Taliban strongholds in the south, holding ground and working with locals.

Meanwhile intelligence showed that the Taliban continued trying to create a shadow government in parts of eastern Afghanistan.

For O'Neill, the most dangerous operation so far in this deployment had been bringing back an important insurgent who had been captured in the remote Kunar Province. O'Neill was asked to coordinate the handoff. He went along, just to be sure everything went smoothly.

Even a simple prisoner exchange was fraught with peril. As O'Neill's van approached the designated spot for the exchange, he became concerned about a setup. Was there a suicide bomber waiting near the designated exchange site? When his van approached the other vehicle, the men transporting the prisoner looked at O'Neill and hesitated—with his long red beard, he looked more like a local than a SEAL. But O'Neill didn't hesitate. When the vehicles stopped moving, he jumped out, grabbed the prisoner, threw him into his van, and took off.

Here at the Jalalabad base were all the comforts of home. The place had been upgraded significantly since he was there last. He now had his own dormitory room with a private bathroom and personal computer. In the past, his days had started at sundown, but now he rose at the break of dawn. He was almost safe here. Once in a while, a mortar might land inside the perimeter, but the base was so fortified that injuries were unlikely.

O'Neill's family still worried about him. When his dad called, O'Neill couldn't tell him much, but he tried to sound optimistic. He turned the conversation to news from home, and usually asked his father to send something he couldn't get on base—like tins of chewing tobacco. He was just then looking out for a delivery of Velveeta cheese and Rotel salsa, to make hot nacho dip for their upcoming Super Bowl party. No one knew yet which teams would play in Super Bowl XLV on February 6, as the NFL playoffs were still going on. He knew it wouldn't be the Washington Redskins, his favorite team. They'd had another miserable season.

This morning, like the others, O'Neill walked into the Operations Center and grabbed some espresso. He checked his emails and looked at reports from Operations. It was important to keep his commander informed of what was happening in different spots. The war was slowly moving nearer to the Pakistan border, where the Taliban and Al Qaeda were dug in.

The bad guys didn't play by American rules. They were waging guerrilla war, crisscrossing the border without any restraints. Meanwhile, U.S. forces had to have a good reason to launch a strike inside Pakistan. It was a frustrating, sometimes infuriating game of whack-a-mole.

O'Neill didn't hold out much hope they'd ever find bin Laden. By now, the head of Al Qaeda had become a ghost, a punchline. Sometimes when they found an insurgent, an interrogator would jokingly ask, "Where's bin Laden?" The insurgent never knew. No one knew, right? The answer was always "You'll never find him." But even after all these years, bin Laden was bigger than life, the spiritual leader. As long as he might be alive, the terrorists had hope.

O'Neill read through the reports. The night had passed quietly. He debated whether to go to the gym now or later. He tried to keep his mind focused on here-and-now Jalalabad, but sometimes he thought about home, his family, the future.

He had been in the military for fifteen years. He'd decided to go for twenty, to work his way up to master chief petty officer. That would mean more money when he retired. And when he retired, what then? Where would he live? Virginia Beach? San Diego? What would he do there?

O'Neill couldn't be a SEAL forever. He wasn't in the same kind of danger as the previous deployments, but you never knew what might happen. The roads outside the base were sown with IEDs, and it wasn't unusual for people to be blown up just driving out to pick up prisoners. Enemy snipers lurked in the hills overlooking the base, and now and then somebody would take a hit in the head.

How many more deployments did he have in him? How long could he keep saying goodbye to the people who loved him?

His family. His wife . . . sometimes her voice, a little phrase she'd said on the last phone call, would skitter across his mind. He'd shut it down instantly. In Afghanistan, he kept his personal life neatly compartmentalized.

He had to get through the day. He focused on what he had to do, and he did it well.

After hours he sometimes thought about home. He let his gaze linger on the drawings and photos his kids gave him. He wondered what they'd learned in school that day, what they'd had for breakfast, if their teachers were nice. When they thought of their dad, what did they remember?

O'Neill never went too far down that road. It was too many goodbyes, he knew. One of these years his kids would be gone, grown up, and he'd have missed out on most of being their dad.

Being a SEAL wasn't a job or a career. It was a way of life. It took over everything.

O'Neill knew he was good for maybe one more deployment. As far as Afghanistan, who knew when Americans would leave? It certainly wouldn't be anytime soon.

For now, he was taking it one day at a time. He kept his mind off that other shit. He sighed, signed off the computer screen, and rose from his desk. The gym. A good workout would clear his head.

COUNTDOWN:
107 DAYS

January 14, 2011
Langley, Virginia

Panetta returned from his vacation just in time for the Arab Spring to break out. On a screen by his desk, he watched the celebration in the streets of Tunisia. For almost a month, protesters had called for longtime President Zine El Abidine Ben Ali to step down. They'd suffered under his authoritarian rule for years, and wanted to taste freedom for themselves.

And now the old autocrat was on the run. Panetta and much of the intelligence world were stunned to learn that Ben Ali had fled Tunisia and was seeking refuge over the border in Libya.

The CIA director wondered which Middle East regime might be next in the pro-democracy sea change. His money was on Egypt, a country ruled for decades by strongman Hosni Mubarak.

Everybody loves a move to democracy, but Panetta was worried that regime change chaos might create a power vacuum in the Middle East. The sudden loss of a longtime leader left an opening for fanatical anti-American groups to step in and take over—creating a danger to U.S. interests.

It had happened before and led to one of the greatest failures for the U.S. military. In Iran in 1979, massive protests against Shah Mohammad Reza led to his overthrow. The Shah's repressive regime was replaced by an Islamic republic led by Ayatollah Ruhollah Khomeini, a fiery Islamic fundamentalist who had been expelled from Iran for speaking out against the Shah.

Khomeini's extremist Revolutionary Guard had cracked down on anyone opposed to their strict new religious rules. The Shah, who had been suffering from cancer, fled to the United States for medical treatment. On November 4, 1979, Islamic militants stormed the U.S. embassy and took fifty-two Americans hostage. They demanded the Shah be returned to Iran to face trial for his reign of terror.

President Jimmy Carter refused. Operation Eagle Claw, a military rescue operation, was mounted to free the hostages. In April 1980, an elite team was organized to take back the embassy compound. But at a rendezvous point in the Iranian desert, a severe sandstorm caused several helicopters to malfunction, including one that veered on takeoff into a large EC-130 transport plane. Eight American servicemen were killed, and the mission was aborted. It was an international humiliation that likely cost Carter his reelection.

The hostages were finally released on January 20, 1981, a few hours after the new U.S. president, Ronald Reagan, was inaugurated. All told, they were held 444 days.

That failed effort still cast a pall over the U.S. military. Panetta knew that if The Pacer was bin Laden and they had to go in and get him, they wouldn't make the same mistakes. By all accounts, the U.S. military—especially Special Operation units—had come a long way since 1980.

But history had a way of repeating itself. Panetta understood they had to closely monitor the outcomes of this Arab Spring. What if it spread to nations like Libya, where the U.S. was already despised, or Iran, where another ayatollah was now the nation's supreme leader? Worse, what if it spread to pro-American nations like Egypt?

Mubarak was Egypt's ruthless dictator, but one of America's strongest allies in the Middle East. Over the years, he had kept the peace between his nation and its neighbor, Israel. His government was stable until protesters began demanding reforms, clashing with Egyptian police and military, demanding that Mubarak step down. It was a crisis Panetta and the administration were monitoring closely.

He pulled out the briefing files. Egypt and Mubarak—just one of the stack of issues waiting for Panetta now that he was back from vacation. He went over them, one by one. He got the latest updates about the surveillance of the compound. Nothing new on that front. Analysts said they were working on several leads in the drive to identify The Pacer.

Meanwhile, Panetta continued quietly informing key congressional leaders about the bin Laden case. Panetta was trying to build trust at a time when the agency's relationship with both political parties was frayed. He believed and preached to everyone inside the CIA that they should tell both Republican and Democratic congressional leadership details about the agency's operations, including the new one. "You shouldn't try to spin anything. You shouldn't try to hide anything. You should be completely transparent with them," Panetta said.

And congressional leaders responded. Panetta had known many of them for years, since his own days on Capitol Hill. During meetings with the oversight committees, Panetta sometimes greeted members with an embrace. He liked to have them all sit around a table and chat. It was more informal, and made them feel more comfortable—it reminded everyone they all were on the same team.

Panetta took account of the shifts in the power balance over at the Capitol. The GOP now controlled both chambers of Congress, so he asked Mike Rogers, the new chair of the House Intelligence Committee, and the committee's new staff director, Michael Allen, to join him for dinner in his private dining room, just down the hall from his office.

By now, the seventh floor of CIA headquarters had become Panetta's home in Washington. He certainly spent more time there than in his attic apartment. So in the quiet of his office with his dog by his side, Panetta briefed Rogers and Allen on everything intelligence analysts had uncovered. He told them about the compound in Abbottabad and the CIA's efforts to find out who lived there. They listened in silence. And before they left, they promised not to say a word.

Morell was one of the few people who knew that Panetta had briefed congressional leaders as well as the military. He told Panetta he supported his decision, but it was fraught with risk. How long until the president found out? And what then?

Right now, Panetta had other concerns. In the presidential briefing in December, Obama had asked him to explore options for an attack on the compound. Now Panetta was putting together a plan for how the CIA's special operations team would go after bin Laden, once they could prove he was The Pacer. But Panetta knew the CIA's paramilitary force could only go so far. They needed more people to advise on logistics—the experts at the Pentagon.

Panetta didn't know it yet, but someone there was waiting for his call.

COUNTDOWN:
93 DAYS

January 28, 2011
Washington, D.C.

With the late afternoon sunlight fading over Washington, D.C., Vice Admiral William McRaven caromed from CIA headquarters to the Pentagon, from luncheon to briefing to meeting. It would almost be a relief to hop on a military plane in the evening and wake up again in Afghanistan.

As the man in charge of the U.S. Joint Special Operations Command, McRaven planned missions for the military's elite counterterrorism units, like the SEALs, Delta Force, and the Green Berets. He'd been summoned to the nation's capital by the Pentagon's top brass to meet with the CIA's Morell, who wanted to brief him about something important.

He had been expecting the call. As much as Obama wanted to keep the bin Laden case a secret, McRaven had already heard bits and pieces. In December, during a visit to Afghanistan, Mullen, the chairman of the Joint Chiefs of Staff, pulled McRaven aside. The CIA might have a lead on bin Laden, he said. "They may call you to come back and take a look at the intelligence."

McRaven shrugged. Yeah right, he thought. He had seen a lot of leads before and they all seemed to evaporate.

But a month later, here he was, at CIA headquarters with Vickers, the undersecretary of defense for intelligence. One of Morell's assistants greeted them in the lobby. He led them straight to his boss's office, where

Morell, Gary, Sam, and Mike were waiting. McRaven and Vickers grabbed chairs while Morell shut the door.

Morell didn't waste any time. His team told McRaven and Vickers everything the CIA knew about the compound and The Pacer. They handed out surveillance photographs of the compound and The Pacer so they could see for themselves. Morell explained the painstaking research that led them to the Abbottabad fortress and the man who lived so secretly inside.

"We believe The Pacer is bin Laden," Morell said. "We're working hard to confirm his identity."

McRaven paid attention to every word. When Morell finished, he smiled. "Congratulations to you all," he said. "This is an incredible piece of work."

Morell shared other details, too. In a meeting before Christmas, Obama had asked Panetta to keep up the surveillance of the compound, and to start putting together options for a possible raid. One option involved using the CIA's special operations teams. That plan called for agency operators to gradually work their way into position close to the fortress, then, at night, charge the compound, capture bin Laden, and smuggle him out of Pakistan.

But after evaluating details, agency officials told Panetta they didn't think the CIA could take the compound and capture the occupants all on their own. Panetta came to the same conclusion. An operation of this size and complexity would require the skills and experience of military Special Forces.

Panetta had explained that to Obama a few days earlier, during a January 24 meeting in the Situation Room. Obama agreed, and asked Panetta to bring military leaders into the bin Laden case. Panetta let out a great, silent sigh of relief. The president didn't know that a month earlier, Panetta had informed the Pentagon's top military leaders.

"That's why you're here," Morell said to McRaven. Then he asked the admiral a question, "If you had to take down this compound, how would you do it?"

McRaven shrugged. This raid wouldn't be much different than thousands of others he had conducted in his long career, he said. They'd need a team of special operators, Delta Force or SEALs. Under the cover of darkness, helicopters would hover over the target while the men fast-roped to the ground and methodically worked their way into the compound. They'd kill everything that got in their way until they reached the target. If he surrendered, fine, they'd capture him. If he resisted, they'd kill him and get the hell out of there. Pretty simple, right?

But there was a twist that would make this mission a great deal more complicated. They were flying into another country without permission. "It might be harder getting out than getting in," McRaven said.

Morell nodded. That was something they'd have to discuss—what would happen if Pakistani police or military responded during the raid? How would they handle that?

They'd work that out later. For now, McRaven said, he would be happy to help with the planning. The briefing was over. McRaven and Vickers left the building. But outside, as he walked to the SUV, McRaven knew this mission was right in the special ops wheelhouse.

America's War on Terror depended more and more on special operations units than regular U.S. forces. There hadn't been a traditional battle—with major U.S. forces in an all-out assault—since Tora Bora in December of 2001.

Special units went in after high-value targets, the people who were leading the insurgency that had planted IEDs and terrorized the people of Iraq and Afghanistan. These small units could drop in and get out of dangerous, remote places quickly. They hit their targets and disappeared into the night.

McRaven was the perfect choice to lead this new kind of warfare. He had literally written the book on special operations. He was tall and handsome, with a rugged, friendly face, a Texan who was outgoing but not loud.

Admiral William McRaven.

He was a son of the regiment. His father, Colonel Claude McRaven, had flown Spitfire fighter planes in World War II, appeared in Wheaties commercials, and played two seasons of pro football with the then Cleveland Rams of the National Football League, before continuing his career as a U.S. Air Force officer.

Bill McRaven, his only son, was born near Fort Bragg, North Carolina. The family soon moved to Lackland Air Force Base in San Antonio, Texas, where young McRaven excelled at sports. He attended the University of Texas, and signed up for the Navy ROTC while he explored his career options.

He fell in love with a pretty young woman from Dallas named Georgeann Brady. He decided to take up his ROTC commission in the navy, but he didn't want to be a regular officer. McRaven wanted to be a SEAL.

He graduated in 1977, married Georgeann, and began his journey.

Although McRaven was a good athlete, BUD/S pushed him to the edge. He managed to make it through, and worked his way up the command structure.

It was an excellent time to be a keen young officer. Ronald Reagan was inaugurated as president in 1981, and initiated a military buildup meant to counter Soviet expansion. His Cold War budget likewise fortified the SEALs and other Special Forces programs.

The Soviet Union began to crumble in 1989, but other threats to the United States quickly filled the vacuum. Iraqi leader Saddam Hussein invaded Kuwait in 1990, and President George H. W. Bush put together a coalition to fight the dictator. McRaven was part of Operation Desert Shield, which liberated Kuwait and sent Hussein's troops straggling in retreat back to Iraq.

After the war, McRaven earned a master's degree at the Naval Postgraduate School in Monterey, California. He saw a need for a graduate-level program in special operations warfare—not just for the navy, but throughout the armed services. McRaven helped create the school's special operations and low intensity conflict curriculum, and in 1996 was the program's first graduate. His master's thesis, "The Theory of Special Operations," broke new ground.

McRaven's paper reviewed a series of daring twentieth-century commando operations, including a 1943 glider rescue of Mussolini ordered by Hitler, and the 1976 Israeli operation to free hostages in Entebbe, Uganda. It detailed how a small group of highly trained, well-rehearsed soldiers can use stealth to maintain short-term superiority over larger or better-armed forces. The keys to successful missions, he wrote, are simplicity, security, repetition, surprise, speed, and purpose.

His master's thesis was published as a book. It quickly became the bible for military special operations units throughout the world. McRaven used those principles to develop a model for special operations to shape U.S. military strategy.

Still, McRaven was not an academic theorist. During his long career, he had personally commanded or carried out more than a thousand special operations in some of the most dangerous places imaginable, mostly going after high-value targets in Afghanistan.

While parachuting in 2001, McRaven was knocked semiconscious and plunged four thousand feet before his chute opened. The accident broke his pelvis and fractured his back. He took months to recover, but the accident only bolstered his die-hard reputation.

He was in charge of the 2009 rescue of Richard Phillips, a ship captain who was captured by Somali pirates. President Obama described McRaven as a "can-do guy. Plain spoken with a dry sense of humor."

Now McRaven leaned back in his seat as the SUV weaved in and out of traffic. It was only a short drive from the CIA to the Pentagon, but it gave McRaven enough time to think over what he'd say to his bosses.

Here was another high-profile mission, a challenge he could get his teeth into. The intelligence was interesting, but McRaven also knew there had been dozens of bin Laden sightings over the years, in places all over the world. Bin Laden was the Middle East version of Elvis Presley. Still, this lead seemed the most compelling of the lot.

McRaven shifted into planning mode. He'd keep the operation simple, and once they had a team in place they'd rehearse like crazy. This mission would be extra complicated, but if he followed the steps in his own hand-book, maybe—just maybe—they could pull it off.

He and Vickers made their way to the defense secretary's office, where Gates and Mullen were waiting. McRaven glanced out the window at the stunning view of the Potomac and the historic center of Washington, D.C. Portraits of Lincoln, George Washington, and old soldiers looked down on them from the walls.

"What do you think, Bill?" Gates said.

"Sir, it's a compound. We do compound raids every night in Af-ghanistan," he said. Arriving at the target undetected might be the most challenging part, but once they got there, it would be "pretty straight-forward."

"How many men would you need?" Mullen asked. McRaven thought about that. It was a large compound, around thirty thousand square feet.

"Probably twenty-five to thirty men," he said.

Mullen nodded. "OK, Bill. I don't know that we need to do anything right now. The CIA has the lead." At some point they might ask for Mc-Raven's help with planning the mission, Mullen said.

"No worries, sir. We'll be standing by to help with whatever they need," McRaven said.

"How long are you in town?" Mullen asked.

McRaven said he was headed back to Afghanistan in a few hours. But he said he could return to the United States whenever they needed him.

He rose from his chair. Mullen stopped him. He had something impor-tant to say. "Bill, you can't tell anyone else about this mission. If word were to leak out, it would be disastrous."

McRaven said he understood. "But if I put together a mission, I'll have to bring some others in."

McRaven and Vickers left the Pentagon and went their separate ways. McRaven settled into the military plane for the long flight back, and pon-dered the mission for much of the next seventeen hours.

The last year had been a bumpy ride. He'd been diagnosed with chronic lymphocytic leukemia, a type of blood cancer. He had refused to leave his command in Afghanistan. They were fighting the Taliban. He had a job to do.

This mission might take a whole lot more of his time and energy, and McRaven was already fighting cancer. He could pull himself off the mis-sion now and no one would say a word.

But he might have a shot at getting bin Laden.

No, he was going to keep going. This was no time to quit.

COUNTDOWN:
75 DAYS

February 15, 2011
Langley, Virginia

Another day, another crisis. Panetta prepared for a day filled with meetings. The pace had picked up in the last couple of months with the Arab Spring, and now a CIA agent was facing murder charges in Pakistan. An Al Qaeda bomber had been arrested in Abbottabad of all places, and that turned up the heat on the bin Laden lead. Panetta laid his hand on Bravo's head and felt the big dog's tail slowly wag under the desk. Pure stress relief, that dog.

He had just returned to his office after a White House session with Tom Donilon and John Brennan, two of Obama's top national security advisors. Panetta met with them once a week to update them on issues facing the United States, as well as covert CIA operations. They in turn would relay the information to Obama.

But today, Panetta had something special to communicate. Time was running out for The Pacer in his Abbottabad courtyard—they'd have to move soon or risk losing their chance.

Panetta was taking the next step, meeting up with "Hoss" Cartwright, the vice chairman of the Joint Chiefs of Staff, to create "a real set of options" for the president's decision-making.

Over the last month, so many major events had unfolded that it was hard to keep on top of them all. The bin Laden operation was the top priority, but there were other serious issues, too.

Pro-democracy uprisings had been spreading across the Middle East. In Egypt, President Hosni Mubarak had been driven from office that month, after his military units refused to use force against protesters. Mubarak was a corrupt old dictator, but Egypt had kept the peace with Israel for thirty years.

What would happen next in Egypt? If radical Islamists took over, the entire Middle East would light up—Egypt was one of a handful of Arab nations that recognized Israel as a legitimate country.

Now protests were starting up in Morocco, as well as Libya and Syria and Yemen.

While Mubarak had been quick to use the military and secret police to silence opponents, his rule paled in comparison to Libya's Muammar al-Gaddafi and Syria's Bashar al-Assad. Both men were brutal dictators. They didn't hesitate to kill opponents. Peaceful protests? No way. It was likely that only armed revolt would remove Gaddafi and Assad from power.

Panetta's other months-long diplomatic nightmare was Raymond Davis, a CIA contractor in Pakistan. A security expert hired to protect American officials, Davis had been stuck in traffic in Lahore the previous month. Two armed men on a black motorcycle stopped by his car. One jumped off the bike and pointed his gun at Davis.

Davis pulled out a Glock 9-millimeter pistol and shot them both dead. He jumped out of his car, photographed the dying man who had pulled the gun on him, then called the American consulate.

A crowd of people rushed to the scene, surrounded Davis, and refused to let him leave. Meanwhile, a consulate car rushing to the scene struck and killed a pedestrian.

When Pakistani police searched Davis's car, they found the pistol, five magazines, a GPS device, and a Motorola radio. They concluded that Davis was a CIA officer.

The Pakistani public was calling for Davis's execution. Obama asked Panetta to defuse the situation. The relationship between the United States and Pakistan was rocky enough already.

Panetta called his counterpart, Ahmad Shuja Pasha, Pakistan's intelligence chief. He told Pasha he would hold him personally responsible for Davis's safety. Meantime, Davis languished in a Pakistani jail, charged with two counts of murder.

Then things got weird. Umar Patek, an Indonesian Al Qaeda terrorist implicated in a 2002 bombing in Bali that killed more than two hundred people, suddenly turned up in Pakistan. After nine years on the lam, he was picked up by Pakistan's ISI authorities at the end of January . . . in Abbottabad.

What the hell was he doing in Abbottabad? Was he hoping to meet with bin Laden? If so, would he disclose that to Pakistani officials?

Gary told Panetta that time was running out. "We have to act now," he warned Panetta.

Panetta didn't need Gary to remind him. These operations took time. Everyone was already working long hours, looking at all the options. They weren't hitting a house in Brooklyn. They were going into a heavily armed fortress in a nation ten thousand miles away.

Everyone had to be on board with the operation. And that meant endless meetings with all the parties. They were still drawing up plans to get bin Laden if they could prove he was in the compound. McRaven had just joined the team. After meeting with Morell, he sent two aides to the CIA to draw up plans for an assault on the fortress in Abbottabad. Panetta hoped to present all the options to Obama soon.

At his meeting with Donilon and Brennan, Panetta filled them in on everything the CIA was considering. They were Obama's gatekeepers. Panetta knew they'd take the latest news to their boss. It would show the president that the spy agency was doing the "nitty-gritty work" as promised.

Obama was a stickler for updates. He didn't micromanage. He just wanted to make sure everyone was doing their job, and reported their progress to him in a timely manner.

More than anything else, he wanted to make sure there were no leaks. Now, with the Defense Department involved, the circle of information was widening. Obama still demanded the fewest possible people know details about the man in Abbottabad.

Donilon and Brennan heard it all at the session. Panetta described several proposals but reminded them that they were still working out the details. The men said they understood. After an hour, Panetta left.

The bin Laden operation was moving along, and Panetta let himself feel good about that. But his mind kept returning to Davis, the CIA man in the Lahore lockup. They had to get him out of there before the bin Laden hunt picked up too much momentum. If he was still in Pakistan when the United States went after bin Laden, Panetta knew he'd have another horror show to handle.

COUNTDOWN:
70 DAYS

February 20, 2011

Virginia Beach, Virginia

With another deployment in the rearview mirror, Will Chesney was home and already restless. Family, friends, maybe some vacation—he had a few weeks to burn. He'd do another round of training in Florida before moving on to his next assignment. Where that would take him, and when, he didn't know.

It was silly, spending his downtime on base, but Chesney was headed to the kennels again, to visit his buddy. One thing was certain about the near future: Cairo would not be with him on his next overseas tour. Chesney could only do two tours as a dog handler. For the next round, Chesney would go back to being a shooter.

Cairo was close to six years old, and had lived through two deployments. The injuries he'd suffered were starting to take a toll, Chesney could see. But the navy, in its wisdom, thought Cairo still had more to offer. He was being scaled down to backup canine, a spare dog. He'd spend most of his days in a kennel in Virginia, or on training exercises, but Cairo would still be available for deployments if he was needed.

If things went right, Chesney would continue to play a role in Cairo's life. In a year or two, Cairo would retire from the military. Then, Chesney would do everything possible to adopt him. Dog handlers in the military—like in law enforcement—were given the "right of first refusal" when their dogs' careers came to an end. Chesney wanted nothing more than to keep Cairo with him for the rest of the dog's life.

The two had become brothers in arms. They'd served in war zones together, gone after the bad guys together. Hell, how many times had Cairo saved his life, sniffing out insurgents before they opened fire, or detecting bombs before they exploded? Cairo deserved to have a little peace in his old age, and Chesney knew when the dog retired, he would be there for him.

Chesney didn't have many ties in his life, no steady girlfriend or wife or children. The big black-and-tan dog had become his near family, by his side through good times and bad. How many times had Cairo jumped into Chesney's lap when he sensed the SEAL was having a bad day? And how could Chesney stay angry when Cairo was wagging his tail? The SEAL always felt good when the dog was around. Just remembering the fun they'd had . . . like the time in Afghanistan when he dressed up the pooch and brought a load of joy to the whole barracks.

Chesney had overslept that morning. When he got up from his cot, Cairo was pacing around the hut with a guilty look on his face.

"What's up, buddy?" Chesney asked.

When Chesney put on his boots, he found them "practically swimming in a puddle of liquid." Cairo had peed in Chesney's boots.

"What the hell?" he grumbled.

Apparently, Cairo had wanted to go outside to relieve himself, but Chesney had taken an Ambien tablet to help catch up with sleep between missions. Cairo had tried to wake him, but to no avail—so the dog did what he had to do. Chesney knew Cairo was well trained. He had never had an accident before. But if he had to go, why did he do it in Chesney's boots?

Chesney took Cairo outside. When they got back inside the hut, he decided to turn the tables on his pooch.

"Let's do a little boot work," he said.

Military dogs had little shoes to protect their feet from broken glass when they worked in urban areas. Cairo hated his. Putting them on his feet would be a fitting but harmless punishment, Chesney thought.

Once Chesney got the boots on the dog, he struggled not to laugh. The big dog took one step forward, two steps back. He looked like he was tiptoeing across the hot sand on a crowded beach. Chesney grabbed a pair of earmuffs—the kind they used to block out the sound from loud explosions—and slipped them over Cairo's ears. Then he placed Cairo's "doggie goggles" over the dog's eyes. Now Cairo looked like a comical cartoon superhero. No one in particular. Maybe a military Scooby-Doo.

Some of Chesney's buddies walked into the hut and saw him laughing so hard he couldn't catch his breath. One look at Cairo and they joined Chesney. The room filled with laughter.

Finally, after snapping a few pictures, Chesney removed Cairo's boots, earmuffs, and goggles. He gave the pooch a big hug and apologized.

"Sorry about that," Chesney said to him. "I know you didn't mean to piss in my boots. It was totally my fault."

The SEALs took Cairo outside and played fetch until they all felt worn

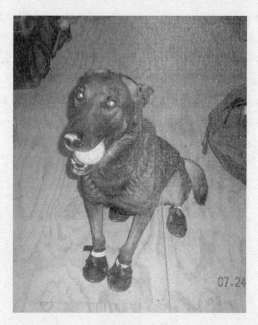

Cairo dressed up.

out. Yes, Cairo had become more than his teammate or friend. He was almost like a shrink. How many times did Chesney find himself talking to
the dog, bouncing ideas off him? Chesney felt empty when Cairo wasn't
around. He didn't open up to many people. There were times when he felt
a little depressed and anxious—early signs of post-traumatic stress disorder. He had seen a lot of action in Iraq, some of it brutal urban warfare. He
had always been resilient. He wasn't always the best athlete or swimmer,
but no one worked harder than he did. He had enough inner strength and
self-will to thrive under all kinds of pressure.

But for some reason, this separation from Cairo, this goodbye—
although temporary—was harder than before. His friend Angelo would be
Cairo's handler through the months until Chesney could adopt him. But it
still didn't make it any easier.

For now, Chesney resolved to distance himself slowly from Cairo.
With time, maybe he'd feel better. He would be headed to Florida in a few
weeks for ocean training. He could scuba dive during the day and relax
at night with his buddies. He'd fill up on good seafood. Maybe he would
drink a little. Nothing too crazy.

Chesney pulled up to the kennel and jumped out of the car. A few moments later, there was Cairo, his tail wagging madly. Chesney grinned. It
was going to be hard leaving Cairo. But for now, he wasn't going to think
about it. He was just going to relax and enjoy the day with man's best friend.

COUNTDOWN:
65 DAYS

February 25, 2011
Langley, Virginia

Friday night, late winter. The CIA headquarters was almost dark and largely empty.

A group of black Chevy Suburbans rolled through quiet Washington suburbs, headed west, and pulled up to a secondary entrance. Most of the thousands of men and women who kept the federal government ticking over the course of each day were home with their families. Courthouses, offices, monuments, and museums stood silent in the winter chill.

Panetta thought it was the perfect time to hold an important meeting.

The CIA director was spinning a web like a seasoned spy, or a wily politician. And by now he was both. He knew how to navigate the complicated bureaucracy and schmooze the right people, and he left nothing to chance. This session was characteristically strategic.

Panetta knew his team was right—they had to push hard and get things in place soon. If they were going to get The Pacer, they had to act fast. They couldn't do anything without the president's go-ahead, and Donilon, who had been promoted to national security advisor in October, was the key to the president.

Panetta told Donilon he wanted to meet on March 4, to update him on the latest bin Laden developments. He had a list of options for the president to consider, ways to get The Pacer if he turned out to be bin Laden.

Panetta wanted to be prepared for the Donilon briefing, so he'd called in the military. Tonight he would share everything he had—all the intelligence his analysts had collected about the compound at the end of a dead-end street in Abbottabad. This was his dress rehearsal.

The first SUV opened up, and out came General Cartwright, a four-star general and a cyberwarfare and nuclear weapons expert. In another Suburban came Vickers and McRaven, just back from another trip to Afghanistan.

Cartwright, Vickers, McRaven, and some of their staff headed to the large conference room down the hall from Panetta's office on the seventh floor. Panetta and Morell met them there, along with an impressive replica of the fortress in Abbottabad.

Officials with the National Geospatial-Intelligence Agency (NGA) had analyzed all the satellite images, then built a scale model of the entire compound. Four feet long by four feet wide, it was accurate down to each bush and tree.

McRaven immediately stepped over to the compound at the far end of the conference table. It's one thing to talk about a raid in the abstract; another to see the target right in front of you.

Panetta tried to keep his information sessions informal. Tonight was no exception. He was going to "talk about what makes the most sense in terms of the operation," or, as he put it: "How the hell would we get him out?" He knew the session could go on for a while, so he had sandwiches and soda on hand. Some of the visitors helped themselves to food and sat at the long wooden table.

The military officials already knew bits and pieces. But tonight, Panetta told them everything the CIA knew about the compound, The Pacer, and the civilians in the neighborhood.

This meeting would prepare them for Donilon and the president. It also, Panetta hoped, would eliminate any interagency distrust or competitiveness. In the ongoing hunt for high-value targets in Iraq and Afghanistan, there was often tension between the military intelligence teams and the CIA agents on the ground. Panetta went out of his way to ensure every-thing ran smoothly and communication channels were clear. This wasn't the time for turf wars. They were on the same side.

This mission, no matter who carried it out, was going to be dangerous as hell. Abbottabad was a city of two hundred thousand people, about two hours north of the national capital of Islamabad. By Pakistani standards, it was affluent. It was home to the Pakistan Army's military academy, a large ammunition depot, a barracks that housed a Pakistan Army infantry bat-talion, and several police stations.

If that wasn't bad enough, the compound was a half mile from a main highway that cut through the city. There were several houses near the com-pound, and a densely populated neighborhood not too far away.

While Panetta talked, McRaven stood up and circled the model. The main house was three stories tall. To get to it, you'd have to scale high con-crete perimeter walls.

The walls surrounding the north, east, and west sides were twelve feet

Scale model of Abbottabad compound.

tall. The south-facing wall was a full eighteen feet high, blocking the interior from the view of anyone in the city. The driveway came in from the north, through a metal double door.

Inside was the main house and small guest quarters, and a smaller building on one side of the driveway. A few goats and chickens were kept in a courtyard. McRaven noticed that one could not easily move from the courtyard to the living areas without passing through several locked metal gates.

What worried McRaven most was what he couldn't see. They didn't have a layout of the interior of the living quarters. Who knew what kind of measures had been put in place to protect bin Laden? Were there tunnels? Were they booby-trapped? Surely if bin Laden lived there, he had an escape route. Were the grounds or interiors laced with explosives that could be triggered against invaders? And what about security guards? Were they in the house, or living nearby, ready to rush in to save the terrorist leader?

"If we determine The Pacer is bin Laden, and the president says 'go get him,' how will we do it?" Panetta asked, rhetorically.

The CIA had come up with several possible Courses of Action (COAs). Panetta went over each one of them—even ones that he had privately ruled out. He discussed the pros and cons of each proposed operation.

One option: "Inform Pakistan." They would tell the Pakistanis what U.S. intelligence had uncovered and urge them to take action. This was the safest move from a diplomatic standpoint.

Option two: A joint operation with the Pakistani military. The risk to U.S. forces would be vastly reduced, Panetta said. CIA leaders had bounced around the idea, but Pakistan's intelligence service—the ISI—had a reputation for leaks and divided loyalties. Many ISI agents had ties to the Taliban. It was impossible to trust them with the information.

That raised another possibility—what the agency called "Compel Pakistan." Tell Pakistani authorities the U.S. was conducting a raid that night, and press the Pakistanis to come with them.

The problem with all of these COAs, of course, was that they relied on assistance and secrecy from an uncertain ally. Panetta now laid out three other options, based on the U.S. acting on its own.

America could launch an air strike. The benefits of simply demolishing the compound were obvious: No U.S. lives would be risked on Pakistani soil. But how could they be sure that bin Laden was there and had been killed? If Al Qaeda denied their leader was dead, how would the United States explain blowing up a residence deep inside Pakistan in the middle of a crowded city? Intelligence estimated that five women and twenty children lived in the compound. The strike would annihilate the buildings and adjoining residences, too. No one could say how many innocent civilians would die.

Another choice was to authorize a special ops mission. A team would fly into Pakistan by helicopter, raid the compound, and get out before the Pakistani police or military had time to react. That would take a lot more planning.

They'd have to pick a team. They'd have to pull off the operation inside another country without being seen—or at least, without being stopped. To preserve secrecy—and maintain deniability if something went wrong—the mission would have to be conducted under CIA authority rather than the Pentagon's.

Panetta said the final option was using CIA operators—the agency's paramilitary unit. They were mostly former special operators or Marines who helped train and run covert operations around the world. The CIA guys would come in on the ground, raid the compound, capture the target, and find some way to sneak him out of Pakistan.

No matter which option they chose, there would be dangers involved. No one knew if the building was booby-trapped, or if Al Qaeda fighters were living there or billeted nearby, ready to strike.

The briefing dress rehearsal went well. McRaven was impressed by the depth and detail of the intelligence. Ultimately, President Obama would make his decision. If he decided to use Special Forces, McRaven knew he'd have to start planning now. On the surface, this was like a thousand raids they had conducted in the past, but there was one big difference. This raid would take place 160 miles inside Pakistani territory. That changed things and created all kinds of potential problems.

When the military folks had left, Panetta invited Morell and Bash back to his office. The director was excited. Everything was coming together. He broke out a bottle of Dewar's Blue Label Scotch, the good stuff, and poured them each a generous glass.

"I think we've developed good options," Panetta said.

The plans were ready to present to the president. They just had to get by Donilon. Panetta didn't think that would be a problem.

They sipped their Scotch, but no one felt any sense of celebration. They knew the hard part was just starting.

COUNTDOWN:
58 DAYS

March 4, 2011
Abbottabad, Pakistan

Dr. Shakil Afridi sat in his car on the dead-end street in Abbottabad and watched a nurse from his vaccination program ring the bell and wait. The gates were big, set within a massive, blank concrete wall. The doctor wondered if the rooms inside were luxurious, hung with silks; if the garden was a shady green oasis. From out here, the big house looked like a prison. Afridi hoped the occupants would let the nurse inside. Would anyone there be interested in a hepatitis B vaccination?

The nurse didn't know that the vaccine program was part of an elaborate CIA ruse to gain access to the compound. And Afridi only knew bits and pieces of the agency's plot. He was parked outside the most watched house in the world, a top priority of U.S. officials from the CIA to the White House.

The CIA plans were taking shape. All they needed was proof that bin Laden was there. Afridi was the perfect operator. A prominent surgeon, no one would suspect he was working for the CIA.

While government doctors were well respected, they were often underpaid, and some, like Afridi, supplemented their income with work in private clinics. Maybe that's why the CIA had contacted him in the first place. They knew he needed money.

His CIA handler told Afridi they'd pay him tens of thousands of dollars for his help. Afridi recruited female health workers to attempt to gain access to a "prominent house"—a three-story villa—in one neighborhood.

Now, here he was, in front of that house, risking it all to help the Americans. He shook his head. Afridi was worried about putting his family in danger.

His wife, Mona, was the principal at a government school. They had two boys and a little girl, a good life. But it was too late to back out.

Afridi had started the vaccination project in a poorer part of Abbottabad to make it look more authentic. He said he had procured funds from international charities to give free vaccinations for hepatitis B. Bypassing the Abbottabad health services, the doctor paid generous sums to low-ranking local government health workers, who took part in the operation without knowing they were part of the CIA plan. He used a vaccine made by Amson, a manufacturer in Islamabad, and had posters put up all over Abbottabad to promote the program. It was a worthy enterprise, even without its ulterior motive.

Compound in Abbottabad.

Slowly, the health workers began administering the vaccine around the city. They were ready to move in on their target. It wouldn't look out of place for health professionals to canvass this affluent neighborhood, too.

The gate opened, and the nurse stepped inside the compound. The gate closed behind her. Afridi's heart raced. Could she do it?

A few minutes later, the door opened again and the nurse left. The man inside had told her to come back another day, that maybe then they would get vaccinated.

Afridi swallowed the lump in his throat. It was a start. And at least he had something to tell the CIA man.

White House

Panetta and his team arrived at the White House for another briefing, a dress rehearsal for the big session with Obama on March 14. The CIA director was feeling confident. He'd update Donilon and other members of the president's national security team about the compound. He'd show them the tabletop model of the fortress. He thought it would be routine.

When he walked into the Situation Room, everyone was there already—Donilon, Brennan, and a few others. But this meeting of the National Security Principals Committee was Donilon's show. He was the chairman of the committee, the official who oversaw the National Security Council staff. He was responsible for coordinating and integrating the administration's foreign policy, intelligence, and national security efforts.

Donilon was perfect for the position. He was sharp and tireless, a Washington insider who had years of foreign policy experience. He had advised three U.S. presidents since 1977. A lawyer by trade, he rose to prominence in the Clinton State Department. He even looked like a Washington attorney—he was in his fifties, tall, balding, distinguished. He dressed in power suits and ties, hobnobbed with world leaders, and tolerated no nonsense. He was a by-the-book bureaucrat who didn't like surprises.

National Security Advisor Tom Donilon with President Barack Obama.

Before Panetta arrived, Nick Rasmussen, National Security Council senior director for counterterrorism, was responsible for sneaking the model of the compound into the Situation Room.

The model was designed like a diorama, so it folded into a big suitcase. When Rasmussen got it inside, he placed the suitcase on the long rectangular table, then opened it up with a flourish. With miniature farm fields carved of clay and walls made of Styrofoam, the elaborate mockup of bin Laden's compound unfolded and became the centerpiece on the table.

Brennan marveled at the highly detailed model. He wondered about the people who lived inside the actual house, their possible escape routes, and the people living nearby. How would anyone get inside there, and then get out again?

Meanwhile, the security for bin Laden meetings was unprecedented. Only a handful of people in Obama's inner circle knew about the operation. Key players were excluded—including Secretary of State Hillary Rodham Clinton, Attorney General Eric Holder, FBI Director Robert Mueller, and

Secretary of Homeland Security Janet Napolitano. And those who knew were told not to inform others what they were doing. They had to keep it from their closest aides and immediate staff. The conferences were never listed on their daily calendars. (On Brennan's calendar, it just said "Mickey Mouse meetings.") When they met, the Situation Room's closed-circuit surveillance cameras were turned off. Brennan knew that Donilon wanted to make sure the room was "hermetically sealed from sound, video." Every piece of paper distributed at the beginning of the meetings was collected before the participants left. They were leaving nothing to chance.

When the doors closed, Panetta and his team got down to business, updating everyone on where they stood with trying to identify The Pacer. He then went over all the options they'd present to Obama at the next briefing.

Donilon was pleased, and he knew Obama would be, too. The CIA had followed the president's orders. He knew Obama was a stickler for detail and procedure, and kept a binder of notes about the bin Laden case. If Obama asked someone to get a job done, he didn't forget. At some point, he'd ask that person what they'd found out, or how they'd followed through with his suggestion. Donilon's job was making sure everyone met the president's expectations.

Before he adjourned the meeting, Donilon told Panetta it was time to let congressional intelligence leaders know about the bin Laden operation. And that was when Panetta said something that stunned Donilon: "I already told them."

"What?" Donilon stammered. "When?"

Before the national security advisor had a chance to say anything else, Panetta explained. Yes, he knew the president told them to keep this secret, but he'd started briefing key congressional leaders in December to "build goodwill." Congress held the purse strings, and the CIA needed massive money to continue this intensive intelligence operation.

Donilon's face turned red. He raised his voice. Time and again the president had made it clear: No one outside the small circle was to know.

No one. Panetta should have waited until a decision was made before he briefed anyone.

"We're still evaluating intelligence," he shouted at Panetta. "There's no activity here to brief anybody on! We haven't decided anything, and you're briefing Congress?"

But Panetta didn't back down. "What the fuck did you expect me to do? That's my fucking job," he yelled at Donilon.

Donilon shook his head. Too many damn people knew about the bin Laden operation now. Something was going to leak. Obama would be livid.

The room was hot and silent. Rasmussen knew they had implemented every security measure to ensure nothing leaked. Very few people in the president's own cabinet knew about the bin Laden meetings—not even Secretary of State Clinton. They couldn't bring unauthorized deputies or staff members to the sessions.

"I need to keep the intelligence committees in the loop," Panetta explained. "We have to trust them. This could be the most important operation they'll ever oversee. We can't blindside them. We can't afford any animosity there."

Donilon sat silent, his face like thunder.

"I have to do this," Panetta said. "This is part of my responsibility with the oversight committees. This is a significant intelligence activity. I'm bound by law to report significant intelligence."

Rasmussen understood both sides. Still, it was concerning that so many people knew. Brennan took a deep breath. This mission meant a lot to Obama, and a leak could compromise everything.

Panetta and Donilon exchanged more words—tough words—before they adjourned.

Watching from a distance, Gary couldn't turn away. Seeing these two "super experienced, super deep, super powerful men" battle was like watching the political equivalent of King Kong versus Godzilla. All he needed was some popcorn.

There was no personal animosity between the two. Donilon was wondering why Panetta was bending over backward for Congress. He thought that could restrict the president's options—Obama still hadn't decided what he was going to do and he certainly didn't need any outside pressure. But Panetta was thinking that if you bring Congress along, they become a partner. They'll be more supportive of the outcome—good or bad.

After the session, Donilon went straight to the president. Obama was angry. He had Brennan call Jeremy Bash and get a list of every congressional member Panetta had briefed.

A day later, Donilon phoned Panetta. The president wanted to move quickly on the bin Laden operation, he said. Panetta hung up the phone and smiled to himself. He'd thought the decision would take months. The fire was lit. He'd have to act fast.

COUNTDOWN:
48 DAYS

March 14, 2011

White House

Vice Admiral McRaven walked down a White House corridor and entered the Situation Room. He was early, the first one there. In a few minutes, high-powered members of the military and Obama's cabinet would join him. He stood for a moment, looking smart in his Navy Service Dress Blue, a double-breasted uniform with gold stripes on the sleeves. He sat down at the far end of the long conference table and waited.

This meeting was as important as it got. Panetta would brief the president and his national security team about the compound—what they'd found and what they could do if bin Laden was there. The intriguing scale model was on the table for everyone to see. McRaven wondered how the spooks had gotten it in here without anyone asking what it was.

Everything about this operation was shrouded in secrecy. Most of the few officials who knew about The Pacer were on their way here, to the Situation Room.

Just a few moments before, McRaven had been caught unawares. He could easily have blown it. As he'd approached the entrance to the White House, he heard someone call his name. When he turned around, he saw it was an old childhood friend—someone he'd met in the fifth grade but hadn't seen in decades. "Bill, how are you doing? What are you doing here?" asked Karen Tumulty, a top *Washington Post* reporter who covered the White House.

McRaven was struck dumb. He mumbled something about "lot going on in the world."

"Is it Libya?" she asked.

Libya was the latest development in the Arab Spring. Peaceful protests had morphed into an all-out civil war. Gaddafi loyalists and rebels were engaged in fierce fighting, and civilians were caught in the crossfire. Obama was ready to order military air strikes against Gaddafi's forces.

McRaven tried to change the subject. He didn't want her to ask why he wasn't in Afghanistan, so he asked Tumulty about her family and career. They chatted for several minutes about children and mutual friends, then McRaven said he had to go. He promised they'd stay in touch.

He picked up his badge from a Secret Service agent and took a deep breath. He'd dodged that one.

One by one, the others walked into the room. Defense Secretary Gates. Admiral Mullen arrived with General Cartwright. Vice President Joe Biden arrived, then Panetta, Donilon, and Brennan. Soon, Jim Clapper, director of National Intelligence; Denis McDonough, deputy national security advisor; and a small briefing team from the CIA, including Gary.

And the meeting had someone new: Secretary of State Hillary Rodham Clinton, who had just been informed about the bin Laden operation. A week earlier, Panetta said he wanted to talk to her in private. Her first clue something was up was when Panetta said, "Make sure the meeting is totally off your schedule." When they met at the State Department, Panetta shared everything, adding that Clinton would be part of a very small group that would advise Obama so he could make "the best decision—whatever that is."

Clinton quickly discovered the bin Laden operation was "completely off the books." She usually relied on her staffers for advice and support. But now she knew she wouldn't be able to discuss bin Laden with them—or even her husband. It was so closely held she knew she wouldn't be able to put the meetings about bin Laden on her calendar. She'd have to make up something to explain why she was going to the White House, so her aides wouldn't suspect anything. The same rules applied to the other high-powered members in the room. They didn't have any staff with them. They had to hide the meetings, too. In the end, they were on their own.

Moments later, the president slid into the chair at the head of the table, directly facing McRaven at the other end. The president leaned back, almost in a reclining position. McRaven sized up the president. He noticed that Obama looked tired. It was no surprise to McRaven—not with so much unrest in the world: the Arab Spring, wars in Iraq and Afghanistan. Raymond Davis was still in a Pakistani jail. A few days earlier, a powerful earthquake had hit northern Japan, killing thousands and triggering a series of large tsunami waves that caused widespread damage to coastal areas—and a nuclear power plant. Now this, trying to decide what to do about bin Laden. It had to be weighing on him.

Morell had sensed that this was going to be one of the most important meetings of his career. So he came even more prepared than usual. The CIA team had put together a PowerPoint of the possible options. Morell handed out three-inch-thick binders with details about the possible courses of action, to make it easy for everyone in the room to follow along. They had maps associated with each COA, including where bombs would fall during an air strike or where the special operations forces would be inserted during a raid.

The president was ready, and Panetta began with a quick rundown of everything their intelligence analysts and agents on the ground had uncovered about the fortress at the end of the street in Abbottabad.

Yes, al-Kuwaiti lived there. He had once worked as a courier for bin Laden. The place was fortified in such a way that made it difficult to see inside the compound or the house. All of that strongly suggested that someone was hiding inside. The Pacer lived in the main house and only came outside for laps around the yard. He never, ever left the compound.

The evidence pointed to bin Laden, but, Panetta noted, it was not conclusive. It could be that al-Kuwaiti was protecting bin Laden's family—not bin Laden himself. It could be that al-Kuwaiti was protecting another terrorist, or a wanted criminal.

The uncertainty of who was inside only made the risks of a military action more serious. But doing nothing carried its own set of risks, Panetta warned: "We could miss our best chance in a decade to capture or kill bin Laden."

After Panetta finished, the president quickly ruled out a joint operation with Pakistan. That was out of the question, he said. Although Pakistan had cooperated with the United States on a number of counterterrorism operations and provided vital supply routes to U.S. troops in Afghanistan, it was no secret that some factions within the government were pro-Taliban.

The region was complicated. With a weak central government, Afghanistan was unable to align itself with India, Pakistan's rival state. The fact that a major military academy was so near the compound only heightened the possibility that anything the United States told the Pakistanis would end up tipping off The Pacer.

But whatever the course of action, Obama knew it would raise the diplomatic stakes between the United States and Pakistan. The State Department would have an epic diplomatic cleanup job on its hands. But that was something to think about later. Right here, right now, the president was listening, weighing the options. Hell, they might not do anything at all. Without concrete proof, should they even go in?

After taking the U.S.-Pakistan options off the table, the president turned to Cartwright, a general who had been a flight officer and pilot. As Obama stared at the model, the general went over the details of an air attack.

The air force had proposed using thirty-two 2,000-pound bombs in a massive air strike. But a bombing would "leave a large smoking hole in the middle of Abbottabad."

Obama knew the pros and cons of that idea, but what really disturbed him was the number of women and children inside the compound who would die. And what about all the families living in the residences nearby? With all the uncertainty about whether bin Laden was even there, Obama was uncomfortable ordering an air strike that would kill so many noncombatants.

As the meeting continued, Obama zeroed in on a possible special forces operation. The team would covertly fly into Pakistan by helicopter, raid the compound, and get out before Pakistan's military or police had a chance to respond. If they did that, Obama knew McRaven was the one to carry out the mission.

McRaven was prepared, with plans in hand. He had spent the previous day at CIA headquarters with Panetta and his senior staff, getting their parts of the presentation ready to roll.

McRaven liked the CIA director. He thought Panetta was a real leader, "the consummate team player, gregarious, bawdy at times, with a laugh that was contagious." More important, Panetta never made things about himself—he was always about doing the right thing for the nation. With his deep connections to the Washington establishment, he proved he could get things done.

In Panetta's office, they'd once again discussed their options, including the possible CIA "snatch-and-grab." It was a frank discussion. No one held back. Even Panetta's aides believed the military should handle the mission—not officers from the CIA's covert action division.

They'd all agreed they shouldn't say a word to Pakistan. "That option should not even be on the table," one advisor said.

Another said he believed that Pakistani authorities knew Osama bin Laden was hiding in plain sight. "The ISI must know bin Laden is there. For God's sake, he's a fucking mile down the road from their West Point," the analyst said.

Finally, Panetta had turned to McRaven. "I think the only real option here is the special forces raid." It was exactly what the admiral had been thinking, for weeks.

Now, in the Situation Room, McRaven walked the president through what the raid might look like. After dark, a select special operations team would fly one or two helicopters for nearly an hour and a half from Jalalabad, Afghanistan, to the compound, landing inside the high walls. They would secure every perimeter entry point, door, and window before breaking into the three-story main house.

Once inside, they'd search the premises and "neutralize" any residents they encountered. They would apprehend or kill bin Laden, then fly back out, stopping to refuel somewhere inside Pakistan before returning to the base in Jalalabad.

Panetta jumped in. "Mr. President, Bill is looking into the use of some special helicopters we have that may be able to get past the Pakistani air defenses."

McRaven nodded and pulled up on a big screen in the Situation Room a picture of a stealth Black Hawk, a chopper that had been modified to mask heat, noise, and movement. "Sir, it's possible that these helos can avoid radar detection and make it to the compound," he said. "There's still a lot I don't know about their reconfiguration."

When Obama asked McRaven to elaborate, he said he didn't know how many men the helicopters would be able to carry.

"How many do you need?" Obama asked.

"At a minimum? Twenty men and their equipment," McRaven said.

Obama examined the picture on the screen as McRaven continued. A lot goes into determining the lift capacity of a helicopter, including fuel and altitude.

"For example, sir, if the temperature is one degree different than what we forecast, it could change the entire load and fuel requirements. If the time on the ground is longer than anticipated, then the helo will have to refuel. That is another element of risk," McRaven said.

McRaven's words echoed in Gates's ears. Gates knew bad shit happened on dangerous missions. Hell, he was right here, in the Situation Room, that night in 1980, when he learned the mission to rescue fifty-two American hostages at the U.S. embassy in Tehran had turned into a disaster. So Gates knew they had to be certain that bin Laden was in the compound. Otherwise, it wasn't worth the risk.

McRaven could feel the enthusiasm draining out of the room. He knew he had to be stark. Truth, no bullshit. They had to know everything—pros and cons. McRaven said he still needed to nail down precise details. But to do that, he said he had to bring in experts to help with the air and ground planning phase.

"How many more people do you need?" the president asked.

The admiral felt a flutter of excitement. "Five," McRaven answered. Obama approved the request. And when McRaven was finished, Obama looked at him and asked, "Do you think you can pull it off?"

McRaven could have said yes. No problem. Special forces are badasses who can do anything. But McRaven wasn't going to bullshit the president. That wasn't who he was. He was going to lay it all out there—the good, bad, and ugly.

He said he'd only "sketched out a concept." He wouldn't know the answer until he picked a team, put together a game plan, and ran through some rehearsals. "What I can tell you is if we get there, we can pull off the raid. But I can't recommend the mission itself until I've done the homework."

Obama smiled. "Let's do the homework then."

Before they adjourned, Donilon reminded the president their next meeting was March 29. When everyone got up to leave, McRaven bounded from the room. He wanted to get started. He knew he didn't have much time to complete his assignment.

COUNTDOWN:

35 DAYS

March 27, 2011
Jalalabad, Afghanistan

McRaven had been working around the clock putting together a plan for the raid. After the meeting with Obama, he knew he had to act fast. There were a lot of moving parts to any major operation, but McRaven knew he'd first have to decide who would carry out the raid: Navy SEALs or Army Green Berets.

Either of the elite special operations units could get the job done. Hell, collectively they had conducted thousands of missions in Iraq and Afghanistan. They were well-oiled machines. And while McRaven had been a SEAL, his decision would ultimately depend on availability.

Most of the units were stationed in Afghanistan, and McRaven couldn't simply pull an entire active Special Forces unit out of there without raising suspicion. The country was full of Taliban and Al Qaeda spies, and his own officers would start asking questions, too.

McRaven would have to spend a lot of time away from Afghanistan, putting together the mission and training the team. (He already had a cover if anyone got suspicious about why he was traveling so much to Washington, D.C. People would assume he was going to Bethesda Naval Hospital to get checked out for his cancer. He'd write on digital travel logs: "Commander going into Washington." No one would ask personal questions of a commanding officer.)

But if McRaven and an active unit suddenly disappeared from the radar, his command center would suspect a big operation. People would start talking and snooping around. He didn't want that.

McRaven checked the deployment schedule. A Green Beret squadron had just landed in Afghanistan. Meanwhile, a Navy SEAL squadron had just returned to the United States. They were on leave for three weeks. Perfect. SEALs it would be.

He called Captain Rex Smith and Colonel John "JT" Thompson, two trusted officers. Smith was cool and poised, a dead ringer for tough-guy 1950s movie star Robert Mitchum. Thompson commanded the special operations aviation unit and knew everything about helicopters. Both were "extremely experienced in combat, superb tacticians and consummate team players." This kind of high-profile mission always created plenty of drama and interpersonal tension. The admiral wanted officers who could build teams and thrive under the pressure.

During his late February visit to Washington, McRaven had briefed Smith on the bin Laden operation. He swore him to secrecy and asked him to help the CIA agents plan a mission. He said they had developed several COAs, but only one involved a raid.

"So what do you want me to do there?" Smith asked.

"Nothing. Just listen. The last thing we want is for the agency to think we're taking over the mission," McRaven said. "Only speak up if they ask for your insight. Then be totally honest with them . . . and stay away from implying that we could do it better."

McRaven was back in Afghanistan the following day. But over the following weeks Smith called him almost every day with an update. He proved invaluable. And now, following the Situation Room meeting with the president, McRaven called on Smith for another kind of help.

He asked him to gather several key SEALs and get them to Washington by the next day. Then he called Colonel Thompson and requested air planners. He wanted the most experienced warrant officer to lead the tactical part of the air planning, and the lead pilot from the special Black Hawk unit to provide technical information about the aircraft.

McRaven didn't disclose the details of the mission or even say who the potential target was. But as Thompson listened, he sensed something big was up. He understood not to ask too many questions, but whatever it was, he wanted a piece of it. He jokingly asked if McRaven needed a personal assistant—someone to tag along. McRaven laughed. He knew what Thompson was up to—and McRaven would have made the same offer if the tables were turned. The admiral knew he'd need a superb helicopter pilot soon, however. . . .

"Not now," McRaven told him. "But stay around, JT. Don't go anywhere soon."

The following day, Smith brought four people to the sprawling CIA complex. Smith hadn't told them a thing about the mission. But they suspected something was up when they didn't go in the agency's main building. Instead, they headed to the printing plant, a small building that produced phony documents—birth certificates, passports, driver's licenses—that agents used on secret missions. McRaven greeted them at the door. When they walked inside, Smith and his men viewed the model of the compound in the middle of a long table. A few minutes later, several members of the CIA team arrived. After a round of introductions, the analysts gave Smith and his men a rundown about the compound, The Pacer—all of their intelligence.

When they finished, McRaven took over. He told them about the options before Obama.

"Gentlemen, in less than two weeks the president expects a fleshed-out concept for the raid option. Your job is to tell me whether or not we can do it," he explained.

He said that he had explored several options to get to the target. They included starting the mission from several jumping-off points inside Pakistan instead of Afghanistan, and parachuting in just outside Abbottabad and driving to the compound. McRaven said he quickly dismissed the ideas as unfeasible. He'd give them a day or two to look at his analysis, "but then we have to decide on one course of action and start planning."

Smith spoke for the team. "OK. You know what the boss needs. Let's get to work."

For the next two weeks, Gary, Sam, and other CIA officers and analysts worked with the SEALs. They reviewed every bit of intelligence. They brought in experts on Pakistani air defense and radar systems. Image analysts answered every question about the compound: the height, the thickness of the walls, the outdoor lighting, what they could tell about The Pacer's living conditions. They discussed the possible number of women and children in the compound, and the location of Pakistani military and police units.

It wasn't only about Abbottabad. Analysts provided information about how the Pakistani military would respond if American forces were detected over the border. In the past, when the U.S. military chased insurgents into Pakistan, the military there activated and engaged American helicopters and ground forces as invaders. Intelligence analysts provided answers to every one of the SEAL planners' questions except one: Was it bin Laden in the compound?

After all the analysis, they came to one conclusion: Their only raid option was a direct path from Afghanistan to the compound. Now they had to determine if the right number of helicopters could get the right number of SEALs into the compound without being detected.

McRaven knew the only way to do that was to practice the plan in simulated Pakistani conditions. That meant bringing in a lot more people. He needed more time to chase down all the little details that would help them avoid disaster.

And time was running out.

COUNTDOWN:
33 DAYS

March 29, 2011
Washington, D.C.

McRaven was back in the Situation Room and ready to go. Since his last visit, he had devoted hundreds of hours to putting together a mission plan. Now, all he had to do was wait his turn.

Obama had been thinking a lot about The Pacer, the compound, Pakistan. But it seemed that every day there was another crisis somewhere in the world or at home that needed his immediate attention. Civil war had engulfed Libya. It was unclear if Gaddafi would survive. In Syria, protesters marched in Damascus and Aleppo, demanding democratic reforms and the release of political prisoners. President Bashar al-Assad responded by cracking down on the protesters, leading to widespread violence.

At home, the newly emboldened GOP majority in the House and Senate tried to repeal Obama's flagship achievement, the Patient Protection and Affordable Care Act, known as Obamacare. They didn't have enough votes to override a presidential veto, so some two dozen states filed lawsuits, arguing that guaranteed health care for all Americans was unconstitutional.

But now, sitting in the Situation Room, surrounded by his national security team, Obama shut out the noise and zeroed in on the subject at hand: the compound.

Almost the entire national security team was in the room, including

Secretary of State Clinton, Defense Secretary Gates, and Admiral Mullen. This was serious.

Panetta knew that despite their best efforts, two questions remained: Who was inside the compound? And if they determined it was bin Laden, how would they get him?

Since the last meeting with the president, Panetta had been refining their options, adding more details. They had looked even closer at bombing the compound.

He'd brought in a group of "flyboys" to CIA headquarters, specialist airmen from the 509th Bomber Wing at Whiteman Air Force Base near Kansas City. They made a great impression with their short haircuts and leather jackets, and they wasted no time in describing how they could conduct a mission to kill The Pacer: Two B-2 bombers would leave Whiteman and fly halfway around the world to the Afghanistan-Pakistan border. There they'd "stealth up," switch on their radar-blocking technology, and bank right. Minutes later, they would be over their target.

Each bomber would drop sixteen JDAMS (joint direct attack munitions). Each bomb weighed two thousand pounds.

Jeremy Bash had a few questions for them. What would they see after the bombs dropped?

"Nothing," one of the flyboys responded.

"Nothing? What does that mean?" Bash asked.

The compound would be reduced to rubble within moments, he responded.

Bash wanted him to elaborate. Would anything be left over? A flyboy shook his head.

"Would we be able to collect DNA from the bodies?" Bash asked.

That was highly unlikely because all the bodies would be nothing more than "dust," a flyboy said, adding that they wouldn't be able to contain the damage to just the compound and a few "rows of houses across the street."

"Everything would be blown to smithereens," he said.

So, if bin Laden was there, he'd be killed, along with everyone else in the compound and the surrounding neighborhood. Panetta and Bash knew that would create another problem: They'd have almost no chance of ever proving they had killed bin Laden. It was unlikely that the Pakistanis would invite U.S. officials to the smoldering ruins to search for DNA.

The flyboys were confident they could successfully carry out the mission. Panetta talked to John Brennan about it. They shared misgivings. "It's a bad plan," Brennan said. "There would be too many casualties."

While the bombing wasn't off the table, General Cartwright, an old naval aviator, had plotted out what he called a more "surgical option for an air strike."

Why not use a drone? It would fire a small, thirteen-pound missile directly at The Pacer while he was strolling in the courtyard. Collateral damage would be minimal. The U.S. military regularly used drones to kill terrorist figures. He was positive they could take out The Pacer, and that would eliminate all the inherent dangers associated with a ground assault.

Panetta had problems with that plan, too. They only had one shot. What if the drone missed? If The Pacer was bin Laden, he'd vanish again. If the missile took him out, they'd be facing the same problem they had with the bombing option: They wouldn't have a way to get DNA. And the Pakistanis would still be angry as hell.

Anti-American sentiment in Pakistan was on the rise. The public was outraged that more and more U.S. drone strikes were taking place inside Pakistan along the Afghanistan border. The Raymond Davis case certainly didn't help.

After two months, America had finally paid his way out of jail. He was released in the middle of March after the victims' families received several million dollars as compensation. Many in the community, though, believed it was a miscarriage of justice fueled by "blood money." Add a United States bomber attack with noncombatant victims, and U.S.-Pakistani relations could be damaged beyond repair.

In the Situation Room, Panetta laid it all out for Obama. He told the president that he was taking the CIA-led raid off the table. He doubted they could carry out that kind of operation.

They discussed the proposed B-2 bombing mission. Obama examined the plan closely, then eliminated it, too.

General Cartwright described his drone attack plan.

Obama said he'd consider it. The president then turned to his national security advisors and widened the focus.

How would this military action serve the overall goal of defeating Al Qaeda? It simply wasn't enough to kill bin Laden to settle a score. A mission so costly and risky would have to measurably advance U.S. strategy, or make Al Qaeda less effective. The president wanted a full analysis. He needed the full policy underpinnings to make a good decision, he said.

The room fell silent.

The president turned to Panetta. "Are you ready?" he said. "The raid. Tell me what you've got."

Panetta looked over to McRaven. He wanted the admiral to explain the details to Obama. So McRaven stepped up, ready with the "homework" he'd been assigned at the end of their last meeting. The admiral respected Obama. He had the strong leadership style McRaven would expect from somebody who'd spent years in the military, which Obama hadn't. The president had confidence as well as a level of humility—he admitted when he didn't know something—and a deference to the experts around the room. Obama asked the right questions. More important, he stayed calm. He had a sense of humor.

McRaven had the same quiet confidence as Obama, but he was more colorful and animated. He said the plan was pretty simple. He'd assemble a team of twenty-four SEALs, a CIA officer, and specially modified Black Hawk helicopters in the United States. If Obama approved the mission, he'd move the team to Afghanistan.

They'd also have two dozen SEALs waiting in two MH-47 Chinook helicopters inside Afghanistan near the Pakistan border. He would only deploy this quick reaction force to Abbottabad if the SEALs in the compound needed help.

McRaven switched on his PowerPoint presentation. A map showed the 162-mile distance between the Afghanistan border and Abbottabad. Another image showed the Pakistani air defense radar coverage. The red lines on the map were places where U.S. helicopters were likely to be detected. The green lines were spots that were clear. Everyone could see, there wasn't much green.

Obama studied the path of the mission. "Can you get by the air defenses?" he asked.

McRaven said he couldn't answer that question right now. "We're still studying the problem. But if we can use the mountains as a shield, there's a possibility we can get pretty close to the compound without being detected."

"How close?" the president asked.

Once they broke from the mountains, it would be two minutes to the compound. But that didn't mean they were home free. "At that point, the sound of helos will give us away," he said. "It's very likely that someone in the compound will hear us."

McRaven flipped to the next image, an overhead photo of the compound with arrows showing their proposed routes of entry. Twelve men would fast-rope from the first helicopter into the center of the compound, clear out the small guesthouse, and then breach the bottom floor of the main building and clear it from the bottom up.

The second helicopter would drop a small team outside the compound to cover all escape routes. Then the chopper would drop the rest of the team onto the roof of the main house. They would methodically work their way down. During the raid, the two Black Hawks would wait at a designated spot on the outskirts of the city.

"What about the women and children?" Clinton asked. Intelligence said there were up to a dozen children in the compound, and maybe five women.

"This is a challenge we deal with every day in Afghanistan. The men know how to handle large groups of noncombatants," the admiral said.

"But what if one of them poses a threat?" someone asked.

In his typical direct, no-nonsense style, McRaven answered. "If they have a suicide vest or are armed, or if they threaten the assault force, they will be killed."

McRaven wanted to make sure everyone in the Situation Room understood the stakes. "Anyone in the compound who poses a threat to the operators will be killed. It will be dark. It will be confusing."

And even if bin Laden wasn't in the compound, there were "still likely to be dead Pakistanis as a result of the raid."

Obama nodded. He understood.

The raid could be executed, McRaven said. Getting the men back out would be dicey.

Obama had more questions. What if Pakistani authorities intercepted the U.S. helicopters on their way in or out? What if bin Laden was on-site but hidden, thus extending the amount of time they'd be on the ground? What if they encountered resistance? How would the team respond if Pakistani police or military forces surrounded the compound?

It was an uncomfortable question, but one that had to be discussed and answered.

McRaven didn't miss a beat. "Sir, we have a technical term for that in the military." He paused for a moment. "We call that 'when the shit hits the fan.'"

"Exactly," the president said.

Gates and Mullen smiled broadly, but the others weren't so amused.

McRaven said he'd built his plan on the premise that his team should avoid a firefight with Pakistani authorities. If confronted, his inclination was to hold the team in place until U.S. diplomats negotiated a safe exit.

Obama appreciated his candor, but with U.S-Pakistan relations in an especially precarious state, the president had serious reservations about this strategy. No, he would not put the fate of SEALs into the hands of the

Pakistani government, especially if bin Laden wasn't found inside. Public outcry would land them all in jail, or worse.

The president knew he couldn't rely on the Pakistanis. He knew he couldn't rely on diplomacy. He didn't want McRaven's men "rotting in jail." So Obama decided to make sure that McRaven had clear and concise instructions on what to do if the Pakistani police or military arrived at the compound. He needed to make sure there was no confusion how he wanted them to handle such a scenario.

"Fight your way out," the president directed.

McRaven smiled. The president's words meant McRaven could put together combat air support to protect his men in the compound, or during their return to Afghanistan. His "gorilla package" would include everything in his military arsenal, including fighter jets and AC-130 gunships. McRaven then showed a few more slides, including the helicopter route out of Pakistan. If everything worked well, McRaven estimated the mission would take three and a half hours—ninety minutes of travel each way and a half hour for the mission. No more.

"How quickly can the Pakistanis react?" Gates asked.

McRaven didn't know yet. They were still gathering intelligence. When the presentation wound up, Obama turned to McRaven with a solemn face.

"Can you do the mission, Bill?"

McRaven said he didn't know yet. It was still just a concept, a sketch. But he said he'd put together the assault team and start running rehearsals. Builders in rural North Carolina were already creating a full-sized replica of the compound. It would be ready soon, and then his team would start preparing. If Obama approved the raid, the optimal time would be the first weekend in May, when a couple of moonless nights would provide the SEALs with extra cover.

"How much time do you need to train?" Obama asked.

"Three weeks."

Obama paused for a moment. He knew it was still early to decide anything. McRaven was on a roll and he didn't want to kill the momentum, but with every step, more and more people were being brought into the circle, increasing the likelihood of a leak. Obama wasn't ready to approve a raid, but he knew they should prepare like it was a go.

"I think you have some work to do," Obama said to McRaven.

The meeting ended. Everyone got up and began to leave. For McRaven, the real work was about to begin. But Donilon knew McRaven had just passed a critical test.

The national security advisor could tell that Obama was impressed by McRaven's honesty. When the president asked whether the mission was doable, McRaven could have said, "Yes sir, Mr. President. No problem." But he didn't. Instead, McRaven said he didn't know, but promised to come back later with an informed answer. McRaven didn't bullshit the president.

After that, Donilon knew that the president—and everyone in the room—would have complete confidence in McRaven. No one knew whether the president would authorize an operation and, if he did, whether it would be a success. But after today's meeting, they were all sure about one thing: With McRaven, they had the right commander.

COUNTDOWN:
26 DAYS

April 5, 2011

Miami, Florida

After seven combat deployments and two weeks back home visiting with family and friends, Robert O'Neill was finally in paradise: Miami! Palm trees, clear skies, and blue water. He was enjoying some sand and surf with his team after a day's work performing a new combat diving training exercise at a nearby base.

He smiled every time he thought about it. Sometimes he loved his job.

This was the perfect assignment, an opportunity for everyone to decompress. They were navy, after all . . . and had spent the last five months inland, in eastern Afghanistan's mountains and deserts. They needed to get back in the water and work on their tactics, in case they had to conduct another high-seas life-or-death operation.

Two years earlier, O'Neill and his team had taken part in a high-profile rescue in the Indian Ocean that unfolded on live television. In a short time, the daring rescue of Captain Richard Phillips from Somali pirates had become etched in SEAL Team 6 lore.

Phillips, a U.S. merchant mariner, was taken hostage by four Somali pirates after they seized his cargo ship. The pirates removed Phillips from the ship and placed him in a eighteen-foot-long enclosed lifeboat. They were either going to extort money from the United States for his safe release or sell him to a group of extremists with ties to Al Qaeda. Either way, the pirates hoped to make millions.

But things didn't go as planned. U.S. warships quickly arrived and blocked the pirates' escape route. Phillips was stuck in the tiny vessel while the pirates tried to figure out their next move. The situation was tense. The pirates threatened to kill Phillips. To defuse the situation, the U.S. Navy struck a deal with the pirates. The USS *Bainbridge*, a destroyer, would attach a one-hundred-foot line to the lifeboat and tow it to shore.

Meanwhile, a SEAL team in the United States began planning a rescue. O'Neill was at his four-year-old daughter's preschool Easter party when his pager beeped and up came a top-secret code. He had to get out of there, fast. He called his wife, Amber, with the news.

She didn't ask any questions. She could easily guess where her husband was headed, as the hostage drama was all over the news. O'Neill had an hour to get to the military base where a Boeing C-17 Globemaster transport plane was waiting. Amber picked up their daughter. O'Neill gave them both a hug and kiss, then hurried to his car.

It was a twenty-minute drive, and O'Neill was already in uniform. He had time enough to stop at the 7-Eleven outside the base and grab a few necessities. He parked, got some cash from the ATM, and chose a couple of cans of Copenhagen and a carton of cigarettes. He would have made it in and out with time to spare—except for a lollygagging guy in front of him in the checkout line. The man wandered back to the newspapers, scanned the headlines, and finally pulled a copy of *USA Today* off the rack. The Captain Phillips ordeal was the lead story. The man tottered back to the counter, slammed the newspaper down, and said, "Man, I sure wish someone would do something about this!"

O'Neill snapped. "Hey, buddy, pay for your shit and we will."

The man stared at O'Neill. This was Virginia Beach, home of several elite military units. He jumped out of the way. O'Neill bought his things and ran outside to his car. Minutes later he pulled into a parking lot on the base and hurried to the team room.

They didn't have much time. SEAL Team 6 leaders and operators were discussing tactics and finalizing details. A transport plane would carry the squad and four speedboats to a designated area in the Indian Ocean. The SEALs and the boats would drop from a ramp in the back of the plane. Once they hit the water, the men would swim to the speedboats and prepare for the mission.

O'Neill and the others scrambled, grabbed gear bags and supplies from their lockers, and headed to the C-17. They strapped in for the sixteen-hour flight.

The trip passed by in a blur. The racket of machinery roused the men. They were there. The ramp in the back of the plane was opening. O'Neill moved to the edge and looked out. The ocean was beautiful; bright sun glistened on the water. He felt a charge of adrenaline. Forget about being tired. The signal came. O'Neill jumped first. As he dropped from the sky, he looked for the four boats, the landing zone.

But first the plummet, the moments of blindness from the sun's reflection off the water, then there they were, the boats, in perfect position. When they hit the water, the men swam to the vessels and climbed on board. After a quick head count to make sure everybody was safe, O'Neill's squadron headed to the USS *Boxer*, an amphibious assault ship. After all that movement, they were still some five hundred miles east of the *Bainbridge*.

And that's when they got their orders. The plan called for a small group of snipers to head to the *Bainbridge*. O'Neill wasn't called, but his buddy Jonny was. As they loaded up, Jonny spoke to O'Neill. "This shit's ending one way. You know that, right?"

O'Neill nodded. "I know. We didn't come here to talk them out of it."

When Jonny and his fellow SEALs got to the *Bainbridge*, they blended in with a crew assigned to deliver supplies to the pirates on the lifeboat.

The snipers took positions on the fantail of the *Bainbridge*. One of the pirates surrendered, but three refused to give up. Two were visible on the deck of the lifeboat, but the third was below with Phillips. Every once in a while, the pirate's head would pop up, visible in a small porthole window, shouting threats. There was no toilet or ventilation on the little boat, and the pirates were short on sleep. Phillips's life was in danger.

It was time to take action.

Jonny kept his gun sights trained on that empty porthole, while two other SEAL snipers focused on the pirates on deck. Jonny knew if they didn't take out all three pirates at once, the survivor would almost certainly shoot the hostage. Jonny told his buddies that when he next saw the pirate in the porthole, he'd "go hot."

And that's what happened. When the pirate's head appeared, Jonny fired. The two other snipers fired virtually simultaneously. One, two, three! The pirates all dropped.

Within seconds, rescuers slid down ropes from the *Bainbridge*, climbed aboard the lifeboat, and found all three pirates dead. They freed Captain Phillips, ending the drama at sea that had riveted much of the world's attention.

O'Neill knew that kind of precision attack was the result of relentless practice. All that training and planning paid off in the "flick of an index finger." When they returned to the *Boxer*, O'Neill and the others greeted Jonny and the other snipers with smiles and back slaps.

But Jonny wasn't in the mood to celebrate. He told O'Neill he wanted to be left alone for a while. O'Neill kept an eye on him. The ship wasn't big enough for much solitude, but Jonny walked to the far edges, alone. He'd talk when he was ready, O'Neill thought.

He understood. SEALs are background players, anonymous triggermen. Now Jonny was in the spotlight, the cool-under-pressure sniper, the guy who took out the main pirate. He was a hero. O'Neill wanted Jonny to know that.

When the time was right, he told Jonny, "You realize that you've done one of the most historic things in the history of the SEAL teams, don't you?"

But Jonny said he didn't care. He felt a great weight on his shoulders. He just wanted to go home.

Now Jonny was here in Miami, sitting with a bunch of other SEAL Team 6 members at the next table at the Marriott patio bar. Mack was there, a former rugby player with a missing tooth; and Paul, an assault team leader with a perfectly groomed beard; and Eric Roth, who'd become a commander during his last deployment.

For O'Neill, it felt great to be chatting in the sunshine about Navy SEAL tactical, theoretical stuff, and not just fighting terrorists in the mountains and deserts.

In the mornings, O'Neill and the guys ran on the beach and swam in the ocean. Then they piled into cars and headed to the training site. When they were done, they went back to the hotel, worked out at a nearby Gold's Gym, showered, and hung out. It was perfect.

O'Neill and his friends were getting ready to order their first round of drinks when Roth's cell phone chirped. He got up from the table and walked away. When he returned, he asked O'Neill, Jonny, and Paul for a quiet word.

They moved inside the lobby. Roth didn't waste any time. They'd pack up and check out of the hotel in the morning, head back to Virginia Beach to meet with command leadership. The rest of the men would continue the training, but without them. That was all Roth knew.

O'Neill understood this was serious. He went to his room and packed. Another hostage situation? He hadn't seen anything on the news. Maybe Gaddafi? He stretched out on the enormous bed, closed his eyes, and tried to sleep. His mind raced over the possible scenarios. Nothing made any sense. It was a whole lot of unknowns. But O'Neill kinda liked that.

Yuma, Arizona

Almost two thousand miles to the west in Yuma, Arizona, Will Chesney was thinking the same thing. He'd started out in Miami, training with O'Neill's team, but a few days earlier, two spots in a special skydiving school had opened up. The team leaders sent Chesney and another SEAL out West.

The Military Free-Fall Jumpmaster Course was a great opportunity—something that could lead to a promotion down the road. It was a rigorous three-week program. Chesney knew he'd not only learn to be a better skydiver, but also how to orchestrate a jump for an entire team. Leading a jump was a technical, highly choreographed, and dangerous maneuver. One mistake could be catastrophic.

He was up for the challenge, excited to be there. But before the class even started, his team leader called him off.

"Pack your gear," the voice on the telephone said. "We need you back in Virginia. Now."

Chesney couldn't believe it. He told the man that he just got there.

But the guy was cryptic. Something important had come up and Chesney would find out more later.

After years in the SEALs, Chesney knew better than to ask. Shit happens. Plans change. You get an order, you follow it. And the next one, and then another.

But before the man ended the call, he said he had one more thing: When Chesney got back to Virginia Beach, he had to pick up Cairo.

Chesney was stunned. He'd been trying to put some emotional distance between himself and the dog, but now they were getting him back together with his buddy, sending them into hell-who-knows-where. But so what?

He and Cairo were going to be a team again. He couldn't ask for anything better than that.

COUNTDOWN:
25 DAYS

April 6, 2011

Northern Virginia

Gary pulled his favorite suitcase from the closet, threw it on the bed, unzipped it. He packed button-down shirts, ties, socks, shoes. Another business trip, but this one felt different. After years of chasing bin Laden, he was on the verge of helping launch a mission that could capture or kill the terrorist. It felt final. It felt good.

The operation was still contingent on Obama saying "go." They were preparing as if he would. And while intelligence hadn't yet confirmed that The Pacer was bin Laden, Gary just knew he was. He had always been the skeptical one, but with time his confidence had increased. Everything his team had collected made sense. The pieces of the puzzle snapped together. That compound had to be bin Laden's hideout.

The president had given McRaven three weeks to put together a possible raid. Every detail had to be perfectly planned out, from the weight each helicopter could carry to the amount of fuel needed to get there and back. Weather conditions, ambient temperatures, local religious holidays—nothing was left to chance.

They'd have to know precisely where to land, where to go in. McRaven already had an idea of how he would conduct a raid, based on surveillance photos, the model of the compound, and other information. Gary's job was to make sure they had every scrap of intelligence they needed. He and

Sam were headed down to North Carolina to advise the SEALs as they planned the operation.

There was another critical member of their team who was going to North Carolina: Maya. In her late twenties, Maya had been involved in the hunt for bin Laden for years. Maya was slender, dark, and attractive. She was smart, driven, sometimes intimidating. She was an analyst who knew every fact in a case—and was quick to tell you so. And she knew more about bin Laden than anyone else in the Pakistan-Afghanistan Department.

Gary's wife hadn't been surprised when he told her about the trip. She shrugged. She knew the signs, she'd seen it coming. He'd spent long hours at the office, and when he was home, he was preoccupied. He picked at his food and wasn't interested in going out.

She didn't know what her husband was working on. She never did. The cases were secret, a given in any relationship that involved a CIA agent. But this case was clearly a big deal. The only thing she knew was that while he was gone, she'd be carrying the full load of kids, housework, bills, errands, as well as her own work. He'd promised his family he'd take them all on a getaway trip when he got back. But honestly, he wasn't sure if he would be able to get away until after this mission played itself out.

Everything was shifting into a higher gear now. At the beginning, Gary had briefed officials about the compound, where it was, who was there, and why The Pacer might be bin Laden. Now the meetings were more about strategy: bombs, drones, raids, escape routes, damage estimates.

In those high-level meetings, Gary was a background guy, only present in case officials had questions like "What would fourteen days of additional intelligence collection time do for you?" or "Gary, can we get more access to the compound?" That was OK with him. After all, his team had developed the information that led them to the compound in the first place.

Gary, Sam, and Maya would be the main briefers at the North Carolina base. They were a team made up of very different characters. In his late forties, with his academic-style goatee and scruffy mustache, Gary was the quiet philosophical one. He looked older and more careworn than his colleagues. He'd dropped twenty pounds in the previous months and was thinner than he'd been in years. His 180 pounds hung on his tall frame. Sam was in his early forties but had a clean-shaven baby face that made him look younger. Like Gary, he was quiet and analytical. Maya was the most outgoing of the trio. With her casual clothes and ponytail, she looked like someone who could be your sister's best friend, a woman who was comfortable hanging out with the guys.

The three had been working so hard for so long, and now they were getting so close. They were excited about briefing the SEALs. Their job would be straightforward: Give them the information they need to successfully carry out the mission.

Even though they hadn't identified The Pacer, Gary continued collating daily intelligence from a wide range of secret sources—from the safe house in Abbottabad, satellite photos, intercepts.

They'd monitored the compound twenty-four hours a day for months. They knew every detail. They looked for any possible change. Was The Pacer still there? What about al-Kuwaiti and his family? They were working at an unsustainable tempo, but they'd have to keep it up until the president made a decision.

Now they were striving to figure out as much as possible about the configuration of the interior of the living quarters. And they had some high-tech help. They were able to go "back in time" and look at old satellite images of the main house when it was under construction in 2005. They knew how many doors and windows there were inside, the layout of the rooms, the height of the ceilings. Not much more.

Doors, windows, crawl spaces, the angles of eaves. Gary had never been so taken up with construction details. What they didn't know was what the people in the house had done after the roof went up. Gates, booby traps, underground tunnels—any of those things could have been installed, and they wouldn't have a clue.

As he finished packing, he mused over how much more work remained. Good work. Gary felt positive. When he'd gone to Panetta in August with the big break, Gary wasn't sure. There was only just enough there to tell his boss.

But over time, with more facts and experience, he'd begun to see the big picture. He was getting closer to the target. He equated it to a game of darts. Taking shots that keep landing closer and closer to the bull's-eye, that keep checking out. In the end, if you have a tight group of shots, you know you're on the target. It's there. And that's what happened here, with the compound. Everything seemed to be coming together.

And they were getting the support they needed to make it happen. Gary was struck by Obama. The president had an unbelievably impressive mind. He read every word of every report. And Panetta was a very elite leader. He pushed them hard.

And Gary did the same. He pushed his team. He reminded them that every passing day had a cost. "Every day we wait, there's a price built into it. The opportunity could dissolve and dissipate, and the chance to get him could go away." Every decision had to be made against that ticking clock.

Gary hammered that point home by two numbers he prominently wrote on the window running across the top of his office wall. The one in red Magic Marker represented the number of days since they had discovered the compound. That number went up every day. The point was that with each passing day, the likelihood increased that someone in the compound would discover the surveillance and The Pacer would leave. He'd be gone, just like that. The number in blue represented how much time their bosses gave them to complete a certain task related to the bin Laden operation. That number would go down every day.

When Gary had started writing the numbers on his window, he'd done so out of frustration. But then he continued the practice to build pressure on his analysts. It was the first thing they saw when they entered his office and the last on their way out. It was a reminder that they had to work faster, harder.

The work was exciting, and it was a grind. Gary felt the weight every single day.

He zipped shut his bag, kissed his wife, and told her he'd be back soon. He didn't know just when.

COUNTDOWN:
24 DAYS

April 7, 2011

Somewhere in North Carolina

Gary and his staff set up shop in a clandestine CIA facility in the middle of Nowhere, North Carolina, networking computers and collating top-secret documents for SEAL Team 6 to study. This was going to be a long day, one of many over the next few weeks.

Some of the top brass was already in the room for the big reveal. McRaven was there. So was his boss, Admiral Eric Olson, the head of the U.S. Special Operations Command, which provided command, control, and training for all of the military's elite units. They were joined by Captain Perry "Pete" Van Hooser, the head of the legendary SEAL Team 6. They'd tell the chosen men what their mission was about, then share the classified materials and answer any questions.

This moment was almost surreal for Gary, the culmination of years of work by his team. He knew Sam and Maya felt the same way. The trio understood every detail of the bin Laden operation. They fired up the coffee machine in the adjacent kitchen, tested the microphone up front, and waited.

A few miles away, a van full of SEAL Team 6 members and their gear was rolling in their direction. O'Neill and three of his SEAL buddies, Mack, Paul, and Roth, had been traveling for two days. They flew from Miami to Virginia Beach on April 6. Once back at their headquarters they had walked straight into their commander's conference room, where most of the squadron's leadership was waiting. O'Neill noticed they weren't the only guys who'd been recalled from another assignment—Chesney was there, too.

Willy, the command master chief, rattled off names from a list—SEALs whose personal situations would keep them in Virginia Beach. Willy asked them to leave the room so the remaining SEALs could be "read in," meaning they'd hear details regarding an operation.

The men left and the doors closed behind them. Twenty-four SEALs remained.

"What I'm about to tell you cannot be discussed outside this room," Willy warned. He then told them almost nothing.

They were going to be part of a highly important mission, but he couldn't say where, or what their objective might be. The target would resemble some of the ones they had hit many times in Afghanistan. It was in a sensitive area, and the only access was to literally be dropped on top of the target. The men would be divided into four teams, with four leaders. O'Neill would lead one of the teams.

Willy took questions, but he answered almost every one the same way: "We can't tell you yet."

As the day progressed, Willy disclosed that the top brass wanted only the most experienced guys on this mission. That created a strange hierarchy. Chiefs usually stayed behind at the base, while team leaders directed the mission in the field. For this operation, however, the chiefs would run the teams, and team leaders would do the "sled dog" work, serving as "assaulters, breachers, and snipers."

Three of the teams would handle the assault on the target, Willy said. Meanwhile, O'Neill's team would hold security on the perimeter.

"What kind of air support will be available on this target?" someone asked.

"There will be no air support," Willy said.

Huh? No air support? What the hell was going on? O'Neill thought. Was this some kind of prank?

Chesney sat in the back of the room, listening carefully, feeling proud to be there. The one thing he knew for sure was he was on O'Neill's squad. Chesney admired and respected O'Neill. He had enormous faith in his ability as a leader and a fighter. And as Chesney scanned the room, he smiled. Everybody there had immeasurable talent and experience. This was a Dream Team.

Chesney realized how far he had come from that trailer park in East Texas. He had worked hard, and was helped along, too, by SEALs who'd mentored him. Now he wasn't part of some random SEAL unit. He was counted among the elite. No matter how difficult this mission turned out to be, he'd remember that.

Before Willy wrapped things up, he told everyone they'd have to be at the "The Point" the next day. The SEALs knew Willy was talking about a twelve-hundred-acre CIA paramilitary base about eighty-five miles south in North Carolina. O'Neill made plans to travel with Mack, Paul, and Roth.

The trip was only an hour and a half, time enough for the men to listen to music, share some laughs, and wonder out loud what they were heading into. Pine and oak trees finally outnumbered people and farm animals, and they pulled up to the gates.

Chesney was not far behind them, driving with his four-legged passenger, Cairo.

Meanwhile, the conference room at the base was filling up. Jeremy Bash arrived, as well as Michael Vickers. One by one, the SEALs came in, dressed in casual T-shirts and jeans. They stood among the folding tables, computers, and printers and caught up with their friends. Others followed the scent of fresh coffee to the makeshift kitchen, for doughnuts and hot drinks.

McRaven moved to a stage in the front of the room, which resembled a small theater with raised seating. Everyone stopped talking and took a seat. He stared toward the back and waited until someone shut the doors.

He thanked the men for getting there on such short notice. Then he turned the briefing over to a CIA officer who handed out nondisclosure forms. The mood in the room suddenly changed.

Some guys had been pissed off because they had just come home from long deployments and been called back from family vacations or relaxing training exercises. Their wives and children had been upset. Some believed they might be sent to Libya. Others thought they'd been called in for "some kind of no-notice exercise just to impress the brass." But nondisclosure forms were serious business, almost never issued for training exercises. The room was silent as the men filled out the forms. Whatever was ahead could be some heavy shit.

After the forms were collected, Captain Van Hooser stepped to the stage. He said the CIA analysts would fill in the details, but he wanted to be the one to tell them the mission objective: They were going after Osama bin Laden.

The room was silent. Before the men had a chance to react, Gary came on. He had about seven minutes to give them the big overview of how they had ended up on the road to Abbottabad. It was the appetizer before the main course.

In the past, special ops had been sent on missions to get bin Laden, but they all turned out to be false alarms. Gary wanted to show the men that this time they had the goods. He wanted to say "this is what we know, and this is what we don't know." And if he laid out all the intelligence like that—in clear, honest terms—they wouldn't be skeptical.

Gary told them about the man they'd dubbed The Pacer, who took daily walks in a compound in the city of Abbottabad, Pakistan. But the man, Gary said, never left the property. "We have reason to believe that The Pacer is Osama bin Laden," he said. "You guys are going in to get him."

A number of SEALs glanced at each other with a look that said, "Are they screwing with us, or is this for real?" There were no smiles. No high fives. Bash could tell that this was "a holy shit" moment for many of them. They finally had bin Laden in their sights—and they were the ones who were going to take him out.

The SEALs tried not to show emotion, but Chesney was pumped. Yes, he knew it would be a challenging, dangerous mission, one with a significant likelihood of casualties on the American side. But for him it was the "opportunity of a lifetime."

For six hours, Gary, then Maya, then Sam and others laid out the genesis of their information, and the options President Obama was considering. They went over the couriers, al-Kuwaiti, the slides, videos, inhabitants, maps, and the model of the compound. The operators studied the compound's layout—the walls, gates, driveway, and guesthouse.

O'Neill noticed that The Pacer had arranged things "to keep the world out, and himself in." The compound was built to block every possible view from the outside. That's why the CIA had been unable to confirm his identity.

As the reality settled in, the SEALs realized there was no way they all would get out of there alive. Bin Laden had to have bodyguards, maybe a small army. The house had to be rigged with explosives. Even if they breached the compound, they'd be blown to pieces. Hell, they might not even get there if the Pakistani air defense system brought them down on the way. They might be blown out of the sky by an RPG as they were leaving.

O'Neill's mind kept returning to 9/11, and all the people "who went

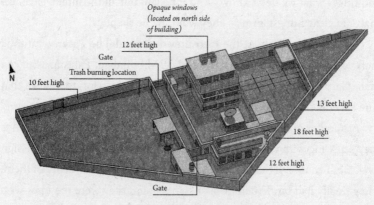

CIA graphic of compound.

to work on a Tuesday morning and then an hour later, decided to jump out of a skyscraper because it was better than burning alive." They were Americans. They were innocent civilians. There was still an empty place at their family dinner tables, a pain that would never heal. O'Neill knew he could die on this mission. But if they could take out bin Laden, it would be worth it.

Chesney knew bin Laden's capture or death wouldn't mean the end of Al Qaeda or the wars in Afghanistan and Iraq. But it would be a "measure of revenge" for the deaths of almost three thousand civilians who perished on September 11, 2001. That's worth something, he thought.

After six hours, the meeting was adjourned, but the SEALs weren't going home. McRaven said they would stay for most of the week and practice, practice, practice. The teams would get together individually in the Operations Center to plan their parts, then they'd head to another part of the base, where the CIA had built a life-sized mock-up of bin Laden's compound. They would spend days at the site working on tactics—how to attack the target—before moving west to another location for a full dress rehearsal.

McRaven told them the mission's name: Operation Neptune's Spear. In Roman mythology, Neptune was the sea god, who carried a trident, a three-pronged spear, a magical weapon that wielded great power. The trident had a deep connection to the SEALs. It was part of the elite unit's insignia, symbolizing the SEALs' connection with the sea.

McRaven hoped it would inspire the men, and perhaps bring good luck on a dangerous mission to get rid of the world's most notorious bad guy. They'd need all the help they could get.

Meanwhile, the SEAL Team 6 members didn't want to waste a minute. After the meeting, they stayed in the building. Bash watched the men examine the model of the compound. He listened as they discussed tactics. The SEALs had been on so many missions that they had a general idea how they'd do this one. It didn't take long before they had sketched out a basic plan: You got a three-story house in a compound surrounded by a big wall. Bad guys on the third floor. A helo would drop guys outside the wall to provide security. Another chopper would hover over the house, where SEALs would fast-drop to the roof and the yard. Then they'd sweep the home.

The team leaders nodded at one another, then approached their commanders. It was time to start rehearsing. And Bash wanted to be there to watch. So after he left the building, he jumped into the back of a flatbed truck with several other people. With everyone on board, the driver headed to a remote section of the base. A few minutes later, Bash glimpsed a clearing behind a thicket of pines. As he got closer, he saw it—a stack of empty shipping containers, arranged at precise angles. Plywood cutouts stood in for stairways, doors, gates, and windows.

It didn't look like a Pakistani luxury villa and its next-door guesthouse, but its dimensions were a perfect match for the original. Chain-link fencing reproduced in exact measure the width and height of the concrete walls surrounding the Abbottabad compound. It wasn't pretty, but it worked. It was the best the CIA could do with the time and resources on hand. Every key feature was accounted for, except one: no one knew exactly what the buildings were like inside. They'd have to guess at that.

Bash's truck pulled into a gravel parking lot. Other vehicles were already there. At the site, Bash paid close attention as the SEALs huddled in small groups. They discussed whether they could fast-rope from a helicopter to the top of the shipping container representing the roof of the house in Abbottabad. They weren't sure whether it was structurally sound enough to hold people. More discussions. Other sidebars. Then the SEALs put on their gear.

It was late in a long day. Bash was bullshitting with the others, waiting to see what would happen next. Then he heard a loud noise. Bash turned around and saw two helicopters, a hundred feet up, headed toward him. About ninety seconds later, the SEALs were on the ground, attacking the compound.

With their guns up, the SEALs weren't running at full speed. No, they were in a "careful hurry" as they moved to their objective. Some went inside the shipping containers. And about ten minutes later, Bash heard someone say, "We've neutralized the object."

After the rehearsal, the SEALs were in no hurry to leave. They were all business. They stood around talking about tactics. Bash heard them say they'd make some adjustments. Then the SEALs called it a day. Bash was amazed at their proficiency. Hell, they'd slapped together and executed a basic plan in an incredibly short period of time. Imagine what they could do with a little practice.

COUNTDOWN:

20 DAYS

April 11, 2011

Somewhere in North Carolina

Colonel John "JT" Thompson rubbed his eyes. Another late night. He had spent hours going over every detail of the aviation plan for the bin Laden mission. Every little detail mattered.

Helicopters had been his specialty for almost twenty-five years. From a tactical perspective, this wasn't the most complicated operation he had ever planned. It wasn't much different from the raids special operation units had conducted every night for years in Iraq and Afghanistan. But Thompson knew it was his most important mission—and that one mistake could take down the entire operation.

The SEALs would be starting dress rehearsals soon at a base in Nevada. McRaven had brought in the best operators in the business, as well as the top operational planners. They had every resource they could need. As a key member of McRaven's staff, Thompson wasn't going to let them down.

Back in February, McRaven had hinted to JT that something big was about to happen. So when the call came a few weeks later in March, Thompson wasn't surprised. McRaven was back from Afghanistan briefly, in Fort Bragg to visit his wife. He wanted to meet Thompson, talk to him face-to-face.

By coincidence, Thompson was already at Fort Bragg for a conference. "Can you swing by?" McRaven asked.

"Not a problem, sir," he said.

McRaven greeted him at the front door of his home. A delicious aroma surrounded them as he led Thompson to the kitchen. The admiral's wife, Georgeann, was just removing a tray of oatmeal-raisin cookies from the oven and offered him some. Who could refuse?

Thompson sat down while McRaven opened the refrigerator. "You want a beer?" he asked.

"No, sir. I have a meeting later," Thompson said.

"How about milk?"

"Cookies and milk is ideal, sir."

McRaven filled up a glass. When Georgeann left the kitchen, McRaven pulled up a chair. A few weeks earlier, he told Thompson he needed air planners but didn't elaborate. He didn't disclose any information—not even the target. Now, he was ready. He leaned over and stared at Thompson. "You need to keep this to yourself," he said. "You can't say a word to anybody."

Thompson nodded, dunking a cookie in the milk. "I understand."

McRaven didn't hesitate. "We think we found bin Laden."

Thompson didn't say a word. He swallowed hard and tried not to show any emotion. Yes, it was a surprise, but Thompson had been down this road a number of times over the years. Once, in 2003, the CIA passed a "bin Laden sighting" along to the military. Thompson recalled "hauling ass" with McRaven from Baghdad in Iraq over to the Bagram Airfield in Afghanistan to track down the lead. Shortly after they arrived, they discovered it was no lead at all. More bad information.

McRaven knew Thompson would be skeptical, so he disclosed all the information he knew about the bin Laden operation. By the time he finished, Thompson knew this one had merit. "I want to be part of it," he said.

"That's why you're here," McRaven said.

Thompson joined the small team planning the mission. He enjoyed working with his old friend. McRaven was a charismatic commander, at ease with anybody—from enlisted men and women to U.S. senators and presidents. The two men had a lot in common, from their work ethic to their backgrounds. McRaven and Thompson both came from military families. Like McRaven's father, Thompson's grandfather had been a pilot in World War II. He was killed when his plane was hit by anti-aircraft fire during a mission over Germany.

Thompson's father, Robert, had been a U.S. Army captain, a helicopter pilot with the legendary 1st Cavalry Division. In August 1969, during his second deployment in Vietnam, Robert's UH-1C was shot down in the Quang Ngai Province. He was just twenty-eight years old. At the time of his father's death, John was two years old.

After Robert's death, his wife moved the family back home to Georgia. She became a teacher, and eventually remarried. She didn't tell her son much about his father, but on his seventeenth birthday, she handed him a letter that Robert had written to the young boy on his second birthday—one that, if something bad happened to him in Vietnam, his son would open someday.

It was a letter filled with the harsh realities of life, but one that inspired hope and optimism and offered sage advice to a boy on the cusp of manhood. It was a letter that would ultimately change the trajectory of his life:

> *Ours is a world beset by perhaps every tragedy imaginable and the majority of them are created by the hands of man. It is in these hands and with God's guidance that our world's salvation lies through, and it is in its salvation and continuance that I pray you participate actively. Your participation will be your desire to strive for what's right.*
>
> *As part of our active life a man has a career and, in all honorable causes, striving for the right is the end result. When you choose your life's work, don't have as your only criteria the fact it's what you like best. I would be a proud father if I thought you also considered that people or mankind in general will benefit from your labors.*

At that point, Thompson was a typical Georgia high school kid. He loved football, chasing girls, and drinking beer. His mother suggested he attend North Georgia College, where she and his father had met. He took her advice. In college, Thompson took aviation classes and learned to fly helicopters, just like his father. When he graduated in 1987, he got his army officer's commission and began his military aviation career.

Over the years, he had been deployed to a number of hot spots. He saw combat during the liberation of Kuwait in Operation Desert Storm. During that period, Thompson could feel his father's presence. He sensed that everything was going to be OK. He was picking up where his father had left off.

Thompson later joined the 160th Special Operations Aviation Regiment unit, an Army Special Forces division known as the Night Stalkers. Their nickname derived from their skill in nighttime airborne operations.

A year before the terrorist attacks on 9/11, John Thompson heard McRaven speak at the U.S. Army Command and General Staff College in Leavenworth, Kansas. The two men hit it off and began working together at the Joint Special Operations Command (JSOC) in 2003. At JSOC,

Colonel John "JT" Thompson.

Thompson helped plan the aviation parts of thousands of missions. Now, here they were, together again.

McRaven knew the expertise of people like Thompson was key to the mission. His skill with helicopter and airborne mission planning was second to none. If there were flaws, he'd find them, as well as every possible solution.

Thompson proposed a combination of "tactics and technology" to evade radar and fly undetected to the target inside Pakistan. Air defense radar systems send out pulses of high-frequency electromagnetic waves. When those waves hit an object, they send a signal back to the radar's antennae for processing. The systems are used as warning devices to detect approaching enemy aircraft or missiles.

He studied Pakistan's air defenses. Pakistan was a nuclear power, with sophisticated defenses set to detect anything entering its airspace. Its rocky relationship with neighboring India, another nuclear power, had prompted development of a first-rate Pakistani military infrastructure, much of it U.S.-made.

The Americans needed to find a work-around. Thompson could use some countermeasures to fool radar—some tricks could even make objects disappear. There were dead spots in the air defense system, but those wouldn't be enough.

Thompson knew air defense systems are designed to look for enemies in the sky. They scan above the clouds, searching for planes flying at a high altitude. They are not designed to detect anything hugging the ground—fifty to three hundred feet above the surface.

The situation called for some really good helicopter pilots, flyers who could navigate near to the ground. The choppers would appear on radar screens as "ground clutter," along with hills and trees and animals. If the pilots flew low and hugged the mountains, that might be enough.

If anyone could do that, it was the Night Stalkers—crack pilots with thousands of "goggle hours."

Technological advances might help, too. Specially modified Black Hawks had a coating that could absorb radar. Engineers had replaced the helo's sharp edges with gentler curves. With that modification, a Black Hawk could scatter radar beams in so many directions that an air defense system would have trouble recognizing the helicopter.

But even with the best pilots and stealth technology, Thompson knew that 99 percent of the time, something goes awry. He had to "prepare for the worst and hope for the best."

He wrote out "mental rehearsals" for the pilots to study, ways to react to engine trouble or stand-down orders or ground fire from the Pakistanis. The pilots would practice so much that their response to any scenario would become instinctive.

But even with all the training, Thompson knew that no one would know for sure how the pilots would react until the big day came and everything went to hell in a handbasket.

Still, Thompson knew he had to provide an instant answer to every question, every scenario the team might encounter, both in the air and on the ground. He started building a "decision matrix," so if something went wrong on the mission, McRaven wouldn't have to think through all the alternatives in the heat of the moment.

The possibilities were almost endless.

McRaven had conducted thousands of missions. And the last thing he wanted to do in the middle of a crisis was to try to figure out "what the hell you're going to do."

As the commander, he knew that he might have to make tough decisions. And this mission, with all its potential pitfalls, only amplified the need for the matrix.

McRaven knew that from the time SEAL Team 6 launched, there were going to be "six or seven decisions" he might have to make. If Pakistani radar picked up the helos right after they crossed the border, would they continue or abort the mission? What if the Black Hawks were detected halfway or three-quarters of the way to the target? Do they stop or keep going? And what happens if they lose a helicopter when they reach their target? Do they bring in another one?

So if they went ahead with the raid, McRaven would have a piece of paper in front of him. He'd know all the answers in advance. He was leaving nothing to chance.

COUNTDOWN:
18 DAYS

April 13, 2011

Somewhere in North Carolina

O'Neill's body was hurting. For days, he and the SEALs had swarmed over the makeshift compound, practicing over and over who'd drop first, second, and third, how they'd take this corner, how they'd secure that cable. They worked through the days and deep into the nights.

They followed the plans their leaders had devised on how they'd attack and take the fortress. But as they rehearsed, they revised some parts to make them stronger. Four teams, four team leaders. The main house was A1, the guesthouse C1. The helicopters that would take them to Abbottabad were Chalk 1 and Chalk 2.

CIA analysts told them that bin Laden probably lived on the third floor of the main building. His son, Khalid, lived on the second floor. There were probably at least one or two wives and a dozen children there, too. Al-Kuwaiti's brother lived on the first floor of the main house with his family.

Under the original plan, Chalk 2 would drop O'Neill and his team just outside the north gate, where they'd set up to provide "external security." His team would include snipers Jonny and Robby; machine-gunner Mack; Chesney and Cairo; and an interpreter. When the helicopter lifted back up above the main house, another team would fast-rope onto the roof, jump down to the third-floor balcony, then work their way inside.

The other helicopter—Chalk 1—would fast-rope the primary assault team into the courtyard between the main house and the guesthouse. This was the most vulnerable spot. The chopper could be hit from any angle while hovering over the compound.

The external security job was one of the most dangerous on the raid. If the guys inside took too long, they'd have to deal with first responders—most likely police, but possibly military forces.

As team leader for external security, O'Neill wasn't supposed to go inside the perimeter. But as he watched the scenario play out in training, he noticed a flaw. If bin Laden was on the third floor, he had to be well protected. The SEALs needed more shooters inside right away, especially as they worked their way through the third floor.

He expressed his concern to Willy, their master chief. He agreed. He put O'Neill, an experienced shooter, on the rooftop with the other team. Jonny stepped into O'Neill's team leader slot on the exterior security crew.

They hit the mock compound for days. O'Neill fast-roped so much he developed tendinitis. Others were feeling it, too, but no one wanted to complain. This was too important, the mission of a lifetime.

When Chesney first saw the mockup compound, he was impressed. When they prepared for missions, the target was almost always "theoretical," only bits of intel until they arrived on the scene. But this model allowed them to actually rehearse their tactics—the approach, insertion, setup, and successful extraction. For the interior, they'd have to use their intuition, based on their past missions inside similar structures in Afghanistan and Iraq.

As long as everyone knew their role, they'd be OK, he told himself. Chesney liked to compare missions to a game of pickup basketball with friends. Sometimes it's all about "read and react"—you go this way and I'll go that way. Everyone knew the mission front to back, and everyone trusted one another implicitly. That would go a long way.

Chesney only had one screwup—but it had nothing to do with the rehearsal.

Cairo always practiced right along with the guys on every rehearsal. But once, when they were practicing using explosives to breach the compound gates, Chesney decided to leave the dog in his kennel inside his Chevy Suburban. Explosives are stressful to dogs, and there was no need to expose Cairo to needless trauma.

He should have known better. Cairo wanted to be at work with the team, and the dog was a Houdini. He had learned to squeeze his foreleg through the bars of his kennel and use his paw to open the latch. He didn't do it often, but that day he did. Even so, he couldn't open the car door.

When Chesney returned, he found Cairo loose in the vehicle, among tufts of white fabric. He had chewed a headrest to shreds.

"Cairo, what did you do?" Chesney shouted.

When he opened the door, Cairo jumped out as if nothing had happened. Good thing they weren't taking that car with them anywhere.

The work wasn't finished when the practice sessions were done. They returned to the Operations Center and examined the model of the compound. They stood around it, running through different scenarios. What would happen if a car left the compound? Which helicopter would chase it? What about crossfire from the guesthouse? Chemical weapons, gas, flamethrowers? What if the bad guys used the children as shields? What if the women were armed? The SEALs tried to account for everything that could go wrong.

They focused on technical details, including how much time would pass between the first sound of a helicopter approaching the compound and the team entering the building. President Obama had asked about that. Right now, it was ninety seconds. They wanted to reduce that. They didn't want bin Laden to have enough time to get up and flee.

Finally, when they finished working, the men headed back to the small, cramped barracks and tried to unwind. That was getting difficult. They had a game room with Ping-Pong and pool tables, but the mood was somber. Everyone was feeling serious. The gravity of the operation was sinking in.

There was a growing feeling in the room that no one wanted to talk about. One night, O'Neill finally broached the subject. The likelihood of them all coming home safely wasn't good. The compound had to be rigged, especially the main building. If the house blew up when they were on the roof, they were dead. If they got that far.

The Pakistani air defense might easily shoot down the helicopters before they even reached the compound. Or the helos would be blown up as they hovered over the target, waiting while the men were inside. (After the SEALs were in the compound, the choppers would wait at a designated spot on the outskirts of the city.) At the most, they had thirty minutes to get in, get bin Laden, and get out. That's it. The military academy was right down the street. They could be surrounded by Pakistani troops. If that happened, what would they do? Would they fight or surrender? What did the Pakistanis do to prisoners?

O'Neill jokingly called his team the Martyrs' Brigade, the most likely of all to die.

SEALs usually never talk about the dangers of a mission or their own mortality. They keep that to themselves. But that night, one guy looked at O'Neill and said, "Once we go on this mission, we aren't going to see our kids again, or kiss our wives."

The men let themselves consider that. The conversation became existential. Why were they doing this? Why were they willing to sacrifice their lives? For what?

The questions finally petered out to silence.

O'Neill spoke up. "We're doing it for all those people who went to work in New York City that Tuesday morning, thinking they would come home, see their wife and children. But they didn't. They were innocent. They had no way to defend themselves. Now we're going to fight for all those people who died that day. We're going to kill the guy who was responsible for all that."

The energy in the room shifted. The men stood up, stretched, smiled. They were fired up. If they could have gone into Abbottabad that night, they would have.

Maybe they would defy the odds. It was a long-shot mission, true, but maybe everything would break their way and they'd all get home. Everybody's got to die someday. At least they would go out doing something noble.

COUNTDOWN:

16 DAYS

April 15, 2011
Langley, Virginia

The SEALs had finished their rehearsals in North Carolina and were headed to Nevada for a full-dress rehearsal, where they'd simulate the entire raid from beginning to end. Mullen and other top leaders would be there. It would be taped so Obama could watch it during the next meeting in the Situation Room.

Panetta was juggling the bin Laden mission and a hundred other issues. He had asked the CIA's National Clandestine Service, an elite corps of secret mission experts, to evaluate the intelligence. They were skeptics, suspicious of any information that didn't come from human beings. They'd argued that the U.S. needed to get "eyes inside the compound" before carrying out the raid, but Panetta had already tried everything he and his team could think of to confirm The Pacer was bin Laden.

They had CIA agents in a safe house in Abbottabad who collected intelligence day and night. They had a doctor running a fake vaccination campaign in Abbottabad, trying to collect DNA samples from the people living inside the fortress. But so far, nothing. None of the family members had been vaccinated. And with the tight deadline, who knew if that would even be possible.

And Panetta was under pressure from other factors, too. A few days earlier, he'd met with Lieutenant General Ahmad Shuja Pasha, the head of

Pakistan's powerful Inter-Services Intelligence. Panetta and Pasha usually got along well. When Panetta visited Pakistan in 2009, Pasha had insisted that the CIA director stay at his house. But lately, the relationship between the CIA and the ISI had gone salty, thanks to the Raymond Davis incident and the ongoing fighting along the Afghan border. The CIA was all over Pakistan, and the country was getting fed up. The four-hour meeting in Panetta's office illustrated just how complicated those issues were, and how much work it would take to repair the relationship.

The U.S. drone campaign was targeting more Taliban positions on Pakistani soil. Pasha wanted more notice before the targets were hit, but that was unlikely to happen—the U.S. believed the ISI would tip off their targets in advance. Pasha also pushed Panetta to cut the number of CIA agents working inside Pakistan. The United States had several hundred CIA personnel—operators, contractors, and special operations forces—in the country. Too many, Pasha had told Panetta.

Panetta pushed back. He said Pasha was doing too little to stop the Taliban fighters' movements in Pakistan. At the end of the meeting, both sides issued a joint statement, saying they agreed to work closely "on our common fight against terrorist networks that threaten both countries."

The statement was all well and good, but sharp differences remained. And if the United States conducted the Abbottabad raid, Panetta didn't know how long it would take to mend fences with Pakistan—or what the fallout would be. Pakistan might well retaliate by tossing all CIA personnel from the country. They could limit or end reliable supply routes the U.S. military used to move equipment to Afghanistan. Was one terrorist worth all that risk?

Panetta couldn't think about that now. His next meeting with Obama was coming up soon, and he wanted to hear from analysts and operators who had been watching the compound. He wanted their latest assessment about who lived in the house. How certain were they that bin Laden was inside? He would soon have to make a decision on what to recommend to the President: "Go or no go."

He waited at the director's conference table on the seventh floor of the main CIA building, as Gary, Sam, Maya, and others pulled up chairs and sat down. Panetta closed the door and took his seat.

There was a sense of urgency in his voice. He reminded everyone of how far they had come, but also of the shortfalls with the intelligence. It was time to make the decision, he said.

Panetta said he knew they had been working hard for years to find bin Laden. But now they were at a critical point in the mission. And if they made the right decision, he said it would justify all the sacrifices they had made.

"I need all of you to give your honest sense of whether you think there's sufficient justification here to put people in danger and send a commando team into that compound," he said.

Then, one by one, Panetta started going around the table.

"Sam, what do you think?" Panetta asked.

Panetta had worked closely with Sam on the bin Laden operation and several other Al Qaeda cases. He knew Sam was cautious by nature, so he didn't expect Sam's answer. "I think there's an 80 percent chance that he's there," Sam said.

Panetta turned to Maya, who had an encyclopedic knowledge of the bin Laden brief and the compound. She had been acting as the liaison between the SEALs and the agency, the go-to person, the one who could tell them what to expect inside and outside the compound.

"What do you think the probability is that The Pacer is bin Laden?" Panetta asked.

She didn't hesitate: "Ninety-five percent." She said she was "supremely confident," and Panetta noticed that it took everyone aback. It was like she was saying, "I don't know what all you weaklings are concerned about."

Panetta continued around the table. Most of the others weren't as confident as Maya. But overall, the team believed they had a strong case. They believed that bin Laden was there.

And so, when it was all said and done, Panetta knew he still didn't have a clear picture. There was no mathematical equation, no algorithm to show bin Laden was there. Maybe that's why he kept coming back to the same question—one that had been keeping him up at night: Without solid intelligence, was it worth the risk? Only by going ahead with the mission would they know for sure the answer to that question.

COUNTDOWN:
13 DAYS

April 18, 2011
Somewhere in Nevada

The aluminum bleachers filled from the top down, with the boots-on-the-ground men taking the top tiers and the higher-ranking operators and officers filing in and filling the gaps. A low buzz of voices echoed down from the rafters of the airplane hangar. The top brass took the places down front, where their view of the floor was not obstructed.

It was show time at the secret air force base tucked away in the highly classified Area 51 in the Nevada desert. Outside it was sunny and more than a hundred degrees. But everyone who mattered was inside the building. McRaven was here. So was Admiral Olson. The CIA guys filed in: Jeremy Bash, Gary and his team, a few other officials, looking nondescript.

They all knew it was Mike Mullen's voice that would carry the most weight. The chairman of the Joint Chiefs of Staff had become Obama's most trusted military advisor. His take on the mission—whether the SEALs could pull off such an audacious raid—would be critical.

A hands-on commander, Mullen had flown out to the final dress rehearsal to show his support for the SEALs. More important, he wanted to see for himself if they were confident about the operation, something he'd only know by looking into their eyes.

Mullen understood this could be the most important mission of his long career. He had been part of the military establishment for decades.

After graduating from the U.S. Naval Academy in Annapolis, Maryland, in 1968, he had worked his way up, earning a reputation among officers and sailors as a "tell it like it is" kind of guy.

In 2007, George W. Bush nominated Mullen to chair the Joint Chiefs of Staff. After he was confirmed, Mullen pushed for shorter combat tours, and stepped up treatment for post-traumatic stress disorder in returning soldiers and sailors.

Now here he was, inside the massive hangar. The noise died down. The rehearsal of concept, known as a ROC drill, commenced. The drill was an important part of any major mission. It was a walk-through of the battle plan. Everyone from the commanders to their subordinates had to know their roles and responsibilities—what they had to do and when they had to do it.

A huge map of eastern Afghanistan was spread out across the floor, with "Operation Neptune's Spear" lettered across the bottom. The tactical plan was there for all to see: the helicopter flight paths, a mock-up of the residential compound. A narrator opened the drill, reading from a script that detailed the mission.

The helicopter pilots were scheduled to speak first. McRaven was a little worried about that because he hadn't had time to tell Mullen about a change he'd made after his team discovered a potential problem while reviewing the flight plans.

A day earlier, Colonel Thompson had approached McRaven with bad news. After his team calculated the weight of the men and the temperatures they expected on the night of the operation, they weren't sure the Black Hawks could make it to the target and back without refueling. Stopping to refuel inside Pakistan could add another layer of danger to an already perilous mission.

McRaven was stunned. All along, they'd planned to fly two Black Hawks to the target. After the SEALs fast-roped into the compound, the helos would fly to a designated spot near the fortress, where they'd wait for thirty minutes on the ground while the men looked for bin Laden. Then, the choppers would return to the compound to pick up the SEALs before heading back to Afghanistan. Every calculation showed they could do it without refueling. Now, right before the ROC drill, there was a wrench in the works.

Refueling the Black Hawks meant bringing in an additional MH-47 Chinook with a forward air refueling pod (FARP), a spare gas tank. That meant another helo in Pakistani airspace. That meant finding an isolated area in Pakistan where the choppers could land and spend twenty minutes on the ground refueling. They'd have to do it without being detected. Mission impossible, right?

Thompson apologized. But he said it was better to plan for this now than to risk running out of diesel in Taliban-controlled Pakistan.

McRaven was frustrated—during earlier briefings with Mullen, Gates, and Obama, he had said they were going to do the mission without refueling. He had pushed Thompson and his planners hard to find an option that only deployed two helicopters to the compound. This was already an incredibly dangerous mission, and adding more helicopters would only increase the risk. Every new obstacle made it more likely that the president would nix the whole operation.

But McRaven couldn't blame Thompson. His team was the best in the world. He had been asking them all along to go over every little detail of the command-and-control part of the mission. Every possible problem had to be identified ahead of time. And that's what they'd done.

"I assume you guys have identified a secure FARP location," McRaven said.

"We have, sir," Thompson said.

"Let's make sure the refueling is part of the rehearsal," McRaven said.

"We've already taken that into account, sir," Thompson said.

McRaven slapped Thompson on his back and smiled. "We'll be fine, JT."

And he meant it. He knew how long and hard his men had worked on the plans and the practice sessions. He understood that was the key to a successful mission. Hell, that was a major part of his master's thesis at the Naval Postgraduate School. Every historical mission he had analyzed showed that when a particular part of an operation wasn't rehearsed, that portion invariably failed. And he wasn't going to let that happen with Operation Neptune's Spear.

The team had rehearsed every individual aspect of the mission multiple times, but they still hadn't put together the entire production. This was why today was so important.

One reason McRaven had picked this part of Nevada was because it looked and felt like eastern Afghanistan and western Pakistan. The flight path in Nevada included high mountains, vast valleys, and long stretches of desert. For the rehearsal, they wanted to reduce from ninety seconds to a minute the time it took the helicopters to reach the compound once they emerged from the mountains. Keeping it to a minute would give the sleeping inhabitants of the house little time to awake, react, and escape.

Another reason for choosing Nevada was privacy. In North Carolina, they couldn't fly two fully loaded Black Hawks 162 miles each way—the distance between Jalalabad and Abbottabad—without raising some suspicion. In Nevada, they wouldn't bother the neighbors.

McRaven wanted to see how many SEALs with all their equipment could actually fit in the helos. The seats had been removed to make each craft lighter, and there was more room inside than most of the SEALs were used to. Still, as McRaven said, he wanted his men to be "crammed in the back so they would get the experience of 'where does my gear go?' and 'is my weapon OK?'"

He wanted them to practice the refueling on the way back. Some men frowned on that. They told McRaven they knew how to refuel a helicopter.

But McRaven was leaving nothing to chance. They were going to refuel. They were going to do every single thing in rehearsal just as they would on the mission.

And sure enough, they discovered a problem. Because of the special configuration of the modified Black Hawk, they discovered that the nozzle from the Chinook's FARP didn't quite fit into the slots for the fuel tanks. They had to jerry-rig it. Better to find that out before the mission than during—especially if they were being chased by the Pakistani military.

McRaven sat stone-faced in the hangar and listened as the pilots walked everyone through the flight path from Jalalabad to Abbottabad. They discussed how they would handle any possible scenario if something went wrong.

Each assault team leader got up and described what they were responsible for during the operation. Chesney listened carefully, but he already knew the details by heart.

A Black Hawk carrying his team and another would land outside the compound. His squad, which included Cairo, an interpreter, a couple of snipers, and a gunner, would get off first. They'd quickly move into position to provide perimeter security while the chopper dropped off the second group inside the compound.

Chesney's job was to hold security outside the fortress. They might encounter Al Qaeda fighters, or maybe Pakistani police or military. Curious locals might come to the scene to see what was going on. Either way, if units showed up and caused trouble, they would do everything to protect the assault teams inside. If the other teams didn't find bin Laden in the house, Chesney would bring Cairo inside to do a more extensive search. For Chesney, it seemed plausible that if The Pacer really was bin Laden, he'd have a few hiding spots worked out.

After each team presented its plan, members of the audience asked questions. Most of them dealt with how the perimeter team would handle onlookers.

"What is your plan if you're confronted by local police or military?" one member asked a team leader.

"Sir, we will de-escalate if at all possible," he said. "First using the interpreter, and then using the dog. As a last resort we will use force."

Mullen paid close attention to all the details, then asked the SEAL chief petty officer a question: "How fast do we think the Pakistanis could react once they know we're on the ground?"

Without missing a beat, the man rattled off locations. There was a police station about one mile from the compound. An entire infantry battalion was stationed four miles from the target.

"We assess that the police will arrive first, but that it would take at least thirty minutes before an armed element from the battalion arrived. Our bigger concern is the locals who live in houses just across this small ditch," he said, pointing to the map on the floor. "With all the noise from the helos, it's highly likely they will come out to see what's going on."

He stepped over to Mohammad, the American interpreter who was sitting with the assault force. Mohammad was fluent in Urdu and Dari, the most common languages spoken in the area.

"If a crowd develops, Mohammad will tell them it's a Pakistani exercise, that they should go back to their homes," he said. He paused for a moment and grimaced. He knew it wasn't a great cover story. "It should buy us a few minutes," he added, "and that's all we really need."

Mullen was impressed by the plan. But it was more than that. He had been around a lot of Special Forces units, but this one stood out. It was a tough, athletic group, a seasoned unit with a "ridiculous amount of experience."

Yes, they still had to conduct the run-through, but Mullen was confident that would go off without a hitch. Before they adjourned for the dress rehearsal, Mullen spoke to each SEAL involved. He looked them in the eye as he asked them the same question: "Are you confident that you can do this mission?"

And each one, without hesitation, responded the same way: "Yes." Then Mullen handed each one a challenge coin, a traditional way for a military leader to show his appreciation for a phenomenal job.

After the briefing, Mullen pulled McRaven aside. "I see that you added another helo."

McRaven nodded. "It might not be necessary if all the conditions are right. But we need to plan and rehearse as though it were necessary," McRaven said.

Mullen agreed.

As the SEALs left the hangar and loaded into the helicopters, McRaven felt confident of Mullen's support. If Mullen believed, the president was likely to give the mission greater consideration.

The day was far from over. Today's full-scale dress rehearsal would be taped and shown to Obama at tomorrow's meeting in the White House. McRaven knew he had done everything to plan the operation, down to the last detail. Still, that wasn't enough. After the rehearsal, he had one more thing to do: He'd prepare his pitch for the White House briefing. It would be his last chance to convince the president that they were more than ready for one of the most dangerous missions in U.S. history.

COUNTDOWN:

12 DAYS

April 19, 2011
Washington, D.C.

The dress rehearsal went off just fine. McRaven and his people flew back to Washington. The admiral was tired, but he didn't sleep. He spent his time going over the plan again. He couldn't let himself get too confident, as he didn't know what Obama was going to do. He might still call off the raid in favor of a less risky drone strike. He might decide to do nothing at all. The intelligence was good, but the CIA still didn't have the key element: No one could say, for sure, that The Pacer was bin Laden.

The stress of not knowing weighed on McRaven. Maybe by the end of today's meeting, he'd have an answer. In any case, he had to be perfectly prepared, able to answer every question—not only from Obama, but from anyone else in the Situation Room, every heavyweight in the administration: Panetta, Gates, Clinton, Biden. Mullen would be there, too, and all the top military brass. There were some great minds among them, and McRaven didn't want to be blindsided.

The room began to fill up. McRaven took a deep breath. He'd have to wait his turn, but he was ready. Finally, the president arrived. Obama greeted everyone, but he didn't waste time socializing. They all knew why they were there.

Obama started with Panetta. The CIA director said the dress rehearsal went well, but he would leave the details to others. Analysts and operators continued to watch The Pacer walk in tight little circles around his vegetable garden every day, but they still couldn't provide a definitive identification.

He pushed the president for action. Panetta said the intelligence community faced "the law of diminishing returns" in gathering any new details about the compound. There was an opportunity cost to waiting. Every day they didn't act increased the chances that The Pacer would disappear. Panetta didn't want to lose the chance to possibly get bin Laden, not after all these years.

And there was another factor, one adding to the sense of urgency. The SEALs wanted to launch the attack under the cover of darkness. Only two or three nights a month were moonless—and they were coming up soon, the first few nights in May. So if they didn't go then, they'd have to wait until June. But by June, the heat might make it impossible to carry off the raid. It was either now or they'd have to wait until September. More time for bin Laden, if it was him, to decide to leave. More time for the trail to go cold again.

Obama didn't want to squander the opportunity. But the president was still weighing the risks and the rewards. He listened to everyone's opinion and read the reports. He wanted to hear the latest—if the SEALs were ready, if the weather was right.

Panetta updated Obama further on the dress rehearsal. The noise signature—the time the people in the compound would have to react after the helicopters emerged from the darkness—was now down to sixty seconds. He told the president that the teams had methodically assaulted the structure standing in for the compound. Once the Black Hawks reached the target, the SEALs fast-roped into the complex, cleared the area, and returned to the choppers with stopwatch precision. That part of the operation took about twenty minutes. It was only a rehearsal, but it was smooth and fast, a good sign.

When Panetta finished, John Brennan spoke next. He said the

consensus among the national security deputies was to go with the helicopter assault.

Gates told the president that Mullen and the Joint Chiefs of Staff agreed that a raid was the best option. But Gates still had doubts of his own, and this meeting was another chance for him to express his concerns.

Gates's opinion carried a lot of weight. He was a soft-spoken but tough-minded career security analyst who had seen it all. He said he had confidence in McRaven's plan, but he felt the risks were too great. He envisioned a nightmare scenario where the Pakistani military would encircle the compound and take prisoners. Operation Neptune's Spear could easily devolve into a disaster of international proportions.

Obama understood Gates's concerns. He had been wrestling with them himself. That's why he'd held off this long. The room was quiet as McRaven took his turn.

He said he had planned for every little detail, every possible scenario. He watched his men work together, coming up with answers to potential problems. That's how they discovered they needed another helicopter. The additional helicopter with the fuel pod would eliminate the risk of emergency refueling inside Pakistan.

After examining and planning for all possible scenarios—and after a flawless dress rehearsal—McRaven said he was confident the SEALs could "get to the target, capture or kill bin Laden, and get back safely."

Obama nodded. The president still hadn't approved the raid, but he wanted to move on to the next phase. He authorized the assault team to move into position in Afghanistan. They would deploy in a week, April 26. The president would still have time to decide. But if they were going to strike, they had to go soon. They couldn't wait any longer.

COUNTDOWN:
7 DAYS

April 24, 2011

Virginia Beach, Virginia

Will Chesney picked up his cell phone. This was the last thing on his list. It was time to call his father. He knew he wouldn't stay on the phone for long. He took a minute to prepare himself.

Chesney had always been an overachiever, a nose-to-the-grindstone type. He was never the flashiest guy in the room, the smartest guy in school, or the best athlete on the field. He was the guy who got things done through sheer will and perseverance. He succeeded when others failed, and his father was a large part of his success. He'd shown Chesney how hard work paid off. He'd encouraged him, in quiet ways. And even though he didn't see his father much these days, the SEAL still felt very close to his dad. That's why this call was so tough. It might be the last time they'd ever speak.

When Chesney and the other SEALs had returned from the drill in Nevada, they were told to get ready, to "get their affairs in order." They were being deployed to Afghanistan. No one knew if they'd actually carry out the mission—that was up to the president. But they had to be in place in Jalalabad just in case.

Chesney didn't have a wife or children. Taking care of business before the deployment meant making sure he paid up his life insurance premiums. It meant saying goodbye to family members, without telling them anything about the mission. He didn't have to worry about Cairo. His dog would go with him.

He never called his mother before deployments. She was hearing-impaired, so telephone calls were hard going. Chesney sent her text messages instead, to let her know he was being deployed and that he'd try to stay safe. If he called her now, she would suspect something was up. No, he had to stick to his routine. Better she didn't worry.

But his father was a different story. It was routine for Chesney to call him and talk before he deployed. He wouldn't deviate from the script. But this time, as he held his phone, he felt different. He wanted to tell his dad how much he loved him, how much he appreciated everything he'd done for him over the years. Chesney started to tear up just thinking about that. He didn't know how he would get through this call.

He didn't waste any time on the phone. "I just wanted to let you know that I'm leaving. It's unexpected, but there's something important going on."

There was silence on the other end of the line. His father knew not to ask him where he was going or any questions about the deployment. But this time, Chesney opened up.

"There's something important going on and I'm part of it. You would be proud." Chesney paused for a moment. "You can't ask me any questions, but . . . I might not make it back."

He didn't have to see his father's face to know he was upset. He knew his father was searching for the right words to say.

"Be careful, OK?" his father whispered.

"I will. And Dad?"

"Yes, boy?"

"I love you."

There was a long pause. Chesney had broken the routine, told him this might be it, told his dad he loved him. He'd never done that. It was time to go. But before Chesney hung up, he heard his father's voice. "I love you, too."

• • •

Meanwhile, in another part of Virginia Beach, Robert O'Neill was sitting at a table in a Chick-fil-A restaurant, watching his four-year-old daughter chattering with a new friend in the play area. As soon as she'd spotted the other girl, she'd left her chicken nuggets and dad behind and jumped into the ball pit. The children laughed as they dived and leapt. O'Neill sat and smiled, sandwich in hand. The other girl's grandmother was talking to him. He smiled politely and made believe he was listening, but all he could think about was the goodbye to come. The mission had cast a pall over his entire visit home.

When he'd returned from Nevada, his wife, Amber, suspected something was up. He had never been able to say much to her about his deployments. She knew not to ask. And these days it was even harder for them to talk about anything at all. The silence and the long deployments had taken a toll on their marriage. Beyond all that, this time felt odd. It was unusual for her husband to return home unexpectedly from training. Why was he being deployed to Afghanistan now, when plenty of other SEAL teams were already there?

A day earlier, O'Neill had taken his daughters shopping at the mall. He was trying to wrap a lifetime with his children into these few days, hoping to give them happy memories. They'd gone from store to store, buying toys and clothes. They'd had a blast. But as much as he tried, there were constant reminders of the mission—the pain in his ankles and his arms.

He was on his way to a suicide mission. The Pacer was Osama bin Laden. He had to be. Of course they wouldn't know for sure until they got there.

As he was leaving the mall, O'Neill spotted a Sunglass Hut. He walked over and spotted a cool pair of Prada sunglasses. He tried them on. They were perfect. The price tag was hefty: $350. O'Neill had never paid more than $50 for shades.

You really shouldn't, he thought. You're an E-7 in the navy. You can't afford it. But standing there that day, his daughters by his side, he decided to splurge. What the hell? A week from now, he might be dead. So he pulled out his American Express card and handed it to the woman behind the counter.

O'Neill glanced at his watch. It was time to go home. His oldest daughter would be home from school in a little bit, and he wanted to be there when she walked in the door. He'd say goodbye to the girls then, and head to the base.

O'Neill gathered up his youngest from the play area and headed home. He felt his heart aching. If something happened to him, who would tell her? Would she remember him? It was too much for him to think about.

Moments after they got home, his oldest daughter arrived. She ran over and gave her father a hug. O'Neill smiled and held her close, inhaled her scent, wondered if this was the last time. Inside he was breaking down. He didn't want to cry in front of his children. They'd know something was wrong, and he didn't want to scare them. He gave each of his girls a big hug and kiss. He embraced his wife, then grabbed his bag and headed to the door.

With his home in the rearview mirror, he let himself cry. For three and a half miles he sobbed like a baby, right up to the guard shack at the front gates. He took a deep breath, wiped away the tears, slowed for the security check. He had to focus. Focus. That was the only way he'd have a chance to see his family again.

COUNTDOWN:

6 DAYS

April 25, 2011

New York City

Jessica Ferenczy woke to the sounds of spring. Birds sang, rain pattered down. It was early on a Monday morning, but she'd taken the day off work. It was Jerome's birthday.

Jerome would have been forty-seven years old. He would have been retired by now from the force, and running his own law enforcement training facility in the mountains. Jessica would probably have been getting two or three kids ready for school. They had planned that for a while. Jerome had wanted a big family. And how many times had Ferenczy heard Jerome's parents say, "We can't wait until you have children."

In a perfect world, Ferenczy would've spent this day rushing around preparing for a big birthday party. The house would be filled with balloons and cake and music—loud music—and laughter. Lots of laughter.

Ferenczy got up and dressed. She was still living with her supervisor, Larry, and his family, but she was planning to get her own place. It was time.

She was moving on, making plans now. She'd retire in less than two years, collect her pension, and move up to that piece of land she'd bought in the Adirondacks. She was only biding her time now. Once she retired, she'd figure out what to do with the rest of her life. She was in no hurry.

Her friends still worried about her, but she assured them she was improving. She was going to therapy, and that helped. It would be ten years soon. Ten years since she lost Jerome.

How long do people grieve? There wasn't a right or wrong answer. Everyone grieved differently, she'd learned. The wound was always there. Yes, a scab grows over it and you can go on. But then something triggers a memory—it could be a song on the radio, or the scent of a toasting bagel—and the emotions come rushing back. The cut will feel as deep as it ever was.

Ferenczy didn't want to wallow in pain, but she didn't want to forget Jerome, either. Some days it didn't hurt so much. Today, she would look at pictures, write in her journal, and strive to remember. Someday she'd be gone, and without children to tell stories to, no one would be here to keep his memory alive.

So this April 25, just like on every September 11 and December 19— the day they met—she'd spend the day concentrating, focusing on "every single little detail of every single minute" of their time together.

The last ten years hadn't been easy. There were times she'd tried to self-medicate. Friends said she was still young and pretty, she should get out in the world again, find a nice guy. Jessica dismissed that idea. What if that man fell in love with her? It wouldn't be fair to him. She was never going to fall in love again. It would be cruel.

That part of her—dating and relationships—was dead. Jessica knew she could never be emotionally available again.

And that was all right. She liked to tell her friends that she'd had her "good shit up front."

"Some people get old together and they have a lifetime of sweet happiness. And when they die, they die together, in their beds. Now, I have to pay for the happiness I had up front. Jerome ruined me for other men," she said.

She didn't want anyone to pity her. This was just the way things had turned out.

Ferenczy smiled and reached for a notebook by her bed. She closed her eyes for a moment, then scribbled for a good ten minutes. It felt good. Therapeutic. Then she put down her pen, closed the notebook. It was time to face the day.

COUNTDOWN:

4 DAYS

April 27, 2011
Washington, D.C.

Obama had had enough. There were so many issues on his plate he didn't have time for this nonsense. A civil war in Libya. Violence in the streets of Syria. A deadly insurgency in Afghanistan. The U.S. economy still struggling to recover from the Great Recession. And of course, the bin Laden decision.

Yet in the midst of all these serious problems, the president was fielding questions about where he was born. Every week, stories about Obama's birthplace had proliferated on right-wing media outlets. Real estate developer and self-promoter Donald Trump had been pushing a wild theory that Obama was born in Kenya, and not in Hawaii. That supposedly meant Obama wasn't really president because only someone born on American soil could be commander in chief.

So, in the middle of everything, Obama decided he had to put the "birther" issue to rest.

Now, the controversy centered over his short form and long form birth certificates. The long form was the actual copy of a birth certificate on file at the facility where a baby was born. The short form was a notarized document saying the long form existed.

Obama had already released his short form birth certificate, issued by the Hawaii State Department of Health. The form was adequate to obtain a passport, a Social Security number, or a driver's license. But to Trump and his allies, the release of the short form meant nothing. They demanded Obama release the long form version of his birth certificate. "What is he hiding?" "Is he a Muslim?" "The short form has been doctored." The non-sense went on and on and on.

To shut them up, Obama told his counsel Bob Bauer to obtain the long form and release it. Bauer and others thought it was a bad idea. But the president said it was the only way to put an end to the lunacy.

And so the day before a critical meeting about the possible bin Laden mission, Obama held a news conference and released the document. The television news networks broke away from regularly scheduled coverage to carry the president's remarks.

Before he discussed the birth certificate, Obama noted that even though he was in the middle of important budget negotiations with House Republican leaders, the news had been dominated by talk of his birth cer-tificate. He said America faced "enormous challenges and big decisions" about the direction of the country, how they can "shape a better future to-gether."

"But we're not going to be able to do it if we're distracted. We're not going to be able to do it if we spend time vilifying each other. We're not going to be able to do it if we just make up stuff and pretend that facts are not facts. We're not going to be able to solve our problems if we get dis-tracted by sideshows and carnival barkers," he said.

Obama was as worked up as this calm, controlled man got in public. He looked at the reporters in the White House briefing room. He said he knew that no matter what he said or did, some people would still believe he wasn't born in America. But he wanted the vast number of people—as well as the press—to know "we do not have time for this kind of silliness. We've got better stuff to do. I've got better stuff to do. We've got big problems to solve," he said, adding that he was going to focus on the problems—"not on this."

"We're better than this. Remember that," he said.

Jalalabad, Afghanistan

Robert O'Neill tried to relax in his bunk, but sleep eluded him. He was simultaneously tired but amped up. He hadn't been able to unwind. That was to be expected with so much on the line.

Days earlier, O'Neill and his team had boarded a Boeing C-17 Globemaster, a large military transport plane, at Naval Air Station Oceana, south of Virginia Beach. No one except the SEALs and mission personnel were allowed on board. The C-17 refueled at the Ramstein Air Base in Germany. They got off, had breakfast, then flew to Bagram Airfield, the largest U.S. military base in Afghanistan. They spent the night in Bagram, then boarded a C-130 for a quick flight to Jalalabad.

They'd had time enough to get over the jet lag, but everyone still felt squirrelly, trying to kill time until they were told whether or not they'd hit the compound. O'Neill knew the window was closing on a raid, that conditions this weekend would be ideal. For the next few nights there would be virtually no moonlight over Abbottabad. After that, it would be another month until the lunar cycle was in its darkest phase. They didn't have another month to wait. Something had to give.

If The Pacer was bin Laden, how long would he stay there? He could bolt at any time, right? The SEALs were in place, on point, ready to strike. And O'Neill was tired of thinking about it. Let's get this over with, he thought.

SEAL Team 6 was placed in special barracks. They still worked out in the same gym and hung out with the other SEALs on the base, but O'Neill's team couldn't tell the others what was going on, and why they were in Jalalabad in the first place.

The team tried to do what they'd normally do on any other deployment. They killed time working out, listening to music, playing card and video games. Much as they tried, they couldn't stop thinking about their own mortality.

With them at the base was Maya, the CIA intelligence analyst O'Neill had come to trust in the last few weeks. It was good to know she was going to be at Jalalabad through the mission. O'Neill knew that if given the chance, she'd fly with them right into bin Laden's lair. But being here for support was the next best thing.

Maya had become the liaison between the spy agency and the SEALs. Along with Gary and Sam, no one had done more over the years to find bin Laden. O'Neill had met Maya at the North Carolina mission briefing, when the SEALs first learned of their role in the proposed mission. They'd hit it off. Both were outgoing, intense, and had the same dark sense of humor.

In North Carolina, she was the one who first said the word "Abbottabad." The word rolled off her tongue with the ease of long familiarity. O'Neill had never heard of the place, but Maya's confident knowledge made him feel like this mission was legit. So many times in his career he had chased bin Laden's ghost. But not this time.

For two hours she'd commanded the room, keeping the attention of grizzled fighters who had seen it all. She showed pictures on a PowerPoint. She pointed to key areas on the photos—the third floor, where she believed bin Laden lived. The balcony outside his room—the one with a security wall. She talked about al-Kuwaiti and his brother, and how they were shielding someone very important. The man who walked back and forth in a garden every day, a man she and her colleagues had dubbed The Pacer. She had satellite images and other information about the compound and its inhabitants.

After that briefing, O'Neill sat down with Maya over coffee. They talked about the intelligence, and how she'd spent much of her career trying to track down information that would lead to the terrorist leader. Others hedged their bets about The Pacer's identity, but not Maya. She was convinced it was bin Laden. Over time, Maya became one of the guys. Although she joked with everyone, she was deadly serious about the mission. If they had a question, the SEALs went to her. She knew every detail about bin Laden and the compound.

O'Neill got up from his bed. He would head to the gym, put on a little Pearl Jam and hit the treadmill, like he did back in high school. The NFL draft was coming up. Maybe tonight he'd watch a preview show, study up a little. The Redskins needed a quarterback, but who would they take? Until they got word about the mission, the football draft would be a good diversion, a way to lose himself for a few hours.

He'd face reality soon enough.

COUNTDOWN:

3 DAYS

April 28, 2011
Washington, D.C.

Leon Panetta headed to the White House to meet with the president. It was spring and the cherry trees lining the streets were still in bloom. A beautiful day in the nation's capital. But with everything going on, Panetta knew it wasn't the best time to meet with reporters.

After Panetta walked into the White House, he headed to the Oval Office, where he was greeted by Obama. General David Petraeus, the top American commander in Afghanistan, was there, too. Obama was going to announce that he was reshuffling his national security team.

He was nominating Panetta to replace Gates as the next secretary of defense, and Petraeus to lead the CIA. The appointments had been set in motion by Gates's impending retirement.

Panetta already knew the president was going to nominate him. Obama had asked him a few weeks earlier if he'd be interested in the position. He said he had a lot of confidence in Panetta.

"I need you, and I need you in that job," Obama had said.

Panetta said yes. He was old school. If a president says he needs you, you do what he asks. But he didn't expect Obama to make the announcement so close to such a delicate and important operation.

He already had so many things to do. For months, Panetta had been juggling the bin Laden operation in addition to his regular duties, which included monitoring developments in the Arab Spring and the war in Afghanistan.

But this morning, Panetta had to focus on his new position. Panetta, Gates, Biden, and Donilon walked into the White House East Room in their dark suits, white shirts, and ties. Petraeus, in his army-green uniform, and Clinton, wearing a gray pantsuit, joined them. They looked solemn as they flanked Obama, who was standing at a lectern that bore the presidential seal.

In a room filled with reporters and television cameras, Obama praised his new team.

"I've worked closely with most of the individuals on this stage and all of them have my complete confidence. They are leaders of enormous integrity and talent who have devoted their lives to keeping our nation strong and secure, and I am personally very, very grateful to each of them for accepting these new assignments," Obama said.

After the announcement, Panetta spent much of the day in the White House, calling members of the House and Senate Armed Services committees, answering questions about his new post, and how he'd hand off the job of CIA director to Petraeus.

But Panetta's heart wasn't in it. He couldn't stop thinking about the mission. Before long, the day had slipped away. He glanced at the time. It was almost 4:45 p.m. He'd have to pivot to the key afternoon meeting with the president, who was still trying to decide what to do about the compound in Abbottabad.

Panetta knew the president was still considering a drone strike. General Cartwright assured Obama that everything was in place for that option, too. He was just waiting for the order.

Panetta had been urging the president to move forward with the helicopter assault. Time was running out. If they were going to strike, it had to be this weekend. That didn't leave a lot of time for more deliberations.

The director had used the long weeks of waiting to tie up loose ends.

He was involved in every aspect of the operation. If there was a meeting—in person or over secure video phone hookup—he was there. He had discussed operational details with the members of the president's national security team. They'd worked out every possible scenario, including what to do with bin Laden if he was taken alive. They'd also planned how they'd dispose of bin Laden's body if he was killed during the raid.

A day earlier, they had talked about whether to inform congressional leaders when the operation was underway. Panetta said it was a good idea to keep them in the loop, but several others worried about possible leaks. How would they notify them over secure, official lines when the members were at home for the weekend? Panetta proposed warning them late in the week that they might get a secure call over the weekend. It would raise the risk of a leak, but it was the right thing to do. That way, no one could say later that they'd been kept in the dark. The group agreed and the calls went out.

Now, as Panetta entered the Situation Room, most of the members of Obama's national security team were already there, including Donilon, Gates, Clinton, and Mullen. They had been together so many times recently it felt like they were roommates.

Over the last month, they had held seventeen meetings to discuss all aspects of the bin Laden operation. Some sessions included the president. Others didn't. They all involved officials from an alphabet soup of agencies—National Security Council, Principals Committee of the National Security Council, the Central Intelligence Agency. They included officials from the Pentagon—the Joint Chiefs of Staff, secretary of defense. As closely held as the deliberations were, Donilon had insisted on a meticulous process.

If the president gave them the green light, the mission would operate under sections of the law that gave the CIA legal authority to run intelligence operations and covert actions in foreign nations.

As Donilon waited for the president, he thought to himself that "history was in the room." It had influenced the views of some key players who were still haunted by the ghosts of Operation Eagle Claw—the failed

Iranian hostage rescue mission. But that operation was also the reason Obama might approve the bin Laden raid. In the wake of the tragedy, the U.S. military had reorganized its special forces, putting them under one command. They had the best training and equipment. The success of the SEALs and other special forces units in Iraq and Afghanistan had shaped a new generation of leaders, like McRaven and Obama, who weren't obsessed by the mistakes of the past. Donilon knew the president was still weighing his options. But he also knew that Operation Eagle Claw wouldn't determine Obama's decision.

When the president opened the meeting, everyone was ready. Mullen had prepared more than a half dozen slides on a PowerPoint presentation. He walked the president through the raid—"from A to Z." He showed them where they would start, what would happen when they got to the compound, and how they were going to leave.

Mullen said he was confident the SEALs could carry out the mission.

Obama then turned to Panetta. The CIA director said they didn't have any new intelligence that could change what everyone already knew about the compound.

In fact, just about everyone in the room believed the analysis they had was pretty strong. But the president wanted to know more—he wanted to gauge everyone's confidence in the mission. To make sure the CIA had "adequately pressure-tested its work," Obama had ordered a fresh team of intelligence analysts to review the available information about the compound. The president wanted to see how their conclusions matched up with the analysts who had been working the case.

Michael Leiter, the director of the National Counterterrorism Center, had led a special group from the Defense Department to review all the intelligence. He set up two "red teams" of analysts not involved in the bin Laden operation to examine every possible scenario. He said they determined there was a 40 to 60 percent degree of certainty that The Pacer was bin Laden. Forty to 60 percent? That was much lower than the CIA team's 60 to 80 percent assessment.

"Even at the low end, we're 38 percent better than we've been in ten years, since Tora Bora, so we have to do something," Leiter said.

Obama was puzzled about why the estimates were all over the place. He asked Panetta to explain. But Panetta turned to his chief deputy, Morell. "Michael, why don't you handle that one?" he said.

Morell was caught a little off guard. He took a deep breath and tried to explain the discrepancy. He told Obama that everyone was working with the same information, but the analysts who had been directly involved in the fight against Al Qaeda were more confident than their counterparts that bin Laden was inside the compound. Their judgment was shaped by their success in recent years in disrupting terrorist plots and taking out senior Al Qaeda leaders.

The analysts who believed that the intelligence didn't support a raid were shaped by the failures of the past, including the mistaken belief that Saddam Hussein had weapons of mass destruction. Morell said in his opinion there was only a 60 percent chance that bin Laden was in the compound.

"Mr. President, I believe the circumstantial case that Iraq had weapons of mass destruction in 2002 was stronger than the circumstantial case that bin Laden is in the Abbottabad compound. Even if I had a source, a human source, inside the compound, telling me that bin Laden was in there, I wouldn't be at 100 percent. Sources get things wrong all the time."

Dead silence. The case for WMDs had been stronger? People in the room were stunned and shifted uncomfortably in their leather chairs. They couldn't believe Morell had said that.

"So, Michael, if you're only at 60 percent, would you not do the raid?" Obama asked.

"Even at 60 percent I would do the raid. Given the importance of who this is, the case is strong enough," he said.

The president leaned back in his chair and said, "Well, what do you all think?" He turned to his right, to Vice President Joe Biden.

Biden said he'd be more comfortable if they had additional information. Why put troops at risk and further damage U.S. relations with Pakistan if they weren't sure bin Laden was there?

Gates said the intelligence was too weak. He recommended against a raid, although he was still open to a drone strike. He was still haunted by the failed mission to rescue U.S. hostages in Iran back in 1980. Hell, he recalled sitting at this same table in this same room three decades earlier as that tragedy unfolded. He was worried about U.S-Pakistani relations deteriorating to the point that it would affect the war in Afghanistan. The U.S. depended on Pakistani supply routes. And what about the Taliban and Al Qaeda fighters operating along the border? Forget about Pakistan's cooperation in rooting them out.

Mullen supported the raid. So did Panetta, who believed this was the most important decision of his career. They would deploy forces into harm's way, but their objective was the world's number one criminal: Osama bin Laden. For ten years everyone had talked about getting bin Laden. They never thought it was possible. But now, here they were with the president, deciding whether to go after him. If they were successful, it would send a powerful message to the world about the United States' ability to track down and stop bad guys. To show everyone that the U.S. will never give up until justice is done. For Panetta, this would be the defining moment for the Obama administration.

Panetta decided to make another passionate plea.

"There's a formula I've used since I was in Congress," he said. "If I asked the average citizen, 'If you knew what I knew, what would you do?' I think in this case, the answer is clear. This is the best intelligence we've had since Tora Bora. I have tremendous confidence in our assault team. If we don't do this, we'll regret it."

Secretary of State Clinton was the last person to respond to the president's question. She had never been in a meeting where the stakes were higher. She knew this would "make or break Obama's term in office." If they were successful—if they got bin Laden—Obama would get the credit. But if it turned out poorly—the Pakistanis showed up and there was a firefight and America lost men—it would be the end of his presidency.

She had worked with Obama long enough to understand that he was a methodical decision maker. He'd look at all the pros and cons and analyze them before making a final decision. She owed it to him—and the others at the table—to lay things out in a methodical way. And so she carefully went through all the arguments for a raid—as well as all the arguments against.

Clinton said she, too, wished they had time to collect better intelligence. She knew the president would be taking a considerable risk. But Clinton said she strongly believed that The Pacer was bin Laden. And after years of searching for the terrorist responsible for taking so many lives, this was a "rare opportunity" to get him. They had to roll the dice. They might not get another chance.

In the end, Clinton said that for her, it was a "51–49 call." Obama should order McRaven to conduct the special operations raid.

Obama listened carefully. He understood everyone's concerns. President Carter never recovered politically from the Operation Eagle Claw disaster. The president knew his national security team believed that he would suffer the same fate if a raid went sideways. For Obama, it wasn't about running for another term. His decision would be based on intelligence, not politics.

Obama had heard enough. In fact, he was getting a little annoyed. "I know we're trying to quantify these factors as best we can. But ultimately, this is a 50-50 call," he said.

As far as he was concerned, there were four outcomes when it came to a raid. They involved going in easy, meaning the SEALs met no resistance, or going in hard, which meant they faced opposition. The men could go in easy and bin Laden would be there. They could go in hard and he would be there. They could go in easy and he would not be there. Or they could go in hard and he would not be there. Obama said there was only one disaster scenario: They went in hard—things got messy—and bin Laden wasn't there. He said he could live with three of the four outcomes.

So after almost two hours, Obama adjourned the meeting. "I'll let you know my decision in the morning," he said.

If he decided on the raid, Obama wanted to make sure that McRaven had enough time to get it right. McRaven would have last-minute things to do. If the president gave the order, the helicopter assault would take place that weekend. He knew everyone around him was anxious, but they'd all have to just sit tight.

COUNTDOWN:

2 DAYS

April 29, 2011
Washington, D.C.

As the sun rose over Washington, President Obama sat alone in the family quarters of the White House, thinking it over one last time. This was it. He couldn't keep McRaven or his national security advisors waiting any longer. If they were going after The Pacer, they had to move now.

For months, the president had heard all the evidence, studied all the intelligence, read all the memos. He knew every detail of McRaven's plan. He'd watched a video of the SEALs' dress rehearsal. He'd sat through endless meetings where the best minds in the country had argued for and against moving on the Abbottabad compound.

Now it was time. Obama didn't say anything to his advisors, but he'd narrowed his decision weeks earlier. He wasn't in favor of a drone strike because there wouldn't be a body.

The intelligence community didn't need more time to collect information. They'd learned all they could from outside the compound walls. With all the planning going on, with so many people in the loop, information was bound to leak soon.

The only question before the president was whether to order the raid. The stakes didn't get any higher. As Gates had said from the start, something always goes wrong in these kinds of operations. U.S. service members could be killed. They could get into a firefight with Pakistanis. SEALs could be taken prisoner. U.S.-Pakistan relations could be irreparably harmed. A single screwup could cost Obama everything.

The president understood Gates's trepidation, but Operation Eagle Claw had happened in 1980, thirty-one years ago. This was 2011, and U.S. Special Forces were much better trained and equipped. They'd been conducting these kinds of missions for years in Iraq and Afghanistan.

The president had utmost confidence in McRaven. He was the consummate professional. If they were making a movie about a special operations raid, he'd be the star. And he'd play himself.

Obama didn't make big decisions on the fly. Whether it was saving the automobile industry during the financial crisis, or increasing American troops in Afghanistan to help stabilize that nation, he had always done his homework. He was always deliberate. He stayed up late at night studying the issues and evaluating the odds before coming to a decision. It drove some people crazy, but he didn't care. He had to get it right.

And last night, he'd been up late again. He had dinner with Michelle and his girls. They laughed and teased him, how he always wore his "ratty old sandals around the house" and how he "didn't like sweets" because there was "too much joy" in "delicious things." After tucking his daughters in, he went to the Treaty Room, his office in the family quarters on the second floor of the White House, and turned on a basketball game—the Los Angeles Lakers with Kobe Bryant were playing the Charlotte Hornets. And in that room, by himself, Obama made a decision, then went to bed.

Now Obama was ready. Nothing had changed. So he sent an email to Donilon, Brennan, and two other advisors, asking them to meet him in the White House Diplomatic Reception Room. When they arrived, he'd give them his answer.

White House

Tom Donilon rushed from the West Wing over to the residence. It was 8 a.m. and he had just gotten an email from the president. This was it.

He knew the president was getting ready to board the helicopter Marine One to begin a trip to Tuscaloosa, Alabama. Obama and his family were going to look at the damage caused by devastating tornadoes that had swept across the South, killing more than three hundred people.

Donilon had to get there fast. He didn't want to keep the president waiting. Other members of Obama's team were on their way, too, including Brennan. They arrived at the Diplomatic Reception Room at about the same time. When they did, they formed a semi-circle around the president. He usually wore suits, but today he had dressed down: He was wearing casual brown pants, a white shirt open at the collar, a windbreaker, and brown shoes. His family was already on the South Lawn, headed to Marine One.

It was hard to hear over the din of the helicopter, but Obama didn't waste any time. He said he approved the raid, adding that McRaven would have full operational control. And there was one other thing: McRaven would determine the exact timing of the mission.

With that, Obama turned around and walked out the door. Donilon stood there for a moment, watching the president and his family board Marine One. In the distance, Donilon could see the Washington Monument and the Jefferson Memorial. Then it hit him. Now that the mission was a go, he had binders filled with things he had to do, calls he had to make. If he thought the last few weeks had been hectic, just wait.

Kabul, Afghanistan

McRaven checked in with General Petraeus for his weekly Friday meeting. He liked Petraeus, who headed the International Security Assistance Force in Afghanistan. He had just been nominated by the president to replace Panetta at the CIA.

But the general had been kept in the dark about the planning for Operation Neptune's Spear. McRaven knew that decision was probably made by someone in Washington who was afraid of expanding the inner circle to too many people. After the last bin Laden meeting, General Cartwright was supposed to fill in Petraeus about the operation. So when McRaven walked into Petraeus's office, he assumed he had been briefed. But McRaven quickly realized that Petraeus wasn't told everything.

"Cartwright mentioned something about a cross-border operation," Petraeus said.

McRaven took a deep breath. "Well, it's a little more than that."

"What is it?"

McRaven pulled out slides with plans of the mission and laid them in front of Petraeus. "We're going after bin Laden."

Petraeus was stunned, "What?" he said and laughed.

Slide by slide, McRaven walked the general through the plan. When he laid down the slide of the compound, Petraeus said, "Holy shit." He repeated the same phrase as McRaven showed him more pictures.

"We're just waiting for the president's approval," McRaven said.

After the meeting, he took a chopper for the short hop from Kabul back to Bagram, where he greeted members of a congressional delegation. He'd thought about canceling the visit, but went ahead with it. No one wanted the politicians snooping around, but here they were.

He finally finished giving them a tour of the special operations headquarters. It was late afternoon, cocktail hour for the senators. McRaven went back to his office. There really wasn't much he could do for the moment, but that was OK. He'd been taking care of business since he'd touched down in Afghanistan.

His deputy commander, Brigadier General Tony Thomas, had traveled with the assault force to Jalalabad to ensure everything there was ready to go. When the time came—if they got a go from the President—McRaven would fly to Jalalabad and oversee the raid from the air base there.

Weeks earlier, he had asked Colonel Erik Kurilla, one of the most aggressive special operations combat leaders, to assemble a quick reaction force of two dozen SEALs in case Team 6 got into trouble. During the raid, two Chinooks carrying the QRF would wait in place inside Afghanistan at the Pakistani border. Two other Chinooks would fly into Pakistan and land in a remote area about thirty miles north of the compound. Then they would set up a refueling site where the Black Hawks would stop on the way back to Afghanistan. If the SEALs had any trouble with one of the helos at the compound, a Chinook at the refueling site would peel off to Abbottabad.

Now he told Kurilla to have the QRF on standby. McRaven also put his "gorilla package" on standby—the fighter planes and AC-130s that would protect his forces in case they were pursued by Pakistani aircraft.

He finished his decision matrix. If the helos were spotted as they crossed the Pakistani border, they'd abort the mission. The same if they were detected all the way up to the halfway point to the compound. After that, they'd keep going.

Yes, everything was ready. McRaven was just waiting for a call.

Langley, Virginia

Panetta paced. The president was deciding. If it was "yes, move forward with the raid," Panetta would relay word immediately to McRaven.

It was early. The president had a busy day ahead. Panetta knew Obama was traveling to Alabama, then to Cape Canaveral, Florida, with his wife and daughters to watch the final launch of the Space Shuttle Endeavour. Later in the day, Obama was giving the commencement address at Miami Dade College.

Morell walked into Panetta's office just in time for the phone to ring. Panetta picked up. It was Donilon. "It's a go," he said. Obama had said yes.

Panetta smiled. "OK, I'll get on it."

Morell stood by as Panetta phoned McRaven. "We got the approval. We'll go this weekend," he told the admiral.

Just when they would hit the compound was McRaven's call. He'd have to look at the weather. McRaven said he was leaning toward Sunday instead of Saturday, but he'd let Panetta know more that afternoon.

"I'm praying for you," Panetta told McRaven. "For the mission, for all of you to get home safely. And one more thing."

"Yes sir?"

"Get in, get bin Laden, and get the hell out of there. If bin Laden's not there, get the hell out of there anyway!"

After he hung up, Panetta sat in his office with Morell and let himself breathe. So much had happened since Gary told him about the fortress in Abbottabad. No one could have known it would lead to a special operations strike to take out the son of a bitch. The scale of the president's decision almost overwhelmed Panetta. So many lives at risk. America's prestige on the line. Who knew what would happen over the next forty-eight hours? One way or another, history was about to be made.

At that moment, before he did anything else, Panetta decided he wanted a "command record" for historical sake. So, in longhand, he wrote a brief note:

Memo for the Record—

Received phone call from Tom Donilon, who stated the President made a decision with regard to AC1 [The code name for the compound.] The decision is to proceed with the assault. The timing, operational decision making and control are in Admiral McRaven's hands. The approval is provided on the risk profile presented to the President. Any additional risks are to be brought to the President for his consideration. The direction is to go in and get bin Laden and, if he is not there, to get out. Those instructions were conveyed to Admiral McRaven at approximately 10:15 a.m.

Leon Panetta, DCIA

He took a deep breath. It was done

Meanwhile, everyone had to maintain a sense of normalcy. They couldn't do anything that might spark suspicion.

Panetta looked at his calendar. Obama had a busy day planned. It was a good thing he didn't cancel his events. But then he noticed Saturday night's schedule. It was the annual White House Correspondents' Dinner. It was part celebrity roast, part fund-raising gig for journalism scholarships. The president would be expected to show up, sit on the dais, and poke fun at Washington personalities.

The president would have to attend, even with such a weight on his shoulders. Panetta didn't envy him. But right here and now, Panetta had to get on the phone and spread the news to everyone in the loop. They were going ahead with the raid.

Pentagon, Washington, D.C.

Gates was finally on board. Before the president announced his decision, Mullen; Michael Vickers, the assistant secretary of defense for special operations; and Michèle Flournoy, the undersecretary of defense for policy, had visited Gates in his Pentagon office.

They thought it was important to have Gates support the raid. Maybe it would help persuade Obama to green-light the mission. The three officials understood why Gates opposed the operation. He had lived through the failed 1980 Iranian hostage rescue.

The secretary sat impassive as Vickers went over the intelligence in the bin Laden operation one more time. He told Gates the evidence was "really quite strong."

"Our forces can do this," he added.

Then it was Mullen's turn. He and Gates had known each other for decades. Gates once told Mullen that Joe Biden hadn't been right about an important issue in forty years. After yesterday's meeting with the president, the two had shared a ride back to the Pentagon. That's when Mullen turned to Gates and reminded him about his Biden comment.

"What's going on here?" Mullen said. "Over the last forty years, he's got it all wrong and now you voted with him two days in a row?" They both laughed. In Gates's office, Mullen made the same pitch as Vickers: They could pull this off.

At the end of the meeting, Gates thanked them for the briefing. He didn't say what he would do. But after they left, Gates called Donilon. "Tell the president I'm all for the raid."

"Obama made the decision to go," Donilon told him.

Bagram, Afghanistan

McRaven hung up the phone. The mission was on. It was morning in D.C., but in Kabul, eight and a half hours ahead of Washington, it was already late afternoon.

McRaven was businesslike. He'd start to let his inner circle know about the president's decision. All the training was done. The SEALs were prepared.

McRaven felt remarkably calm. Had they been 100 percent certain that bin Laden was there, maybe he would have felt more excited about the mission. But he knew they might fly to Abbottabad, raid the compound, and come up empty. He had learned a long time ago to "never get too high, never get too low."

His main job right now was to watch the weather. If it cooperated, the operation would go off on Saturday as planned. If not, they'd go on Sunday. Either way, he'd be up early, ready to go.

Washington, D.C.

The day was packed with meetings, but Donilon and Panetta called another one. The president was on the road. Still, they gathered the major players in the Situation Room anyway, just to make sure everyone was on the same page.

The room filled up as the afternoon stretched on. Panetta said Mc-Raven would decide when the operation would begin and how it unfolded. They went over who was responsible for what, but they weren't going to micromanage the mission from this distance.

This was officially a CIA operation. It had been classified as a "Title 50," referring to a section of the U.S. code that authorized the agency to carry out covert missions. This way, if something went wrong, the United States could deny it had anything to do with the raid. But everyone knew the mission was McRaven's to direct.

Someone brought up the White House Correspondents' Dinner. The president was expected to go. But should he be laughing and glad-handing with a major military operation unfolding half the world away?

"Fuck the Correspondents' Dinner," Hillary Clinton snapped.

Everyone stopped. Clinton explained. The dinner was set for 8 p.m. Saturday night. Pakistan was several time zones ahead of Washington. If things went according to plan, they'd know long before the dinner started whether the mission was a success or not.

If Saturday was the best night for the raid, McRaven should go for it, Clinton said. Would it be difficult if something went wrong? Yes. But it would be more difficult if they said, "Oh, sorry, you can't go after bin Laden because we have a dinner that night. If we ever let a political event get in the way of a military operation, shame on us." That was absurd.

In the end, they agreed the decision was McRaven's to make. The timing of the operation had been delegated to him. Now they could only wait.

Meanwhile, Donilon and Brennan had some important unfinished business. Several key cabinet members still had no idea about the bin Laden operation. Now it was time to tell them.

The two White House advisors expected blowback. They knew some officials might ask why they had been excluded. Weren't they critical members of Obama's team? Donilon and Brennan read in FBI Director Mueller and Attorney General Holder. Both men said they understood. Brennan "drew the short end of the straw" and had to brief other members of the national security team.

When he told Susan Rice, the United Nations ambassador, she said, "Way to go." But Janet Napolitano, the homeland security secretary, was less than thrilled. Her job was to stop terrorist attacks against America. If the raid was successful, Al Qaeda might try to retaliate against the United States. Napolitano said she wished she had more time to prepare, but her department would be ready.

COUNTDOWN:

1 DAY

April 30, 2011
Jalalabad, Afghanistan

Word quickly spread across the base: A briefing! O'Neill, Chesney, and other members of their team hurried to the squadron building. This was it. Either the mission had gotten the green light, or they were packing up to go home.

Captain Van Hooser, the top SEAL Team 6 commander, didn't waste any time.

"The president authorized you guys to launch," he said. "It's either today or tomorrow."

O'Neill was excited. They were going! They were really going to do it! Logistically, this was the best time for a raid. Conditions would be perfect—the moon was in its first phase, a new moon, meaning the skies would be dark. Perfect cover.

Within the hour, McRaven decided to postpone the raid until Sunday. Meteorologists predicted low-lying fog along the route. Fog probably wouldn't cause major problems for the Black Hawks, but the temperature was getting close to sixty-eight degrees Fahrenheit. If it went higher, they'd have to take men off the helicopters to save fuel—and they barely had enough soldiers to begin with.

And McRaven took something else into consideration: the White House Correspondents' Dinner. He wondered what would happen if they launched the operation on Saturday and they ran into trouble? If the president was at the event and had to be pulled out, the entire press corps would start asking questions. Why take any unnecessary risk, especially when conditions were supposed to be better on Sunday? So McRaven decided to delay for a day.

He called Panetta and told him. Panetta, in turn, contacted everyone on his team. Word spread among the SEALs.

With the delay, O'Neill decided to do something he'd been putting off. He headed back to barracks, but veered into the admin offices for a pen and paper. On the way out he ran into Maya, the CIA liaison.

"Hey, what's going on?" O'Neill asked.

"I'm nervous. Aren't you?"

O'Neill shook his head no. "I do this every night. I fly somewhere. I fuck with some people. This is just a longer flight," he said. "But you? Now I see. You need to be right, since we're about to invade a country to take out someone we're only guessing is there. Based on years of your work. So, yeah, I understand why you're nervous," he said.

He didn't stay around to talk. He went to his cubicle and sat down in the chair at the small desk by his bed. He spread out the paper and drew squiggly lines to bring the pen to life. It was time to write letters to his children.

Even with all the military planning and firepower behind him, O'Neill felt this was the end. There were just too many risks. If The Pacer was bin Laden, the house had to be booby-trapped to kill invaders. There had to be escape tunnels and Al Qaeda fighters ready to give their lives to protect their leader. The Pakistani military had all sorts of monitoring equipment to protect their airspace.

He was on a team that would land on the roof of the main house. For weeks, they'd been jokingly calling themselves the Martyrs' Brigade, because they knew the building was going to blow as soon as their feet hit the roof. O'Neill had no regrets about the mission. This was his job. And if there was even a slight chance of getting bin Laden, he'd sign up for that anytime. And he had. So had the other guys on his team.

He had to say goodbye, in letters to his children and family members— letters that would only be delivered if he was killed in the raid.

O'Neill didn't write to his four-year-old and seven-year-old daughters. He wrote to their adult selves, his girls as twenty-four- and twenty-seven-year-old women. They were pages filled with apologies—for not being there for their graduations and weddings, for missing out on their celebrations and heartbreaks. He thanked them for being there for each other, and for standing strong by their mother. He knew they'd grow up to be wonderful women.

As he wrote, tears fell on the paper. He had to stop at times to compose himself. This was one of the hardest things he'd ever done.

When he finished, he wrote to his wife, brother, sisters, his mom and dad. When he finished those, he put all the letters in a manila envelope then walked back to headquarters. He had to find someone who would drop the letters in the mail if he didn't come back alive.

He couldn't give them to his companions to mail. If something happened to him, they probably wouldn't be coming back, either.

Washington, D.C.

President Obama stabbed a tiny Old Glory pin into the lapel of his tuxedo jacket and chuckled at one of the funny lines he'd rehearsed. He was less than thrilled about going to the White House Correspondents' Dinner. It had already been a long day.

Earlier in the afternoon, he'd met with Panetta and the national security team to go over the final details—where everyone would be when the raid happened. Some would watch events unfold in the Situation Room. Panetta, Morell, and their staff would watch from CIA headquarters in Langley. But no one was fooling themselves. Once the helicopters took off, it was McRaven's show.

After the meeting, Obama started going over his material for the dinner. Every president since Calvin Coolidge had attended the event at least once since it began in 1921. Back then, it was a small gathering, an event where politicians and the journalists who covered them for newspapers set aside their differences for one night and poked fun at each other.

Over the years it had morphed into a big Hollywood-like production, a black-tie event broadcast to the nation, where hundreds of journalists, politicians, business leaders, and stars mingled in a hotel ballroom. Usually featuring a comedian, the dinner had turned into a celebrity roast of sorts. And for one night, the president was expected to become a stand-up comic.

It was the last thing Obama needed. The following day he'd oversee one of the greatest military gambles attempted by the United States in decades. What he needed right now was a good night's sleep. But Obama had attended the last two Correspondents' Dinners. If he blew this one off with such little notice, it would raise red flags—in a roomful of nosy reporters. He had to attend. But no one said he had to like it.

A few days earlier, Hawaii had released Obama's long form birth certificate to the press, proving the president truly was born in the United States, and not Kenya. That seemed to have silenced Donald Trump and his fellow "birther" conspiracy theorists—at least for the time being. The birth certificate was still on his speechwriters' minds when they gathered in the White House to help Obama with his monologue. None of them knew anything about the planned operation.

He did ask them to change a line that made fun of the birthers. Minnesota Governor Tim Pawlenty was considering a run for the GOP presidential nomination in 2012. So they wrote that Pawlenty had been hiding the fact that his full name was "Tim bin Laden Pawlenty." Obama suggested they change "bin Laden" to Hosni, the name of the embattled former Egyptian president. The writers didn't like the "improvement."

After the writers left, the president called McRaven. The admiral assumed Obama wanted to talk about the mission. "We're all set,

Mr. President, but the weather in Pakistan was a bit foggy so I decided to wait until tomorrow. We'll be good to go on Sunday."

"Well, don't push it until you're ready," Obama said, adding that he wanted to wish McRaven and his men good luck.

"Tell them that I am proud of them. Make sure you tell them that, Bill," the president said.

"I will, sir."

Then Obama asked McRaven one more question: "Well, Bill, what do you think?"

"I don't know, sir," McRaven said simply. "If he is there, we will get him. And if he's not, we'll come home."

The admiral paused for a moment. He wanted to let the president know that he appreciated his leadership. "Thank you for making this tough decision."

The call was over. Now all McRaven had to do was live up to his promise.

That evening, the motorcade pulled up to the Washington Hilton. When the doors of the presidential limousine, known as "The Beast," opened, Obama and his wife, Michelle, stepped out, looking glamorous.

In a few minutes, they would be hobnobbing with the Washington press corps, celebrities, and billionaires. Inside, they posed for pictures with some of the guests, and made small talk with media magnate Rupert Murdoch, actor Sean Penn, and actress Scarlett Johansson.

The president smiled as he "quietly balanced on a mental high wire." His thoughts were on Jalalabad, McRaven, the two dozen Navy SEALs, and the compound.

As he sat on the dais, he scanned the glittering crowd. There at a nearby table sat Donald J. Trump. Perfect. Half of the president's material was aimed at "The Donald."

Leon Panetta was in the crowd, too, sitting at the *Time* magazine table. He was tense in his tuxedo, but trying hard not to show it. It was surreal, he thought. Actor George Clooney and director Steven Spielberg were seated at his table, and everyone was laughing and enjoying themselves. If these people only knew what the hell is about to happen, what kind of mission we're trying to conduct . . . , he thought to himself.

When it was Obama's turn, he opened with a video segment called, "I Am a Real American," which poked fun at the controversy about his birth certificate. When it was over, he stood up. He faced the audience, flashing his big wide smile.

"My fellow Americans," Obama began, emphasizing "fellow."

He rattled off joke after joke. About halfway in, he focused on Trump. After weeks of attacks, the president got his revenge.

"I know he's taken some flak lately," Obama said, "but no one is prouder to put this birth certificate issue to rest than Donald. That's because he can get back to the issues that matter, like, Did we fake the moon landing? What really happened in Roswell? And where are Biggie and Tupac?"

Obama also took a jab at Trump's plans to run for presidency in 2012.

"We all know about your credentials," he snarked.

Trump didn't laugh. He sat there with a sour face.

But Obama wasn't done. He said the billionaire businessman could bring change to the White House, transforming it from a stately mansion into a tacky casino with a whirlpool in the garden.

"Donald Trump owns the Miss USA pageant, which is great for Republicans. It will streamline their search for vice president," he joked.

The audience howled. Donald Trump seethed.

Obama couldn't imagine what was going through Trump's mind during the few minutes he laid into him. And he didn't care.

But the same reporters who laughed at Obama's jokes that night would continue to give Trump plenty of airtime. And what the president could not have envisioned was that—as preposterous as it sounded—Trump would one day sit in Obama's chair in the Oval Office. In fact, the beating he took at the dinner may have been part of his motivation.

COUNTDOWN:

10 HOURS

May 1, 2011

Jalalabad, Afghanistan

At dawn, the little plane landed at the sprawling base in Jalalabad. Mc-Raven grabbed his gear and bounded down the ramp to the runway. A young petty officer saluted crisply and drove him to the SEAL compound.

They rolled up to the Joint Operations Center, a glorified name for a squat, rambling plywood barn. One end of the building was set up as the Tactical Operations Center for this mission, with banks of computers, telephones, and flat-screen monitors on the walls. Van Hooser greeted McRaven at the door and gave him a quick rundown.

They'd have a final briefing later in the day, he said. After that, the boys would get some rest until it was time to suit up.

McRaven smiled. He knew he could count on Van Hooser to keep things running smoothly. He'd be in direct contact with the SEAL ground commander and provide McRaven with updates as the raid unfolded. Colonel JT Thompson, the man in charge of the helicopters, would report directly to Van Hooser.

Others in the building had their defined roles to play. McRaven had assembled fifteen people from the CIA, air force, and his own staffers who would provide intelligence, surveillance, and reconnaissance—"ISR" in military-speak.

The room was about thirty feet from one end to the other, and perhaps fifteen feet wide. With everybody packed inside, the command center would be tight and noisy. His staff had built McRaven a tiny office just inside the front door—a space no bigger than a closet. This gave the admiral some privacy if he needed to talk to Panetta and the team in Virginia. From inside his alcove, McRaven could still see the action unfolding on the monitors and hear the radio communications. For the most part, he expected to keep the door open. But if the big room got too loud, he could shut himself away with his telephone and computer screen.

McRaven was impressed at the setup. They were up and running. It looked like the weather was going to cooperate. Meteorology had just sent an update: The valleys were clear of fog; the temperature would be 18 degrees Celsius, or 64.4 degrees Fahrenheit. Perfect. Those were the final pieces of the puzzle. The mission was a go. That's what he'd tell the SEALs at the briefing. There was no turning back now.

COUNTDOWN:
9 HOURS, 30 MINUTES

Northern Virginia

Gary jumped up from his bed and glanced out the window. It was still dark, but he had to get to the office. No chance to stop and say anything to his wife and children. They were gone, off on the "mini vacation," the trip he'd hoped would make it up to them for all the time he'd been away from home. It figured the mission would go off this weekend. The house felt very empty.

Gary had laid out his clothes the night before, to save time in the morning. He didn't want to waste time searching for a shirt or tie or shoes. He'd chosen his best. This could well be his last day on the job. If so, he would go out in style.

The SEALs were as ready as they'd ever be, but Gary and his analysts were still working around the clock, monitoring the compound, making sure the people inside didn't leave. No one knew that corner of Abbottabad like Gary's operators. They watched for any possible change, anything that might seem out of place, out of the ordinary—something unexpected that could jeopardize the mission or the SEALs' lives. They were on twenty-four-hour alert, available at a moment's notice to answer questions from military or national security officials.

Gary thrived on the pressure. Eight months earlier, they had briefed Panetta and Morell concerning the lead they'd uncovered on a possible high-value target in Abbottabad. Since then, Gary had become the CIA's point man on the bin Laden operation. He'd examined the intelligence and connected the dots. He'd pushed his analysts, attended countless meetings, sat in rooms with high-profile players, ready to answer any question.

For eight months, he'd experienced gut-wrenching highs and lows, suspended on twin poles of excitement and energy with long stretches of tedium in between. But finally the puzzle pieces had all snapped together. He was working with a team of exceptional players, and the positive energy kept him charged up. It was rewarding, both professionally and personally.

But there was that one potentially fatal flaw: What if The Pacer wasn't bin Laden? Gary would be the big failure, the person who'd oversold it, the person who'd led them all the wrong way. When he was feeling down, it was easy to drag out those doubts.

A lot of people in his position would "paddle in a circle" and hand off the big decisions to the next person. But that wasn't in Gary's DNA. If he was going to do something, he was all in. This had become his truth. He was gambling his career—and a lot more—on it.

Maybe in the end all the hard work, cajoling, and late nights would pay off. If it did, today would be a pretty good day. If it didn't—if it turned into a disaster—this would probably be his last day at the CIA.

Gary wore his blue suit with a chalk pinstripe, a crisp white shirt, and a gray silk pattern tie. He clipped his old-fashioned Montblanc pen into the breast pocket, for good luck. He was ready.

He turned to scan the room, the hallway. He whispered a prayer. He didn't pray that bin Laden was the guy in the compound. No, Gary was confident of that. He prayed for the SEALs. He asked that no good guys die on the mission. Gary took a deep breath and headed for the door. Whatever happened today, hero or zero, his life was going to change. He hoped it would be for the better.

COUNTDOWN:

7 HOURS, 30 MINUTES

White House

The president had gone straight to bed after the Correspondents' Dinner and was up early the next morning, ready to hit the links with Marvin Nicholson, the White House travel director. He had to get outdoors for a while, even if it was just for a quick nine holes of golf at Andrews Air Force Base. Otherwise, the mission would consume him.

Obama was a night owl. He usually worked late into the evening in his Treaty Room office. The phone didn't ring nearly so much at night, and he could think things through without interruptions.

It was a quiet, cool spring morning. His staff had already canceled the public tours of the West Wing for the day. Obama often played golf with Nicholson on Sunday mornings. He wanted to maintain his usual routine. He didn't want anything to seem out of the ordinary. He put

Jalalabad out of his mind. There would be enough time for all that later in the day.

COUNTDOWN:
6 HOURS, 39 MINUTES

Washington, D.C.

Leon Panetta was seated in a pew in the back of Saint Peter's Church on Capitol Hill. If there was ever a day he needed the Lord's help, this was it.

Panetta was a devout Roman Catholic. He often prayed during Mass, usually for his family, the typical health, happiness, success stuff. But today he knelt and bowed his head and focused. He asked God to bless the operation, to put bin Laden in that house, guide those helicopters, to ensure that everything they had planned over the last few months would succeed. Please.

Panetta was confident. He had weighed the pros and cons of the operation a thousand times. No matter how often he and his staff examined the intelligence, it always said there was a damn good chance bin Laden was in Abbottabad. Now they were going to find out. He felt a sense of relief that, after all these months, it was finally going to happen.

He hadn't slept well. He couldn't get the mission out of his mind. When he woke, Panetta knew he had to go to Mass before he headed to the office.

When the Communion hymn finished, the congregation stood for the final blessing. Panetta felt good. The day and everything in it were in God's hands.

COUNTDOWN:

4 HOURS

White House

The Situation Room was set up for a long day. Denis McDonough, the deputy national security advisor, had ordered sandwiches, drinks, and cookies from Costco.

Everybody was in place. Brennan had slept only a few hours the night before. From the time he got up, he went over everything in his mind, asking himself the same questions: What did we miss? What do we still have to do?

Michael Leiter, the director of the National Counterterrorism Center, hadn't slept much either. Long before anyone had heard of Abbottabad or The Pacer, Leiter had scheduled his wedding for April 30. When McRaven slated an April 29 to May 1 window for the mission, McDonough had remembered his wedding invitation. He'd turned to Leiter and asked, "Isn't that your wedding day?"

"Damn," Leiter had muttered. "I'm in trouble."

So, a week before their wedding, Leiter broke the news to his fiancée that he might have to work that weekend. She was stunned. They had big wedding-related events lined up, things they had planned for months. When the date of the raid changed from Saturday to Sunday, Leiter heaved a great sigh of relief—he didn't have to postpone his wedding. Still, he told her they'd have to put off the honeymoon.

"When you find out why, you'll understand," Leiter said.

The wedding went beautifully. Leiter didn't waste a moment thinking of the mission. He enjoyed the ceremony and festivities, thanks to a trick he'd learned as a navy aviator: Compartmentalize. You might be having a bad day at home, but once in the cockpit, you focus on the mission.

He walked into the Situation Room to a hail of congratulations. "Didn't you just get married a few hours ago?" Mullen asked.

Leiter smiled, held up his hand to show the ring on his finger, and grabbed a coffee. Brennan had prepared the most up-to-date information. Afghanistan and Pakistan were quiet—at least as far as the Taliban, Al Qaeda, and Pakistani military were concerned. Donilon arrived with his three-ring binder, talking points, scripts for various courses of action. They reviewed their game plan: a detailed tick-tock of who would pick up which phone and notify which official once the raid commenced.

Mullen was at the White House to make sure nobody tried to grab the steering wheel of the operation. With the live feeds and audio from the Chat Information Network, he knew that could easily happen in a room full of people accustomed to command. McRaven was running the show in Pakistan, and Mullen wanted senior officials' opinions to stay in the Situation Room. The last thing they needed was backseat drivers meddling with the mission.

COUNTDOWN:

3 HOURS

Jalalabad, Afghanistan

The final briefing. McRaven and Van Hooser wanted to go over everyone's role one last time.

O'Neill stepped inside the huge airplane hangar and joined a crowd of about a hundred people. For a secret mission, there sure are a lot of people here, he thought. Besides the SEALs, the aircrews, the mechanics, and the CIA people were gathered.

McRaven sat in a folding chair in the middle of the hangar. He was facing a couple of rows of chairs in front of him, but many of the military stood in a semicircle behind him. McRaven's props were arranged up by his chair—a model of the compound and a big slide projector with key images of the mission. It was show time. The big steel doors rolled closed. McRaven was calm, cool, and confident.

He had every person taking part in the raid come to him and say his name and what his role was in the operation. They went over a checklist of everything they had to do. Sometimes McRaven stopped and grilled them. They had to answer each question without hesitation. And when one man finished, another would come up and do the same thing—from the lowest to the most important members of the team. It went on and on until the very last man.

The briefing was long. As McRaven wrapped it up, he realized he should say something to encourage the men. In a way, he wasn't just their commander. He was their coach, and these men were his team, going into the biggest "game" of their lives. He could see them looking at him like, "OK, Boss, now's the point where you give us some inspiring words."

It was his role, his duty. McRaven stood up and moved closer to the group.

He told them that one of the reasons Operation Eagle Claw had failed was because the assault force was "overly conscious of operational security." So when the C-130s hit a dust storm, they didn't notify the assault helos. They were concerned that Iranians would pick up their communications.

"Look, here's the deal," McRaven said. "You're out there, you talk to me if you have any concerns at all. I want you to talk to me. We'll talk it out and we'll go from there."

He turned to the helicopter crews. The Black Hawks each had two pilots and a crewman from the 160th Special Operations Aviation Regiment, the Night Stalkers. The choppers had been modified to mask heat, noise, and movement. Even with all the stealth modifications, he urged the pilots to fly safely.

"Don't try to fly so damn close to each other that you create a risky flight profile. Your job is to get the SEALs there safely. If you have problems with the helo, set down in a remote area and work through it. Slowly. Methodically. Safely."

Then he focused on the SEALs. He warned them, "Don't shoot any Pakistanis unless you absolutely have to, to save your life. Is that clear?"

They nodded. McRaven reminded them that the operation's goal was to capture or kill Osama bin Laden. "Capture him if you can, but if he presents a threat at all, any threat whatsoever—kill him."

McRaven had gone over the rules of engagement with them before, but he wanted to make sure there were no misunderstandings. No one knew what they'd encounter. In the middle of the night, in a confusing combat situation, anything could happen. Anyone at the site who appeared to pose a threat—male or female—would die. That's what McRaven had told Obama and the national security team, and that's what McRaven told the men in front of him.

He only had one more thing to convey, a little bit of Hollywood. He reminded the men that he was a big basketball fan. Some people smiled because they had played pickup games with him over the years. McRaven said he loved the movie *Hoosiers*. It was the story of a small-town Indiana high school basketball team in 1954 that defied the odds by making it to the state championship game.

McRaven told them about one of his favorite scenes. The team had just arrived in Indianapolis to play a squad from the big city. Most of the kids on the small-town team had never been to a city. The arena where they'd play the game looked cavernous.

"At one point, the coach, played by Gene Hackman, realizes the boys on the team are intimidated by the size of the gym, that they'll be playing on this big stage in front of thousands of people," McRaven said. "So in that arena, when no one else was there except his team, Hackman grabbed one of his players and handed him a tape measure. He told him to climb up on the shoulders of one of his taller teammates and measure the height of the basket. The player turns to Hackman and says, 'Ten feet.'

"Hackman grabbed another player and told him to pace off the length of the court. The player does so. It's ninety-four feet," McRaven said.

The admiral was on a roll. His passion was contagious. The men gazed at him, nodding their heads. They knew where he was headed.

"The court in the arena is exactly the size of the court at home. The basket is exactly the height of the one at home," McRaven said. He paused, then looked at his men. "Gentlemen, each of you has done hundreds of missions just like this one. This mission is no different. The only difference is that this time, the world will hear about it. It's a bigger stage, but it's exactly the same. Just play your game like you always have, and we will be successful," he said.

McRaven was finished. The men in the front stood up. Some shook his hand as he walked out of the hangar into the warm evening.

It was the perfect message for O'Neill. He loved McRaven. The guy was born to give that speech, O'Neill thought. The men headed back to their barracks to suit up. They weren't going to let the admiral down.

COUNTDOWN:
2 HOURS, 30 MINUTES

Langley, Virginia

Panetta had turned the large conference room across the hall from his office into a makeshift operations center. An RQ-170 Sentinel, a drone with a high-powered lens, would hover over the Abbottabad compound and provide a live video feed of the raid. Panetta would likewise be connected by secure video links to McRaven in Jalalabad and the president in the White House Situation Room.

A bank of laptops was arrayed along the tabletop. Gary would also monitor the operation from the conference room.

Morell was in Panetta's office. They were about to head to the conference room when Panetta turned to him. "Michael, what do you think?" Panetta asked.

"I won't be surprised if he's there. I won't be surprised if he's not," Morell said.

Panetta nodded. "I feel the same way."

The room was starting to fill up. Admiral Eric Olson, commander of U.S. Special Operations, had just arrived. Others were testing the feeds from the drones and the audio links, ensuring clear, immediate communications with Jalalabad and the White House.

Panetta reached into his pocket and fingered his rosary. He'd keep it in his pocket for now. When the mission started, he would hold it in his hand.

Word came in: Another national security team meeting. Obama wasn't in the Situation Room yet, but Donilon wanted a quick update. When Panetta appeared on the screen, Donilon asked if anyone had new information to share. Silence. Panetta didn't have anything. No one did.

The meeting was over. This was it. The mission was a go. All they could do was wait. Everyone in the room felt a little tense. So many people had worked so long and so hard for them to get to this point. Analysts and operators had given up weekends, family dinners, children's school functions—plays, conferences, graduations.

Morell was feeling the heat at home. For years, he had missed family events because of his job, and over the last few months, he'd been working longer and longer hours. Mary Beth was shouldering more of the responsibilities at home.

A few days earlier, a friend had given Morell tickets to the May 1 Washington Capitals playoff game against the Tampa Bay Lightning. When he saw he couldn't use them, he asked his wife to come to his office to pick them up. He wanted her to give them away instead of letting them go to waste.

When she arrived at CIA headquarters, Mary Beth expected to go to his office as usual—but Morell told his security detail to meet her down-stairs and hand her the tickets. With all the activity in the office, he didn't want her to get suspicious. His security team took it a step further: They met her at the front gate. They wouldn't allow her into the parking lot. "This is as far as you go," they told her.

She was upset at that, but she really blew up when Morell told her he couldn't attend their daughter's last high school choral performance.

"It will just take an hour," she said. "Whatever you're doing can't be that important."

"I'm sorry. I can't," he said.

Mary Beth was furious. But what could Morell do?

Maybe if they got bin Laden, his wife would understand.

COUNTDOWN:

2 HOURS, 15 MINUTES

Jalalabad, Afghanistan

O'Neill put on his work clothes. He donned his ceramic body armor and packed his Nalgene water bottle, two protein bars, and his Heckler & Koch 416 automatic rifle with three extra magazines. He put his PVS-15 night-vision goggles on his helmet. He was ready.

The sun was setting. He walked to the fire pit where shooters from both squadrons had gathered. The thundering beat of heavy metal music blasted from the speakers. Usually, guys would joke around, throwing a few barbs at one another. They'd bullshit before heading into action. Not this time. This was serious.

Meanwhile, Command Sergeant Major Chris Faris walked into Mc-Raven's office. "It's about time, sir," he said.

McRaven nodded. Faris had become his right-hand man over the last few years. He was an Army Ranger who had seen action in some of the world's most dangerous hot spots. McRaven bounced ideas off him, and Faris always answered with the truth. He was never disrespectful, and was fiercely protective of his commander.

Together, McRaven and Faris walked to the fire pit. The SEALs killed the music as they approached. McRaven could sense their tension. He understood that. There was always some anxiety before a mission. He'd be surprised if the men weren't amped up.

The SEALs closed in around the commanders. Faris spoke first. He reminded them that the motto of their British counterparts, the SAS, was, "Who Dares, Wins."

"Tonight, we are daring greatly and I'm confident that you will come home victorious," he said. McRaven glanced at the men. They had their game faces on. He knew the men loved one another as brothers. They didn't know what would happen to them tonight, but they knew they were lucky to have been chosen for this mission. They had worked their whole careers for a chance like this. McRaven kept his message short and simple.

"Gentlemen, since 9/11 each one of you has dreamed of being the man going on the mission to get bin Laden," he said. "Well, this is the mission. You are the men. Let's go get him."

No one smiled. No one cheered. Buses rolled up to the fire pit to take the men to the hangar where the stealth Black Hawks were warming up. O'Neill had one last thing to do before he jumped on board.

He'd written letters to his wife, daughters, and family members, but he wanted to talk to his dad one last time. He always called him just before he left on a mission. It always put O'Neill in the right frame of mind. He stepped into a nearby doorway to make the call.

His father, Tom, answered right away. He had just pulled into a Walmart parking lot to pick up a few things, so he sat in the car outside the store and talked.

They had a routine. O'Neill would say he was "getting ready to hop on a bird." His father would respond, "I wish I was there to go with you." O'Neill would reply, "I wish you were, too, Dad."

O'Neill stuck with the script. But after Tom said he wished he could go, O'Neill broke the code. "Don't worry, Dad," he said. "I'm with some great guys."

Tom paused for a moment. Something was wrong. "Everything OK, son?"

"Yeah, everything's good," he said. O'Neill took a deep breath. If this was it, if he was killed in the raid, he wanted his old man to know how he felt about him. How much he loved him.

"Hey, Dad. I just wanted to say thanks for everything. Thanks for teaching me how to shoot free throws. Thanks for teaching me how to be a man. It's nice that we got to know each other as adults," O'Neill said.

His father knew his son couldn't talk about the mission, but he could hear the finality in his voice. He was going into the dark. Otherwise, why would he be saying these things? Tom was scared, but didn't know what to say. O'Neill ended the conversation, "I've got to go to work."

"I love you," Tom told his son.

"I love you, too," O'Neill said. "Goodbye."

O'Neill stood there for a moment in silence. He knew his father was worried, but he'd had to do it. Had to. Finally, he put the phone away and jogged to the bus.

He stared out the window as the vehicle pulled up to the airfield about a mile away. The Black Hawks were out on the runway. Huge stadium lights with blinding beams had been set up around them. They faced outward so no one could see the helicopters on the ground.

When O'Neill got off the bus, he took a leak. No one wanted to be thinking about a full bladder in the hours to come. The men boarded in teams. O'Neill and Chesney were on Chalk 2, which would trail Chalk 1 into the compound.

1 HOUR, 39 MINUTES

Jalalabad, Afghanistan

McRaven was ready. He counted down the seconds, then issued the command: "Launch the assault force. I say again, launch the assault force."

Van Hooser relayed McRaven's message to the SEAL squadron commander on one of the two Black Hawks. Moments later, McRaven peered out of his alcove at the command center and watched on the screens as the Black Hawks lifted off.

Everything was live, including the Chinooks with the QRF, the chopper carrying the fuel, and the helo accompanying it. The gorilla package, with the fighter planes and AC-130s, was in the air—just inside the Afghan border, but ready to cross if needed. It all felt very businesslike. McRaven knew he had done everything he could do—all the right planning, all the right rehearsals, great leaders on the ground and in the helos.

There wasn't much left for him to do but stand by to make decisions if something went sideways. He could see the view from the helicopters and listen to the pilots' voices on the radio.

1 HOUR, 30 MINUTES

Somewhere over Afghanistan

The helicopter was packed. Some of the guys sat on folding camp chairs. O'Neill looked around the chopper.

Chesney sat on the floor with his dog Cairo on his lap. Cairo looked relaxed. He could have been headed for a family picnic instead of a dangerous mission. Chesney had his headphones on and was rocking. Some of the guys were asleep. O'Neill didn't know how they could do that. O'Neill was too wired, too anxious to close his eyes.

COUNTDOWN:

1 HOUR, 25 MINUTES

White House

President Obama didn't want to be in the way. He knew if he was in the Situation Room, he might distract everyone. He told Donilon to notify him when the helicopters were in the air.

The president sat in the Oval Office, trying to read through some papers. He couldn't focus. He kept reading the same lines over again. He was wearing a navy-blue windbreaker, khakis, and a white polo shirt—the same outfit he had worn golfing. He called in Nicholson, his personal aide Reggie Love, and Pete Rouse, who was the deputy White House chief of staff. They had all been told about the raid. So, to kill time, the four of them played spades in the dining room just off the Oval Office.

Word came: The Black Hawks were in the air. Obama headed down to the Situation Room. The atmosphere was tense. All the key players were sitting around the conference table: Biden, Clinton, Donilon, Gates, Mullen. Adjoining rooms were full of assistants and technicians.

Obama was updated on plans for notifying Pakistan and other nations after the raid. If The Pacer was indeed bin Laden, and he was killed during the operation, preparations had been made for a traditional Islamic burial at sea. They were concerned that if bin Laden was buried on land, his grave could become a shrine for his followers.

Obama noticed that, evidently for his benefit, his national security team was going over things they had discussed many times before. Worried that he was distracting them, Obama went back upstairs. McRaven was overseeing the mission from Jalalabad. Panetta was officially commanding the operation from CIA headquarters. Obama was an onlooker. His team promised to let him know when the helicopters neared the compound.

COUNTDOWN:

1 HOUR, 20 MINUTES

Somewhere over Pakistan

With headphones covering his ears and an iPod on his shoulder, Chesney closed his eyes and felt the Black Hawk cut through the evening darkness. He was listening to AC/DC's "Moneytalks."

On missions, everyone has his own routine. Some guys talk. Others go over the operation in their head. And some, like Chesney, listen to music to relax or to pump them up.

Chesney liked all kinds of music, but tonight, on this mission, it was hard rock all the way, AC/DC style. With his headphones blasting, Chesney leaned over and patted Cairo on the head.

It was pretty tight inside the Black Hawk. A dozen SEALs were crammed into the back of the chopper. Cairo arched his head and looked up at Chesney. He was ready, too.

It was a moonless evening, and the pilots flew without lights over mountains that straddled the border with Pakistan. Radio communication was kept to a minimum. Chesney had faith in the pilots, a couple of badass Night Stalkers. A voice crackled over the helicopter's speaker: They had just slipped undetected into Pakistani airspace.

For more than sixty years, Pakistan's military had maintained a state of high alert against its neighbor, India. Because of this obsession, Pakistan's principal air defenses pointed east. Maybe they should have paid more attention to the western border, Chesney thought.

He smiled. They'd be there soon. Until then, he was going to keep singing.

Now that they were over Pakistan, O'Neill's mind began to wander. They could get shot down any minute. How does it feel when a helicopter blows up? he wondered. Do we die instantly? How long does it take to die?

To engage his mind, he would count: one to one thousand and back. So, under his breath, O'Neill began: "One, two, three . . ." And when he hit one thousand, he counted backward: "Nine-hundred ninety-nine, nine-hundred ninety-eight, nine-hundred ninety-seven . . ."

COUNTDOWN:

50 MINUTES

Jalalabad, Afghanistan

McRaven went through his checklist. He tracked the helos' movements from point to point. Everything was going as planned. They were monitoring Pakistani radar systems. The Black Hawks hadn't been detected. He hoped that would continue.

But McRaven knew the serious part hadn't even started yet. A few minutes earlier, the SEAL squadron commander had radioed the Joint Operations Center (JOC) and said that a large spotlight was "emanating from a nearby city, sweeping the mountainside." They were apparently looking for something.

So far, intel hadn't detected any Pakistani chatter. They had no idea why the Pakistanis were using the spotlight. McRaven ordered the assault force to press on. But it was something they'd have to keep monitoring.

COUNTDOWN:

35 MINUTES

Langley, Virginia

Gary was in the conference room, along with all the brass, following the helicopters' progress. Binders full of contingencies and timelines were spread across the table. They all knew exactly when the helicopters would get there. But everyone was on edge. The choppers had only been in the air a short time, but it already felt like an eternity.

Panetta was in his usual spot at the center of the conference room table. Morell was beside him. Morell looked around the room. All the communications equipment made it seem like they were playing an important role. But the reality was they were "spectators, not participants."

That only added to the tension. They knew anything could happen at any moment. And if it did, there was nothing they could do. If this was a movie, everyone would be tempted to fast-forward to the end to see how it turned out.

COUNTDOWN:

20 MINUTES

Jalalabad, Afghanistan

McRaven's eyes were darting from the screens to his checklist, when he was interrupted by an aide.

"General Petraeus is on the MIRChat," said the aide, referring to the military's online chat.

"What does he want?" McRaven said.

"He wants to know if we're still doing the mission tonight."

Petraeus didn't know the status. When he'd asked McRaven's liaison officer in Kabul, he didn't know what Petraeus was talking about. No one had briefed him about the mission.

McRaven laughed. "Tell Petraeus we're about ten minutes out from the target."

"Good luck," Petraeus responded.

COUNTDOWN:

19 MINUTES

Somewhere over Pakistan

The helicopter banked south. O'Neill took a deep breath. They were about to begin their attack run. For some unknown reason, he segued from counting numbers to repeating words that President George W. Bush had uttered just hours after the 9/11 terrorist attacks.

"Freedom itself was attacked this morning by a faceless coward. And freedom will be defended."

O'Neill had no idea why he started hearing that line. All he knew was that at that moment, in this helicopter somewhere over Pakistan, he felt an incredible rush of patriotism. He was proud of the men sitting to his right and left, and even the noble dog on the floor. He would fight and die for them. And no matter what happened today, they were heroes.

As O'Neill repeated the words in his head, he could hear President Bush's voice. He could see his face, telling Americans that the United States would never rest until they brought the people responsible for the attacks to justice. In a few minutes, this team might be face-to-face with the man behind the terrorist attacks. O'Neill was ready.

COUNTDOWN:
12 MINUTES

White House

The president's national security team didn't want to give anyone the impression that Obama was micromanaging the operation. That could pose a political problem if the mission failed.

They tried to keep Obama out of the Situation Room as much as possible. They thought it was better if he "indirectly" followed the developments. The president was of the same mind, but he couldn't think about anything else. As the choppers approached the compound, Obama headed back downstairs. Just before he got to the Situation Room, he heard McRaven's voice coming from a small room across the hall.

When he peeked inside, Obama saw a live aerial view of the compound on a desktop video monitor. He stepped inside and watched, over the shoulder of Air Force Brigadier General Brad Webb, who was monitoring the events on his laptop. When Webb looked up, he saw the president. The general offered Obama his seat, but the president put his hand on Webb's shoulder, "Sit down," he said.

Webb immediately let McRaven and Panetta know the president was watching the live feed with him. When the others in the Situation Room found out Obama was next door, they slowly, one by one, joined him there. Biden, Clinton, Mullen, Donilon.

Leiter was eating pizza in the Situation Room when he discovered that just about everyone was gone. When he finally looked across the hall, he saw "so many people jammed in there, it looked like a clown car." Pete Souza, the White House photographer, slipped in and began snapping pictures.

COUNTDOWN:
11 MINUTES

Abbottabad, Pakistan

The helicopter made a slight turn to the right and the doors opened. O'Neill looked outside and there was Abbottabad, looking exactly like all its photos. They started descending as they approached the target. He noticed they were flying over a golf course!

A golf course. There weren't any golf courses in Afghanistan. And lights! The city had lights. Electricity. This is a resort town, O'Neill thought.

For a moment, he smiled. They don't know we're coming. Soon, all hell would break loose. This is serious Navy SEAL shit we're about to do, he said to himself.

COUNTDOWN:
10 MINUTES

Abbottabad, Pakistan

Chesney turned off his music. He checked his radio, weapon, night-vision goggles. He glanced at a laminated card each SEAL carried, with a layout of the compound on it. The two helicopters had flown in tandem up until this point. Now the other chopper, Chalk 1, veered off to the right. Chesney lost track of it.

COUNTDOWN:
9 MINUTES

Jalalabad, Afghanistan

McRaven's eyes were glued to the screen. He didn't like what he was see-ing. Chalk 1 was in trouble. The helicopter was supposed to hover over a designated spot while the men fast-roped into the compound near the main house. But the pilot was having trouble holding the chopper in place.

The Black Hawk buckled and swayed back and forth about twenty feet above the courtyard. The rotors screamed as the pilot tried to lift, but no matter what he did, the chopper wobbled. Then, without warning, its nose tilted toward the ground. The tail spun and struck the compound wall. The helicopter fell.

White House

The images on the video feed were grainy. Even with the less-than-perfect picture, Obama could tell something had happened to the helicopter.

Obama felt "an electric kind of fear." A disaster reel played in his head—a Black Hawk crashing, SEALs scrambling to get out before the chopper exploded. Neighbors running to the scene before the Pakistani military ar-rived, guns blazing.

Mullen shot a glance over at Gates. It looked like the older man was having a heart attack. This was Operation Eagle Claw redux.

Anxiety swept over the room. Were there injuries? Is the mission com-promised?

"Oh, Lord, Murphy turned up," Biden said.

"What are you talking about?" McDonough asked.

"Come on, Denis. Murphy's Law." Anything that can go wrong will go wrong.

President Barack Obama and members of the National Security team watch the raid, May 1, 2011.

Clinton knew the dangers. She had studied the plan. She knew there were a lot of homes nearby. She thought about what the SEALs might face in those streets, with the residents, police, and military. She held her breath and stared at the grainy figures on the screen.

Abbottabad, Pakistan

As planned, Chalk 2 landed just outside the compound. The interpreter, snipers, Chesney, and Cairo bounded out of the Black Hawk and began moving clockwise around the perimeter. They had to clear the area of possible mines and traps, as well as any insurgents who might be there to protect The Pacer.

When Chesney checked behind him, he noticed his helicopter was still there. The pilot was supposed to lift and hover over the main house, where O'Neill and others would fast-rope either to the roof or into the courtyard.

But then Chesney saw O'Neill and the others jump out of the chopper. They were outside the compound—not inside. What happened? Chesney shook his head. He understood that sometimes things change fast on missions. Still, what the hell? But he had his orders. Unless he heard otherwise, he and Cairo would continue with their assigned role.

Langley, Virginia

Bash watched in stunned silence as the rotors of the lead helicopter slowed, then stopped. His heart was in his throat. This was the lead chopper, carrying the SEALs who were supposed to drop into the courtyard. Everything was going wrong. He had no idea what would happen next.

Morell was stunned. When he heard McRaven's voice, he didn't feel much better. "It's down. Can't use it," McRaven said.

Fuck, Morell thought. Gates was right. Something always goes wrong. Is this the end of the mission?

Panetta was anxious. It looked like the whole damn raid was in jeopardy. "Bill, what the hell is going on?" Panetta asked.

"We have a helo that has gone down," the admiral said.

Panetta's heart sank.

COUNTDOWN:

8 MINUTES

Jalalabad, Afghanistan

McRaven had lost a few helicopters in his day. He knew the difference between a crash and a "hard landing." This was a hard landing, survivable. But it came at the worst possible time.

He'd known the most dangerous part of the mission would be when the helicopter was hovering over bin Laden's room, on the third floor of the main house. If there were Al Qaeda fighters there, they could fire an

RPG at the helo. That's why McRaven had positioned snipers and door gunners on the Black Hawk to face the house.

But even with all the planning, something still went wrong. The chopper went down in the animal pen west of the main house—not in the inner courtyard of the three-story home. The radio noise suggested that the SEALs were banged up, but OK. None of the plan was unfolding the way they had rehearsed it. But McRaven stayed calm. He had his decision matrix. They had practiced for these worst-case scenarios. Thank God they'd added the Chinook.

As soon as the helicopter hit the ground, the assault team jumped out of the Black Hawk and headed toward the main house. McRaven called Van Hooser. "How long will it take for the Chinook to get to Abbottabad?"

"About thirty minutes," Van Hooser said.

"OK. . . . She's going to have to be the extract bird."

Colonel Thompson contacted the commander of the Chinook about the change in plans. It would have to come in and, when they were five minutes from the compound, hide in place until it was time to pick up the SEALs.

With the contingency plan set, McRaven reached Panetta. "The SEALs are continuing with the mission. I'll keep you posted," McRaven said.

Panetta took a deep breath. "God bless you. We're all praying for the best."

Abbottabad, Pakistan

O'Neill wondered why they were on the ground on the wrong side of the compound wall. By now, his chopper should have been hovering above the main house so the SEALs could fast-rope to the roof. But something had happened.

The pilot said there'd been a change of plans. They had to start from here instead of the other side of the wall. O'Neill and his team bounded from the helicopter. It was time for Plan B.

They had to quickly find a way to breach the wall. O'Neill had studied the compound's layout and knew every piece of the real estate—every gate, every entrance.

There was a gate near the northeast corner. If the intel was correct, he was only a few feet away.

COUNTDOWN:

7 MINUTES

Abbottabad, Pakistan

Cairo kept his nose to the ground, sniffing for explosives or insurgents. The dog stayed calm even as the sound of gunfire and explosions cut through the darkness. When Chesney turned a corner of the compound wall, he glimpsed something strange in the distance. "What?" he said aloud.

Sticking up, almost resting on top of the other side of a twelve-foot-high section of the compound wall, was the tail of a helicopter. "Hey, that helicopter looks like one of ours," he said.

A moment later, it hit him: That was Chalk 1. He didn't know what had happened, but he didn't have time to worry about it now. He had to stick to the plan. They still had their jobs to do.

Meanwhile, at another section of the wall, O'Neill spotted a metal gate, just where it was supposed to be. He knew this was the place where they'd have to try to get inside. Another SEAL pulled out a seven-foot charge of C-6 and placed it in the middle of the door. Seconds later, the gate blew open. Behind the gate was a solid brick wall. Another SEAL shook his head, "This is bad," he said.

No, O'Neill said. It was a good sign. Having a fake door meant somebody important lived there. O'Neill sent a message to the field commander: They were going to blow the carport gate to get inside. But a voice crackled over the radio: Stand down. A team was already inside. They would open it. A moment later, "Open Sesame," the main gate swung open. There he was, one of the SEALs from the Chalk 1 crew, giving O'Neill a thumbs-up.

O'Neill and his team ran toward the house and the sound of gunfire. This was bin Laden's house. There had to be Al Qaeda fighters in there. The SEALs probably wouldn't all make it out alive. O'Neill was going to do everything he could to take a few terrorists with him.

COUNTDOWN:
6 MINUTES

Jalalabad, Afghanistan

On the video feed, McRaven could see SEALs moving toward the main house. He could hear the explosions and the rounds being fired. But he couldn't see anything inside the building.

He heard someone say, "One EKIA." The SEALs had killed someone. Then he saw multiple explosions. Dark figures moved across the compound, SEALs methodically clearing the outbuildings. He could see beams of infrared light from their weapons' laser sights sweep across the grounds, through the windows, into shadowy spaces where people could be hiding.

Then McRaven noticed something else—something disturbing. Some locals were gathering near one of the entrances. So far, no police. No military. But he knew that could change in a heartbeat.

White House

Leiter had been a navy pilot for six years. When he saw the helo's tail clip the wall, he knew it was curtains. You can't hit anything that hard and fly again, he thought.

Now that the SEALs were entering the main house, Mullen was

frustrated. Sure, they were getting the video feed of the exterior, but they could only guess what was going on inside the building.

The packed conference room was silent. Mullen had been through this before. He learned a long time ago that there are some moments when you're just not in control. He had a lot of faith the SEALs could pull this off. All he could do was wait.

It was excruciating. Clinton looked at Obama, who was hunched over, chin in hand. He looked calm. She didn't know how he did it. There was so much chaos on the ground, the video was just gray swirls, blinking lights, then nothing. For Clinton, this had become a "really intense, stressful experience."

McDonough couldn't sit there. He knelt on one knee, then stood and left the room. He paced up the hall, then went back inside. Now that the SEALs were inside the house, you could hear the silence, he thought.

Langley, Virginia

Bash stared at the monitor. His heart raced as he watched the SEALs, who moved like ants on the screen. He kept checking the time. They had thirty minutes to get in and out. He heard gunfire. He longed to know what was going on.

Panetta sat quietly, his face pale. If people inside the house were firing weapons, they were protecting somebody important.

COUNTDOWN:

5 MINUTES

Abbottabad, Pakistan

O'Neill glimpsed two bodies on the floor just inside the door of the house, a man and a woman, lots of blood. Someone, more than one, was crying. Children. A SEAL came up to O'Neill, his eyes wide. He'd shot the man, he said, but the woman jumped at him as he was shooting. "I didn't mean to hit her," he said. "Am I going to get in trouble?"

"Let's finish the mission," O'Neill said.

Women martyring themselves was a sign they were in the right place. He checked out the dead man. He didn't look like bin Laden. Probably the courier or his brother. O'Neill moved on.

A few of the guys were ahead of him, making their way down a long hallway with four doors. The SEALs went methodically through each room, bringing out little girls, boys, a couple of women. Frightened but unhurt. The SEALs took them to one of the first rooms to keep them out of harm's way.

O'Neill heard a high wail coming from the final room up the hall, a chillingly familiar sound. He stepped inside. It was a tiny girl, maybe four years old, frightened out of her mind. All hell was breaking loose, the world's most notorious bad guy was hiding upstairs, but he couldn't just leave her alone in there. One of the SEALs picked her up and carried her down the hall to the safe room.

The last room secured, O'Neill spotted two SEALs at the end of the hallway using a sledgehammer to smash down a metal gate that blocked the stairway leading to the second floor. O'Neill's eyes scanned the ceilings, the floors, looking for any signs of a bomb. He couldn't stop thinking the house had to be booby-trapped, that it would explode any second. They had to get through that barricade. The longer they stayed in the house, the more danger they faced.

Standing in one place was driving him crazy. For the moment, there was nothing he could do. He heard one of his teammates say something about a helicopter crash. At first, O'Neill thought it was the Chinook with the reserves. Then he learned it was Chalk 1.

The pilot had encountered a mechanical issue while hovering over the compound, and dropped down hard. The rotors had blasted the muddy courtyard, blowing dust and debris everywhere. The chopper was toast.

Oh, shit, O'Neill thought. How the hell were they going to get out of here? At that point his training kicked in. Forget the helo, he thought. It was time to get upstairs and get the son of a bitch before he blew up the house. The mission had become a race against time.

COUNTDOWN:

4 MINUTES

Abbottabad, Pakistan

Chesney completed two laps around the compound. The perimeter was secure. If this was bin Laden's house, why weren't there IEDs rimming the compound? Where were the bombs and snipers? How could they leave this place so unprotected?

With other SEALs providing security on the perimeter, Chesney took the dog and headed inside as planned. Cairo's job was to detect explosives and find anyone who might be hiding. So far, he hadn't found a thing.

Chesney and Cairo stepped carefully inside the house. It was dark and the electricity didn't seem to be working. Debris was everywhere. They passed by the bodies on the first floor.

Chesney was calm. He could hear shooting above him. There were about twenty SEALs in the house already, and he and Cairo had to work through the first floor, then the second and the third.

He didn't know what Cairo might find. There might be a dozen bad guys hiding in the basement, or behind the walls. He couldn't let his guard down for a second.

By the looks of the first floor, the SEALs had engaged the enemy. Steadily and methodically, Chesney and Cairo worked their way through the rooms. When broken glass crunched underfoot, Chesney picked up Cairo and carried him over the danger.

Meanwhile, at the end of the first-floor hallway, the SEALs gave up on the sledgehammer and set an explosive charge. Seconds later, the barricade blew apart. Now they could sweep the second floor.

O'Neill recalled something Maya told them during the briefings: Khalid bin Laden, Osama's twenty-three-year-old son, lived on the second floor. If they made it up there, he'd be armed and waiting to protect his father.

"If you find Khalid, Osama's on the next floor," she'd said.

The staircase was inky dark. The entire house was dark, but with night-vision goggles, the SEALs had the advantage. Whoever was up there on the second floor could hear them coming, but couldn't see them.

The SEALs started clearing the staircase. Suddenly a figure with an AK-47 appeared on a landing between the first and second floors. His head poked quickly into sight, then disappeared behind a banister.

This wasn't good. The man could toss a grenade down the stairs and the shrapnel could take out several SEALs. They didn't know how many others were up there behind him. But they couldn't just stand there. They had to move.

COUNTDOWN:

2 MINUTES

Chesney headed toward the stairs. Cairo was nose to the floor, sniffing for bombs. Chesney was worried the building was wired to blow. Something was going on overhead, gunfire. Yelling. They were almost done here. . . .

Meanwhile, on the staircase, O'Neill was five guys behind the point man. He was wondering whether he should pull them back, but the point man had thought out a brilliant next move. Before the mission, he had learned how to say a few phrases in Arabic and Urdu.

"Khalid, come here," he whispered.

Confused by hearing his name, Khalid poked his head around the banister and said, "What?"

The point man shot him in the face. He dropped onto the stairs, spattering the walls and floor with flesh and blood. The SEALs quickly moved up the stairs to the second floor, stepping over the body on the way.

The men spread out, clearing rooms on the right and left. Meanwhile, the point man stayed on the stairs, aiming his gun at a curtain covering a doorway on the third floor. O'Neill moved up behind him.

Just before O'Neill reached him, the point man fired a shot at something moving behind the curtain. He didn't know if he'd hit anyone. How many people were up there? Were they suicide bombers? There wasn't much time to analyze the situation. O'Neill laid his hand on the point man's shoulder. With a touch, he could give him the sign to halt or advance.

COUNTDOWN:

1 MINUTE

O'Neill heard the men spreading out all over the house. Some were still on the first floor; others were clearing the second. He and the point man stood still, staring up the steps at the curtain on the third floor.

O'Neill had had enough. Maybe he should wait for a few more guys, or have Cairo run up ahead of them. But time was running out. They had already been in the compound for a good while. The man in the room upstairs might be putting on a suicide vest or getting ready to detonate a bomb to blow up the house. Hell, he might toss a grenade down the stairwell.

O'Neill squeezed the point man's shoulder. They charged up the steps—the point man in front, O'Neill right behind. The point man pulled the curtain to the side and moved straight ahead into the darkness, while O'Neill bolted into a room to his right.

The point man ran into two screaming women. He didn't know what they were shouting, but it didn't matter. Thinking one might be wearing a suicide vest, he tackled them to the ground. This way, if they detonated a bomb, he'd absorb most of the blast. He would die, but O'Neill might live.

O'Neill pressed forward into the darkness of the other room. A few steps inside, he saw a man in the half-light, standing at the foot of a bed. He was taller and thinner than O'Neill had expected. His beard was shorter, and his hair whiter. The deep eyes, the sunken face . . . there was no mistaking who he was. It was the face O'Neill had seen a thousand times before. Osama bin Laden.

The man lunged, grabbed a small woman O'Neill hadn't even seen, and pulled her body in front of his, a human shield. She cried out. O'Neill didn't know if bin Laden had a suicide vest, or if other soldiers were about to burst into the room to protect him.

It would be difficult to get a clean shot. He didn't want to kill the woman, but this was the moment of truth. After all these years, O'Neill wasn't going to leave without bin Laden—dead or alive. O'Neill tuned out the chaos—the screaming, the gunfire. He slowed everything down. He focused on the man holding the woman. He aimed his gun above her right shoulder, then squeezed the trigger. Once, twice. And in that moment, everything changed.

COUNTDOWN:
GERONIMO

May 1, 2011
Abbottabad, Pakistan

O'Neill's shots hit the man above his eyebrow, splitting his face open. Blood and skull sprayed the floor and walls. O'Neill put another bullet in his head, just to be sure.

The woman toppled toward O'Neill. He caught her, then carried her to the bed. Her face was blank, stunned.

No wonder. If the man was bin Laden, this was probably one of his wives. Nine minutes earlier, she had been here in this room with him, probably fast asleep. She had to have heard the helicopters, the gunfire and explosions, all the screaming downstairs and men running up the staircases, closer and closer. What had her husband said to her? Then a soldier crashed into their bedroom, her husband held her hard against him, and the flash of gunfire lit up the room. O'Neill had shot her husband in the face, just inches from her own. She'd felt him drop to the floor behind her. Of course the woman was in shock. If Maya was right, this was Amal, the youngest of bin Laden's four wives.

Someone was crying, a child. O'Neill glimpsed a toddler boy, maybe two years old, in the corner. That had to be bin Laden's youngest son.

O'Neill took a deep breath. The room was dark. Maybe the boy hadn't seen anything. He thought about the child, a baby really, innocent of his father's sins. Yet here he was, surrounded by strangers and screaming women, his father a heap on the floor, his mother lying impassive on the bed.

O'Neill stepped to the corner, tenderly scooped up the boy and placed him on the bed next to his mother. Other SEALs barged into the room. They saw O'Neill standing there, breathless, trying to process what had just happened.

"You OK?" one of them asked. He nodded, then asked, "What do we do next?"

The SEAL smiled at the body on the floor. It was dressed in a white sleeveless T-shirt, loose tan pants, and a tan tunic. Half the head was gone, but that SEAL didn't need DNA to know that the guy on the floor was Osama bin Laden. Before they did anything else, they had to let the squadron commander know they had gotten their man.

Jalalabad, Afghanistan

McRaven continued to monitor the mission from his small alcove. Van Hooser gave him regular updates. The admiral watched the clock. They had been in the compound for fifteen minutes. The longer they stayed, the more likely it was that Pakistani police or the military would show up at the scene. Hell, people were already gathering outside.

Van Hooser told McRaven that the SEAL squadron commander was on the radio with an urgent message. "OK, put him on," McRaven said.

A deep, clear voice said the words McRaven had been hoping for: "For God and country, Geronimo, Geronimo, Geronimo."

"Geronimo" was the code name they'd given bin Laden before the mission. The message could only mean one thing: They'd found bin Laden. McRaven quickly relayed the message to Panetta.

Moments later, Van Hooser confirmed that "Geronimo was EKIA." Enemy Killed in Action.

He passed the information to Panetta. The JOC exploded in cheers.

McRaven wasn't ready to celebrate yet. Neither was Van Hooser. "Shut the fuck up!" he shouted at the others. "We still have to get these guys home."

Langley, Virginia

Panetta took a deep breath. All their hard work had paid off. Bin Laden was there, and they'd gotten him. They still had to positively identify the remains. The SEALs still had to get safely back to Afghanistan. But Panetta was relieved. He had risked so much pushing this mission. He stood up and hugged Morell. Aside from that brief moment, it was all business.

Gary, who had spent years chasing a ghost when others had given up, felt a great sense of pride. The Pacer was bin Laden, just as he, Sam, Maya, and the rest of his team had predicted. But his work didn't end just because bin Laden was dead. The mission wasn't over. They had to make sure Al Qaeda wouldn't strike back, launch a 9/11-style attack in retaliation for bin Laden's death.

But sitting there at the conference table, how could Gary not feel joyful? He had redeemed himself. Years ago, he had been disciplined for telling the truth about an insurgency that threatened to tear apart Iraq. At that point, Gary could have thrown in the towel. He could have moved on to other cases. Maybe he could have left the CIA altogether. But that wasn't his style. He was relentless. When he did a job, he finished his work.

It was perseverance that had led to the fortress at the end of the street in a little-known resort town in the shadow of the Himalaya Mountains. He didn't know if this would bring closure to bin Laden's victims, or save his marriage. He only knew that bin Laden was dead, and the world was a better place.

And at some point, maybe they could celebrate. Maybe they could tap into the stock of alcohol they'd been accumulating for such an occasion. In the past, when they thought they were on the verge of getting bin Laden, someone would buy a bottle of scotch or gin or champagne. Then, when it didn't work out, they'd leave it at the office, save it for a better day. Well, the future was now. They just had to pick the right time to open the stash.

White House

President Obama stared at the screen with the live video feed, but he wasn't really looking at the images. The words sank in.

"We got him," Obama said.

Nobody left their seats. They still had to take bin Laden's body out of the house, secure the women and children, look for computers and Al Qaeda documents that might be stored in the compound. They'd have to destroy the downed Black Hawk. With all its new technology, they didn't want to leave it behind.

There was still a load of work to be done.

Biden began tucking a rosary ring back into his wallet. Mullen touched the rosary ring he wore and said, "Mr. Vice President, I've got fifty guys in a foreign country illegally. I've still got to fly them for an hour and a half through enemy airspace, find out who it is for sure, and then fly him on an Osprey down into the Gulf and bury him properly. Please, put the ring back on."

Biden slipped the rosary back into his hand.

Abbottabad, Pakistan

The compound was secure. The women and children were together in one room. No one else had been found hiding in the house. They ransacked the compound for documents, computers, notebooks, maps—anything that could help them fight Al Qaeda in the future. O'Neill joined fellow SEALs as they loaded everything they could find into bags.

Meanwhile, Chesney and Cairo were headed up the stairs to the third floor when another SEAL stopped him. He said it was "crazy" on the third floor. They didn't need Cairo up there. "It's over. Bin Laden's dead," the SEAL said.

Chesney smiled. The intel had been right. He wanted to go up and see for himself, but he knew he should stay out of the way, help to find evidence down here.

As he exited a bedroom, he spotted O'Neill in the hallway. Chesney had known O'Neill for years, they'd flown dozens of missions together. During an operation, O'Neill was all business, one of the toughest and most disciplined SEALs. O'Neill never showed emotion, but now, as he approached Chesney, he smiled. "Dude, I think I just shot that mother-fucker," O'Neill said.

"Seriously?"

O'Neill nodded. He never said "bin Laden," but Chesney knew who he was talking about. For a moment, they just stood there. Over the years, they had seen the worst combat imaginable, some of the deadliest missions in Iraq and Afghanistan. They saw friends die in front of them in bloody firefights, and had dodged many bullets themselves. They had never celebrated in the field. It was uncool, unprofessional, wrong. But that day, on the second floor of bin Laden's hideout, Chesney held his right hand high in the air and shared a high five with O'Neill. When the smiling O'Neill smacked his hand, Chesney shouted, "Fuck yeah!"

Jalalabad, Afghanistan

Time was running out. The SEALs had been on the ground in Abbottabad for twenty minutes. They had ten to go before they hit the danger zone.

Some of the SEALs started placing explosives in the downed Black Hawk. People were starting to mill around outside of the compound.

Van Hooser told McRaven the men had requested more time on the ground.

"They found a whole shit-ton of computers and electronics on the second floor," Van Hooser said.

McRaven was torn. For all they knew, the Pakistani police or military were on their way to the scene. But the opportunity to seize important Al Qaeda documents didn't come along every day. McRaven decided to give them a little more time. The Chinook was on its way.

As soon as he gave the OK, McRaven realized the Pakistanis knew something was up at the compound. Pakistani civilian and military channels in the city were lit up with chatter. Did a helicopter crash in Abbottabad? Were they Americans? All McRaven could do was watch, listen, and hope the SEALs were getting close to leaving.

Abbottabad, Pakistan

The CIA translation officer waded into the crowd. Several dozen people were gathered outside the compound. He calmly told them that this was a Pakistani military exercise. They needed to stand back, he said. For the time being, they bought the story. They started moving away from the walls. It bought them some time. But how much?

Inside the main house, the SEALs scrambled, stuffing everything they could find into garbage bags. O'Neill pulled a duffel bag from under a bed. Inside was something that looked like "freeze-dried, vacuum-sealed rib-eye steaks." But when another SEAL examined the stash, he realized it wasn't meat. It was opium. Hundreds of pounds.

They continued searching the house, but O'Neill felt their time was running short. They had to get out soon. So O'Neill rushed back upstairs to help move bin Laden's body. He stepped into the room where an Arabic-speaking SEAL was interrogating two of bin Laden's daughters. He asked them who was the dead man on the floor. At first, they lied. Then they said, yes, he was "Sheikh Osama"—bin Laden's nickname.

The SEALs put bin Laden's corpse into a body bag and took pictures to help officially confirm his identity and place of death. O'Neill stared at bin Laden's face. It was a mess, split wide open above the eyebrow. O'Neill bent down and pressed parts of his skull together to try to restore his facial features so the guys could get better pictures. They snapped a few frames, then sent them to the ground force commander, who passed them along to the intel folks in Jalalabad.

They zipped the bag closed. O'Neill and three SEALs carried the body outside to the driveway. O'Neill's friend Jonny was there, waiting for the evacuation helo. "Here's your guy," O'Neill told him.

"You got to be shitting me," Jonny said.

O'Neill said he wasn't joking. Bin Laden was inside, covered in plastic.

Meanwhile, Chesney noticed the crowds were returning, approaching from a different street this time. There weren't enough of them to be a problem, but Chesney knew this was a heavily populated city, and it was just a matter of time before they outnumbered the SEALs. And there was another worry. What about the police? Or military? At some point, they'd show up at the compound, right?

Then things could turn ugly fast. Having Cairo, an attack dog, by his side helped. Nobody was going to venture too close to the guys—not with Cairo there, ready to rip them apart.

As he waited, he spotted several SEALs escorting women and children out of the house. They were taken to a wall at the far end of the compound. They'd have to stay there until after the helos picked up the SEALs.

At the same time, the ordnance experts set the timer for the explosives. The clock was ticking for the downed Black Hawk.

Chesney knew four MH-47 Chinooks had been assigned to the mission. Two carried the quick reaction force. Those choppers had waited at the Afghanistan-Pakistan border, ready to jump in if necessary. Two others had crossed into Pakistani airspace and landed in a remote area. They were there for refueling or to help during extraction. Chesney knew they needed one now to get them the hell out.

He heard rotors, and quickly recognized Chalk 2, the Black Hawk he'd arrived on. It landed in the compound, and the assigned SEALs quickly climbed on board with bin Laden's body and the bags of computers and materials from inside the main house. The Black Hawk lifted and headed west to Afghanistan, while the other SEALs waited in a grassy area just outside the compound for their ride.

As luck would have it, Chesney could see the chopper approaching the compound just as the downed Black Hawk was about to blow up. "Oh shit," he muttered.

The team leader remained calm. He radioed the Chinook pilot and said, "Abort. Do the racetrack." That meant something was wrong below and that he needed to take a lap overhead before landing.

The pilot responded quickly, "Copy that."

The Black Hawk exploded, sending smoke and debris all over the compound. If the Pakistani police and military hadn't known they were there before, they certainly did now.

The massive Chinook flew through the smoke and landed safely. Chesney, Cairo, and the others dashed on board the chopper. As the helicopter lifted into the air, Chesney picked up Cairo and glanced at the scene below. Flames and smoke billowed upward from the compound.

It was hard to hear anything beneath the din of the rotors. It was hard to think. But at that moment, Chesney realized he was still alive. They had left behind a trail of death and destruction, but they had accomplished their goal. Bin Laden was dead.

Chesney pulled out his iPod and scrolled through his music. He stopped when he found one of his favorite songs: "It's a Great Day to Be Alive," by country singer Travis Tritt. He sat down on the floor, and with an exhausted Cairo nestled in his lap, Chesney leaned back, closed his eyes, and sang along with the music.

The SEALs had killed al-Kuwaiti, his brother, his brother's wife, bin Laden's son, and the terrorist leader himself. Aside from a few bruises, none of the SEALs had been injured. So it really was a great day to be alive. As Tritt warbled: "Why can't every day be just this good?" O'Neill strapped in and reflected on the mission. He was the man who'd killed bin Laden. What would he say to people? Could he keep it quiet? He felt his pockets for his chewing tobacco.

Two years earlier, he'd tried to comfort his friend Jonny, who had fired the shot that killed the pirate holding Captain Phillips. At the time, Jonny had trouble dealing with the spotlight. He didn't want any fame. He'd just wanted his anonymity back.

Now Jonny returned the favor. He knew how O'Neill was feeling. When Jonny saw O'Neill had left behind his Copenhagen chewing tobacco, he tossed him a tin.

"Take one of mine," Jonny said. "Now you know what it's like to be a hero."

White House

As the choppers left the compound, Biden placed his hand on Obama's shoulder. "Congratulations, Boss," he said.

Langley, Virginia

Bash thought the good-guy helos lifting away from the flaming compound looked like the end of a Jerry Bruckheimer action movie.

But Panetta knew it wasn't time to roll the credits yet. He still had his rosary clutched in his hand. He was waiting for the other shoe to drop, hoping the helicopters made it out of Pakistan.

With all the gunfire and explosions, there was no question in Panetta's mind that Pakistan would activate its military. The only question was how soon, and if they'd be able to reach the U.S. helicopters before they crossed into Afghanistan.

Jalalabad, Afghanistan

McRaven agreed with Panetta. "We still have a long way to go. I'll keep you posted," he said.

An intelligence office notified Van Hooser that the Pakistanis were about to scramble their F-16 Viper fighter jets. The pilots would be on the hunt for the U.S. helicopters. McRaven's analysts said it was unlikely that

Pakistani radar would be able to find and then direct the F-16s to the U.S. choppers . . . but anything could happen out there.

Obama had directed McRaven to "fight their way out." McRaven had his gorilla package of U.S. fighter planes, AC-130s, radar-jamming aircraft, and attack helicopters waiting on the Afghan side of the border. If a Pakistani fighter jet came close, they'd do what they could to protect the U.S. crews. If it touched off an international incident, so be it.

Thirty minutes after the helicopters left the compound, they approached a remote area of Pakistan for refueling. McRaven was concerned. With the Pakistani planes on the move, he had to get the choppers off the ground and over the border. When they landed, McRaven bulldogged Thompson.

"Refueling done yet?" he asked.

Thompson could sense McRaven's impatience. "Sir, we're almost there. Everything's all right."

Maybe, McRaven said.

Finally, nineteen agonizing minutes later, the helicopters were refueled and ready to go. They lifted off and resumed their journey.

Almost an hour later, McRaven finally left his alcove. The choppers had made it into Afghan airspace and were closing in on Jalalabad. McRaven wanted to be on the flight line to greet his men.

White House

With the helicopters out of harm's way, the West Wing of the White House heaved a collective sigh. Obama stood up, and Denis McDonough gave the president a fist bump. But the mood was subdued.

Jalalabad, Afghanistan

McRaven had one more thing to do. He had to see the body to confirm it was really bin Laden, and let the president and Panetta know right away.

McRaven and the CIA's chief of station jumped into a small Toyota pickup and drove to the hangar. It was 3:30 a.m., but McRaven felt fresh. He wasn't tired at all.

He welcomed the men back. They were hugging and yelling and whooping it up. Just a few weeks earlier, they had been drafted for this suicide raid, and now they'd pulled off the most successful U.S. special operations mission since World War II. They were heroes. They had every right to celebrate.

Inside the hangar, O'Neill and his point man waited for the body bag to be removed from the chopper. They spotted Maya. "You've got to give her something from the mission," the point man said.

O'Neill nodded. When they reached her, O'Neill pulled the magazine from his weapon and handed it to her. "Hey, do you have room for this?"

He'd had thirty bullets when he left for the mission. Now he had twenty-seven. She smiled. "I think I can find a place in my backpack," she said.

The three of them walked over to the body bag on the hangar floor. It was already open, waiting for McRaven. Maya stood and stared at bin Laden's face for a few seconds. She showed no emotion. "Well, I guess I'm out of a fucking job," she snapped. She turned around and walked away.

When McRaven reached the body, he knelt and examined the face. Even with the devastating wounds, he and the CIA officer both thought it looked like bin Laden. McRaven had to be sure before he reported to Obama. He pulled the body out of the heavy rubber bag. The legs were folded in a fetal position. McRaven grabbed the corpse's legs and straightened them out. Now it was at full body length.

McRaven knew bin Laden was about six feet four inches tall. No one could find a tape measure. So McRaven looked around the hangar until he spotted a lanky SEAL.

"How tall are you?" McRaven asked him.

"Six foot two."

"Good. Lay down next to the body," the admiral said.

The SEAL gave McRaven a "you want me to do what?" look.

McRaven repeated himself. So the guy took a deep breath and lay down next to the remains. McRaven could see that the SEAL was a good two inches shorter than the body. It had to be bin Laden. McRaven left the hangar. It was time to call the president.

White House

Obama looked at McRaven over the video teleconference line. The admiral said he had examined the body. They didn't have the results yet of DNA tests or the CIA's facial recognition software, but in his opinion, the body was bin Laden's.

He even told Obama that he had a six-foot-two SEAL lie next to the body to compare his height to bin Laden's.

"OK, Bill, let me get this straight. We have $60 million for a helicopter, and you don't have $10 for a tape measure?" Obama joked.

They laughed, a rare moment of levity.

The president said he knew McRaven still had things to do, but he wanted the admiral to pass along something to his men. "This was a historic night and all of America will be proud of them," Obama said.

McRaven was the ultimate tough guy. He thrived under stress. His men loved him. But that night, the president's words moved him. He fought back tears. "Thank you, sir. I will pass it on," he said.

Soon, Obama and his national security team were passing photographs of bin Laden's corpse around the conference table. Obama knew it was him.

Still, they wouldn't be 100 percent sure until the DNA tests came back. During the mission, a SEAL had used a long needle to extract samples from the corpse's upper thigh. That sample would be analyzed for DNA. Not only that, they had cut off the man's pinky fingers for the same purpose. In fact, Maya would carry one of them back with her to Washington, in a small box. But they wouldn't have the DNA test results back for another day or two.

Langley, Virginia

After McRaven's call, Panetta closed the link to Afghanistan. Panetta, Morell, Bash, Gary, and Sam jumped into a black armored Chevy Suburban and headed to the White House.

It was 6:30 p.m. The sun was setting over Washington. The nation's capital was quiet.

When they got to the White House, they headed to the Situation Room, where an NSC meeting was already underway. Everyone looked up when they entered.

"Great job," Obama said. "Everyone at the CIA who worked on this deserves the nation's thanks."

It was a touching moment. Panetta knew agents didn't always get recognized for their hard work. But here the president was, in real time, offering his gratitude.

Now Obama had to decide what they should do next. Should they

President Barack Obama and advisors in the Situation Room.

announce the raid? Osama bin Laden's death? The president wanted to wait for DNA analysis, but Panetta argued that it would take too long. "This is going to come out," Panetta said. They had turned the compound into a war zone. Hell, they just blew up a Black Hawk in bin Laden's front yard.

Obama said Panetta had a point. He joked that he just might listen to Panetta, because at the moment, his standing with the president was pretty high.

"Today, anything you say, I'm prone to agree with," Obama said.

But Obama said they had to get this right. That included making sure Pakistan was told about bin Laden before it hit the news. Panetta knew this was typical Obama. He was a president who carefully analyzed everything before making a decision.

The meeting was about to adjourn when Morell rushed into the room, carrying the facial recognition report. The analysis measured details like the curvature of his ear, the space between his eyes and the shape of his earlobes. Everything matched.

"We got him," Obama said. Now there was no guessing. Obama decided he would tell the nation later that night. A Sunday night. How many people would tune in? So what? They had to get it out there.

"Let's have a draft of the speech within an hour," Obama said.

The West Wing was up and running. Before they did anything else, they would have to call top U.S. and international leaders to let them know bin Laden was dead. Obama would have to work on his remarks. Speechwriter Ben Rhodes would help him craft the right words.

U.S. officials had to handle each Pakistani leader a little differently.

Mullen reached out to his counterpart in Pakistan, General Ashfaq Parvez Kayani. The men had a good relationship, but he didn't know how Kayani would react to the United States conducting a raid on Pakistani soil—without their knowledge or permission. When Mullen reached Kayani, he apologized for calling so early in the morning there, but he said he wanted the general to know they got bin Laden.

"It's a good thing you arrested him," Kayani said.

"He's dead," Mullen responded.

Silence.

Bin Laden, dead? The general was taken aback by that, as well as by the news the terrorist had been living in Abbottabad. But then Kayani made a request. He asked Mullen if the United States would make the announcement of bin Laden's death in a way that would give the appearance that maybe Pakistan took part in the military action. It was a way for Pakistan to save face. Mullen said Obama was planning to tell the American people in a few hours.

Obama called Pakistani President Zardari and Afghan President Karzai. Surprisingly, Zardari was supportive. He recalled how his wife, Benazir Bhutto, had been killed by extremists with reported ties to Al Qaeda.

Panetta phoned General Ahmad Shuja Pasha, head of Pakistan's intelligence agency. When he picked up, Pasha said he had already heard about the raid. Word spread quickly in Pakistan.

Panetta was frank. He said the United States had made a deliberate decision to exclude him and his agency from the operation. This way he would be shielded from any blowback from the Pakistani people who might think they cooperated with the United States. The raid would only exacerbate the increasingly frosty relations between the two countries. Still, with all the potential problems, Pasha said he was glad America got bin Laden.

Pasha hung up, and Panetta made one more call. When his wife, Sylvia, picked up the phone, he shared all the details. She was thrilled. He didn't have much time, but they talked about all the hard work Panetta had put in to get to this point.

And then, he made a request: Call his friend Ted Balestreri, the owner of the Sardine Factory, and tell him to turn on the news later. Panetta smiled. Balestreri didn't know it yet, but he'd lost the bet they'd made on New Year's Eve. He was going to have to open that very expensive bottle of wine.

Obama had one last thing to do before he went upstairs and got ready for his address. He wanted to call former presidents George W. Bush and Bill Clinton. He made a point of letting Bush know that the mission was the culmination of all the former president's hard work to find bin Laden and destroy Al Qaeda.

When he called Bill Clinton, Obama said, "I guess Hillary told you." But Clinton said he didn't know a thing. When Obama said not to share the information with anybody, she didn't. All these weeks she had kept the secret—even from her husband.

With the calls out of the way, Obama returned to the Oval Office and sat with Rhodes. They worked on the speech. It was getting late. They'd have to finish it up soon.

White House

Obama's national security team scrambled to get ready for the president's address to the nation. But some also wanted to let their loved ones know what was going on.

McDonough called his wife and urged her to watch the news later.

"It should be on at about 10:45," he said.

She'd had a long day and was ready for bed. She stayed up, but at 10:45, nothing happened. No one broke into programming with a special report, so she went to sleep.

Morell didn't know if his wife would pick up the phone. She was still furious about him missing their daughter's concert. By 8 p.m., she still hadn't heard from him.

When Morell called, he said the president would address the nation soon and she'd understand why he had been working so many long hours and missing so many important family events.

Now Mary Beth was worried. "Did something terrible happen?"

"No, it will be good news," Morell assured her.

She paused for a moment, then blurted out, "You got him?" Mary Beth knew that her husband had been working on Al Qaeda cases for so long that maybe it had something to do with bin Laden.

Morell couldn't tell her. Not even now. He just smiled into the phone and said, "Love you, got to go."

Meanwhile, in the West Wing, Obama, Brennan, Rhodes, and others were going line by line over his speech. Obama wanted to strike a positive, uplifting tone. Bin Laden was dead. Of course, Al Qaeda was still a threat. But things were getting better. They had the terrorist group on the run.

President Barack Obama with speechwriter Ben Rhodes and White House Chief of Staff Bill Daley.

Somewhere in the North Arabian Sea

The captain of the nuclear-powered aircraft carrier USS *Carl Vinson* was ready. A Boeing V-22 Osprey had delivered bin Laden's body to the ship. Now it was about to be lowered to its final resting place in the Arabian Sea.

No one would know the exact location of the watery grave. In Islam, the burial takes place as quickly as possible after death. The U.S. officials followed Muslim tradition. They washed bin Laden's body before wrapping it in white cloth. They placed his body in a bag with weights to sink it to the bottom. It lay on the deck while a Muslim seaman spoke the prescribed Arabic prayers.

Only a small group of the ship's leadership was informed of the burial. Most of the sailors had no idea what was going on. And only a handful were at the burial ceremony, including a navy photographer.

The seaman finished and stepped back. Less than a day after he was killed, Bin Laden's body was placed on a flat board, his feet facing the water. Several men tipped the board up, and bin Laden's body slid twenty-five feet into the sea. It disappeared beneath the surface.

White House

President Obama calmly stepped to the lectern in the East Room. Television lights lit up the room. It was 11:35 p.m.—far beyond prime time to address the nation. But Obama wanted Americans to know what had happened that day in a city halfway around the world.

News was already leaking out, so Obama wanted to make sure everyone heard the official version. No rumors, just facts about a daring operation that brought the world's most notorious criminal to justice. And he also wanted to remind Americans why they had conducted the mission in the first place.

Obama's clothes—dark blue suit, crisp white shirt, and red silk tie—reflected the solemn and dramatic nature of his speech. Only a handful of officials were there: Biden, Clinton, Panetta, Donilon, Mullen, Morell, Bash, and James Clapper, the director of National Intelligence.

Obama took a deep breath, then stared straight ahead. He announced that U.S. military and CIA operatives had conducted an operation that killed Osama bin Laden, the Al Qaeda leader, "a terrorist who's responsible for the murder of thousands of innocent men, women, and children."

"It was nearly ten years ago that a bright September day was darkened by the worst attack on the American people in our history. The images of 9/11 are seared into our national memory—hijacked planes cutting through a cloudless September sky; the Twin Towers collapsing to the ground; black smoke billowing up from the Pentagon; the wreckage of Flight 93 in Shanksville, Pennsylvania, where the actions of heroic citizens saved even more heartbreak and destruction.

"And yet we know that the worst images are those that were unseen to the world. The empty seat at the dinner table. Children who were forced to grow up without their mother or their father. Parents who would never know the feeling of their child's embrace. Nearly 3,000 citizens were taken from us, leaving a gaping hole in our hearts."

He reminded Americans how the nation came together in the wake of the tragedy.

"We offered our neighbors a hand, and we offered the wounded our blood. We reaffirmed our ties to each other, and our love of community and country. On that day, no matter where we came from, what God we prayed to, or what race or ethnicity we were, we were united as one American family."

Obama was just getting started. He said America was united in another way: In its resolve to bring to justice those who committed this vicious act. He reminded everyone that bin Laden and Al Qaeda had declared war on the United States.

And so, over the last decade, the United States went to war with Al Qaeda to "protect our citizens, our friends and our allies." He said America had "disrupted the terrorist network and strengthened the nation's homeland defense.

"Yet Osama bin Laden avoided capture and escaped across the Afghan border into Pakistan. Meanwhile, Al Qaeda continued to operate from along that border and operate through its affiliates across the world."

He told the nation that shortly after he took office, he directed Panetta to make the killing or capture of bin Laden the top priority in the U.S. war against Al Qaeda.

White House advisors watch President Barack Obama deliver address to the nation, May 1, 2011.

Obama disclosed that in August 2010, after years of painstaking work, he was briefed on a possible lead to the terrorist leader.

"It was far from certain, and it took many months to run this thread to ground. I met repeatedly with my national security team as we developed more information about the possibility that we had located bin Laden hiding within a compound deep inside of Pakistan. And finally, last week, I determined that we had enough intelligence to take action, and authorized an operation to get Osama bin Laden and bring him to justice."

Then he disclosed that the United States had launched a targeted operation against that compound in Abbottabad.

"A small team of Americans carried out the operation with extraordinary courage and capability. No Americans were harmed. They took care to avoid civilian casualties. After a firefight, they killed Osama bin Laden and took custody of his body."

He was wrapping up the speech, but he wanted to warn the nation that the War on Terror wasn't over.

"There's no doubt that Al Qaeda will continue to pursue attacks against us. We must—and we will—remain vigilant at home and abroad," he said.

Obama reminded Americans that the United States "did not choose this fight. It came to our shores and started with the senseless slaughter of our citizens. After nearly ten years of service, struggle, and sacrifice, we know well the costs of war. These efforts weigh on me every time I, as commander in chief, have to sign a letter to a family that has lost a loved one, or look into the eyes of a service member who's been gravely wounded.

"So, Americans understand the costs of war. Yet as a country, we will never tolerate our security being threatened, nor stand idly by when our people have been killed. We will be relentless in defense of our citizens and our friends and allies. We will be true to the values that make us who we are. And on nights like this one, we can say to those families who have lost loved ones to Al Qaeda's terror: Justice has been done."

The lights were killed, the speech was over. Obama walked toward his group of advisors. As he got closer, he could see Biden clutching his rosary. So were Mullen and Panetta. Obama smiled, then reached into his pocket and pulled out a crucifix. It turned out they all had prayed for a good outcome. They all had sought divine intervention in the success of the mission and the safe return of the SEALs.

Panetta could see that Obama was tired. But he could also see the joy in his face over what had happened. It was a look of great satisfaction.

It was midnight, and Panetta wanted to get home. He waited for Morell, who was talking to the media in a White House "press backgrounder," where senior officials answer questions about sensitive issues. Reporters can't quote the briefers by name, only as "senior administration officials." But with information this juicy, no one would care. Morell explained the intelligence that led to the compound. After Morell finished, Michael Vickers and a State Department official answered questions about the military operation.

The press briefing wrapped up close to 1 a.m. As Morell and Panetta were leaving, they heard a strange noise coming from outside. Voices. When they walked outside into the crisp night air, they heard a loud and raucous chant: "USA. USA. USA. USA . . ."

A crowd of thousands had gathered across the street in Lafayette Park to celebrate. They had been there for a while. Each official in turn heard the chants as they headed for home.

Mullen stood alone in the White House Rose Garden, staring at the stars stretched across the sky. With the patriotic chant echoing into the night and the peaceful scenery above, he finally started to relax.

Clinton was overwhelmed by the response, too. It was mostly young people, students from nearby universities. They were shouting and waving American flags. As a New York senator, she had visited Ground Zero the day after the attacks. She had talked to the victims' families and worked hard in Washington to try to get them the financial support they needed. Clinton was emotionally and physically drained. It had been a rough few months. But for a moment at least, she gained strength from the outpouring of love.

This was the proudest moment of Panetta's professional life. He stopped and listened to the rhythmic chants. He knew it was a rare public expression of joy.

Morell found it surreal. He had heard the chant before, a decade earlier. In the days following 9/11, a patriotic surge swept the nation. He recalled President Bush's visit to Ground Zero a few days after the terrorist attacks.

The Twin Towers of the World Trade Center were still smoldering. Bush suddenly climbed on top of some rubble, put his arm around a firefighter, and grabbed a bullhorn. Someone in the crowd said they couldn't hear the president. So Bush replied with words that inspired the nation: "I can hear you!" he said. "The rest of the world hears you! And the people— the people who knocked these buildings down—will hear all of us soon." The crowd reacted with loud, prolonged chants of "USA. USA. USA."

Now, outside the White House, Morell was listening to the same chant.

He turned to Panetta and hugged him. It was Morell's way of thanking Panetta for his faith in him, for his diligence and relentless drive to get bin Laden. Panetta smiled. Morell released him. "Let's go," the CIA director said. With that, they trudged to their cars as the crowd chanted into the night: "USA. USA. USA."

COUNTDOWN:

AFTERMATH

New York City

Obama's late-night announcement sent waves of patriotism across the United States. The streets erupted in spontaneous celebration. Applause and shouts of joy from Lafayette Park could be heard inside the White House.

New Yorkers cheered and honked horns and waved flags. Thousands headed to Ground Zero in lower Manhattan, site of the World Trade Center, to celebrate the joy, comfort, and closure that came with the death of the terrorist most responsible for its destruction.

New York City mayor Michael Bloomberg gave a speech that recalled America's commitment to bring justice to those who planned and carried out the September 11 attacks. Almost three thousand people died that day, but in the end "Osama bin Laden found out that America keeps its commitments," Bloomberg said.

The Ground Zero celebration was held in the shadow of a new skyscraper under construction, the Freedom Tower. It had been designed to dominate the New York City skyline. As Bloomberg put it, Osama bin Laden was dead, and the World Trade Center site was teeming with new life.

For many, it was a historic moment long overdue. For others, it was bittersweet.

Jessica Ferenczy was excited about the news. They finally got the bastard! she thought. How many times had she imagined this moment, and thought about what vengeance might feel like? Justice had finally been served, but Jerome Dominguez, the love of her life, was still gone forever.

Jessica looked at the time. It was late. She would have to get up early for her shift. But before she headed to bed, she went to Dominguez's Legacy page and wrote a brief message.

I love you Baby. I don't feel any better, even though I waited so long for this day. I miss you so much. Nothing can bring you home to me. I love you now, as I did then, as I did before we met.

Jessie

Elsewhere, national and international leaders expressed their support for the raid. At the United Nations, Secretary-General Ban Ki-moon said bin Laden's death was a watershed in the global fight against terrorism.

"This is a day to remember the victims and the families of victims here in the United States and everywhere in the world," Ban said.

Israeli Prime Minister Benjamin Netanyahu said the result of the raid was "a resounding victory for justice, for freedom, and for the shared values of all democratic countries that fight shoulder to shoulder against terror."

The reaction in the Muslim world was more subdued. "I hope the death of Osama bin Laden will mean the end of terrorism," Afghan President Hamid Karzai said. Few others were so optimistic.

Bagram, Afghanistan

Robert O'Neill was tired. He had been running at full speed for who knows how long. Now, standing by the flight line at the Bagram Airfield, he was trying to decompress. In a few minutes, he and his fellow SEAL Team 6 members would board an empty C-17. The plane usually stopped in Germany to refuel, but this time it was a direct flight home.

After their debriefing in Jalalabad, the SEALs had been flown to Bagram, where they finally had some breakfast in a chilly aircraft hangar.

O'Neill chose an egg and cheese sandwich and squeezed on a little hot sauce. He walked over to a big-screen television in the back of the hangar and munched while he watched President Obama tell the nation what SEAL Team 6 had just done.

Then it hit him. Everyone at home knew. The president said no SEALs were killed or injured, but O'Neill was seized with the need to call his father, to tell him he was OK.

But he couldn't call. He didn't have access to a phone. He couldn't break the "mission silence" yet. O'Neill took a deep breath. This was normal, he told himself. He hadn't had time yet to process everything.

Nearby, Will Chesney was feeling the same jumble of emotions. It was strange, sitting in a hangar, with Cairo, eating breakfast, watching the president on television just hours after the raid. All those weeks of buildup, and now it was over. Chesney was ready to go home. In a few minutes, he knew he'd be on his way. He understood that killing bin Laden was big news. But he didn't know how big it had become—or that by now, the world knew the mission had been carried out by SEAL Team 6.

The C-17 was ready. O'Neill, Chesney, Cairo, and the other newly minted heroes picked up their gear and began boarding the plane. The men hoped they would be able to get some much-needed rest during the long flight. They were going to need it.

Washington, D.C.

President Obama hoped bin Laden's death would become the defining event in the American-led fight against terrorism, a symbolic moment affirming the relentless pursuit of those who attacked New York and Washington on 9/11.

No one could say if bin Laden's followers would turn him into a martyr. No one knew if this could be a turning point in the war in Afghanistan. The exact impact would remain unclear.

For years, American intelligence had said that bin Laden was an important symbol, but that he was operationally less than significant. He was on the run, hindered in any meaningful leadership role. Yet he had remained the most potent face of terrorism around the world, and most of those who played down his role in recent years nonetheless celebrated his death.

Given bin Laden's status among radical Islamists, the American government braced for possible retaliation. Military bases in the United States and around the world were ordered to a higher state of readiness. The State Department issued a worldwide travel warning, urging Americans in volatile areas "to limit their travel outside of their homes and hotels and avoid mass gatherings and demonstrations."

But something strange happened in the days and weeks that followed. Despite threats and saber rattling, there were no terrorist attacks. It was as if Al Qaeda and its supporters were in a state of shock. Their leader was gone. What would they do now?

As the excitement faded, President Obama noticed something else, something positive. The mood of the country had changed. There seemed to be more optimism in America. Bin Laden's death "offered a catharsis of sorts." The American people had experienced a decade of war. They believed that "violent extremism was here to stay." But now they had hope.

The man held responsible for two decades of terror and death was dead now, buried beneath the sea. Maybe the world had turned a corner, and peace was possible. Maybe better days were ahead.

Jalalabad, Afghanistan

Accolades poured in for Admiral McRaven. He had overseen thousands of missions in his career, but none had the impact of this one, or resonated as much with the public.

He became a public figure overnight, the face of the SEALs. So many things had gone right for the mission. Even when they went wrong, McRaven was cool and calm under pressure. Everyone in the Situation

Room and Langley and Jalalabad witnessed his unflappable grace under excruciating conditions. They'd seen how his men responded.

Obama called McRaven "famously cool under pressure." If the president had to pick one person to "represent everything right about our military, Bill McRaven might have been that person."

McRaven didn't like the limelight. He retreated to his office, where he combed through the operation reports to learn the details on the things that had gone haywire.

Why had the Black Hawk crashed to the ground while hovering over the compound? Engineers said the chopper got caught in an air vortex caused by higher-than-expected temperatures and the high compound walls, which blocked the downwash of the rotor's blades. During dress rehearsals, they had substituted chain-link fences for the masonry walls. The air could flow through them instead of being trapped.

McRaven also discovered another problem. The day of the mission, the meteorologists said the temperature would be 18 degrees Celsius, or 64.4 degrees Fahrenheit. That was perfect for the operation. But it turned out they were wrong. The temperature was really between 20 and 23 degrees Celsius, or between 68 and 73.4 degrees Fahrenheit. Flying in that was a mistake. If McRaven had known the real temperature, he might have postponed the mission.

But in the days and weeks after, McRaven felt an incredible sense of pride. He knew the raid was for all the people who were killed on 9/11, the men and women who gave their lives in Iraq and Afghanistan, and those who were wounded in those conflicts. In the end, the mission was for "all those around the world who suffered as a result of this man's evil."

President Obama knew the critical role McRaven had played in the mission—and he wanted to thank him.

A few days after the raid, when McRaven was in Washington, he got a call that Obama wanted to see him. When he arrived at the Oval Office, the president shook hands with him and offered him "heartfelt thanks for his extraordinary leadership."

Obama told McRaven that he had a gift for him. He opened his desk drawer and pulled out a handsome oak plaque with a tape measure mounted neatly in the center. McRaven smiled and recalled Obama's joke once he'd learned McRaven used a SEAL to measure bin Laden's corpse.

McRaven gave the plaque to the Joint Special Operations Command headquarters at Fort Bragg, North Carolina, so they could put it in a display case. A few weeks later, a guy showed up at McRaven's house at Fort Bragg. He told McRaven that the president found out he gave away the plaque.

McRaven protested that he hadn't given it away, but instead donated it.

The man smiled and handed McRaven another one. "The president wanted to make sure you have one that you can pass on to your children."

McRaven was touched by the president's kindness. "Tell him that was very gracious," he said.

Abbottabad, Pakistan

Dr. Afridi was on the run. He had to get out of Pakistan. Fast. He read the newspapers. He watched the broadcasts. He listened to the radio. Americans had raided that home in Abbottabad—the one he had been trying to get inside. They found Osama bin Laden. The terrorist leader was dead. Afridi was worried that he could be next.

When the doctor had talked to the CIA, he didn't know bin Laden was the target. He had no idea who was inside the compound. Bin Laden? He didn't even consider that. Now his heart was racing. He knew if Pakistan's notorious Inter-Services Intelligence found out he had been working with the CIA, he would be in deep trouble.

From the news reports, Pakistani authorities were swarming all over the city. It was just a matter of time before they found out about him. That he had been trying to get inside the fortress at the end of the dead-end street. Word had a way of getting out.

So Afridi rushed home. He told his wife they had to pack. No time to waste. They were getting out of Abbottabad. She didn't ask many questions. But she knew it would look suspicious. She was the principal of a government school. They had three children. They were just going to pull up stakes and leave without explanation? But the terrorized look on her husband's face said it all.

Afridi didn't have a plan. It was hard to even think straight. He just knew he had to find a way to get across the border to Afghanistan. If he could make it there, he'd find a way to reach out to his handlers. They'd help him get to the United States. They had to.

But he didn't have time to think about that now. He had to pack.

Langley, Virginia

Leon Panetta beamed. The day after the raid, he called an agencywide meeting in the CIA auditorium. He took the stage to shouts, cheers, and applause. In typical Panetta style, he stared at the crowd, then deadpanned, "What the hell are you all excited about?" Everyone laughed, and he broke into a broad smile.

Panetta knew he wouldn't be there much longer. He had just been nominated as defense secretary. That morning, in front of the men and women of the world's largest spy agency, personal ambition didn't matter. He just wanted them all to know that this victory was their victory, too. The mission would go down as one of the greatest in U.S. history. He dedicated the operation to every officer who had ever worked in a war zone, and every analyst who had ever helped thwart an Al Qaeda attack overseas or at home.

Meanwhile, Gary, Sam, Maya, and the entire team of analysts knew they had a lot of work ahead. The SEAL raiders had hauled home a treasure trove from the compound. Ten computer hard drives and five computers revealed countless secrets. They included seventy-nine thousand audio files, ten thousand videos, and bin Laden's personal journal. While they didn't uncover an immediate terrorist plot against the United States or its allies, Gary and others began exploiting the information.

Virginia Beach, Virginia

When the C-17 landed in the United States, the SEALs braced themselves for a media onslaught. They understood the raid was big news, and that journalists were scrambling to learn the details. Reporters knew that Seal Team 6 was based in Virginia Beach, so the streets would be full of satellite trucks. Television crews would be hitting bars and other places they thought the guys would hang out. They wanted to know everything about the "elite band of brothers."

O'Neill realized the impact as soon as he turned on his cell phone. *Ping, ping, ping.* He had been bombarded with messages from loved ones. Was he on the raid? Was he back home yet?

O'Neill could hear the other SEALs' phones pinging, too. No one was allowed to say much. The raid was classified. Only the commanders could talk about it. O'Neill knew he could tell his family that yes, he was there, but he couldn't say much more than that.

Their squadron commander was waiting on the flight line when the SEALs stepped off the plane. He gave everyone a handshake and a hug. In the distance, O'Neill could see the buses that would take them back to the base. But as they moved closer, he could see that a couple hundred of their navy teammates had come along to congratulate them, too.

O'Neill walked onto the bus and leaned back in his seat. They'd only left here a week earlier, on their way to that mysterious compound in Pakistan. Now they were back again. Was it a dream? Did it really happen? It was surreal.

O'Neill called his father and told him he was safe. The older man told his son he'd prayed and prayed for his safe return, and now his prayers were answered.

Likewise, his son had to give thanks, too. He hadn't thought he would be coming home this time. He'd believed, like the others, that Al Qaeda fighters were stationed in the house, that the place was wired with explosives. It was almost odd to still be here. The Martyrs' Brigade had made it home alive.

So when O'Neill walked through his front door, he hugged his wife and children with special tenderness. It was finally time to celebrate.

Chesney, full of joy, phoned his folks on the way home to his apartment. Cairo sat in the passenger seat. After a mission Chesney was supposed to take Cairo directly to the kennel. Handlers weren't allowed to bring their dogs home. But forget about rules, Chesney thought—not tonight! The dog had done his duty, right? He deserved to celebrate, too.

Cairo wagged his tail. Chesney opened the door to his apartment, dropped his gear, headed to the refrigerator, and pulled out two filets mignons. Steak dinner!

They feasted. Chesney got cleaned up and went to bed. But this was no barracks room, and Cairo wasn't about to sleep on the floor. The dog jumped up and hogged the bed all night. Chesney didn't mind. It was all good. They both slept like babies.

When Chesney brought Cairo back to the kennel the next day, he got a stern talking-to. He couldn't do that again, the officer said. Chesney understood the regulations. But he'd only taken Cairo home for one night. He didn't regret it.

Chesney knew that he was supposed to go back to separating from Cairo, that this mission was a fluke. Cairo was going to become a training dog until it was time for him to retire.

For now, they were going their separate ways. Before he left the kennel, Chesney knelt, rubbed his hand against Cairo's head, and whispered, "I'll be back soon."

Dallas, Texas

President Obama asked Michael Morell to do him a favor: fly to Dallas, Texas, to give former president George W. Bush a detailed briefing about the raid.

Obama knew Morell had been close to Bush. He'd been responsible for preparing his President's Daily Brief. And Morell was with President Bush on that terrible day, September 11, 2001.

Morell said he would be honored to do it. He took a senior CIA analyst and an officer from JSOC with him. When he got there, Bush was gracious as usual. "Good to see you," he said as he shook Morell's hand.

They sat down and caught up on their family news, then Bush said he wanted Morell to tell him every little detail. Morell nodded his head. Of course.

Morell could never forget the moment he heard the news about the terrorist attacks, or the look on Bush's face when he told him he believed Al Qaeda was responsible—and that all roads would lead to Osama bin Laden.

The CIA man patiently walked Bush through how they collected the intelligence, how it started with a courier and led to a compound in Abbottabad. Then the JSOC officer went into details about the raid, the downed helicopter, and how a SEAL shot and killed bin Laden in a room on the third floor of the compound's main house. It sounded like an action thriller.

At the end, Bush smiled. "You know, Laura and I were supposed to go to the movies tonight, but this is better than any movie I'll ever see," he told them. "I think we'll stay home."

Then, as they prepared to leave, Bush reached out and shook Morell's hand. Morell could feel something in his palm. Bush had given him a special "challenge coin," one with "commander in chief" engraved on it. Morell fought back the tears. Morell and his boss at the agency, George Tenet, had tried to warn others about Al Qaeda before the 9/11 attacks. Morell was haunted by that. Now, for the first time in years, he felt a sense of closure.

Fort Campbell, Kentucky

It had been a remarkable week, an outpouring of patriotism that hadn't been seen since 9/11. Obama knew the mission had had a profound effect on Americans. The nation was unified. How long would it last? There was one more thing he wanted to do: He wanted to personally thank the SEALs.

They gathered at Fort Campbell, Kentucky, home base of the 160th Special Operations Aviation Regiment, the Night Stalkers unit whose helicopters had carried the commandos to bin Laden's compound. There the SEALs' identities would be shielded, and the president could spend a bit of private time with the men who'd pulled off the raid.

The SEALs had just begun to unwind at home when Gates visited their commanders in Virginia Beach and told them all to pack up. They were traveling to Kentucky to meet the president.

For O'Neill, it had already been a whirlwind week. The SEALs were awarded Silver Stars. They'd been dodging television cameras in Virginia Beach. In a way, it was like being chased by the paparazzi. So this is what it's like to be a celebrity, O'Neill thought.

In Kentucky, one of the pilots of the Night Stalker regiment had walked over to O'Neill and gave him a "stiff salute," right in front of the others—a sign of great personal respect.

O'Neill was embarrassed. He knew the other SEALs would be pissed about it. Since he'd returned, some of his close friends had been shunning him. The same thing happened with his friend Jonny after he shot and killed the Somali pirate. There was professional jealousy that O'Neill was the one who'd taken down bin Laden. They all wanted to be that guy. Now O'Neill was learning what it was like to be "a fucking hero."

At Fort Campbell, the president and Joe Biden entered the room with McRaven. The SEALs jumped to their feet. "Hey, everybody," Obama said, with a bright, cheerful tone.

The president described the raid as one of the greatest military and intelligence operations in American history. He told them how proud he was of them, and awarded SEAL Team 6 the Presidential Unit Citation.

Then Obama was shown a PowerPoint presentation of the raid, with maps, photos, and a scale model, narrated by members of the assault force.

Afterward, Obama looked around the room and made a request. "I want to meet this dog."

Chesney was in a separate room with Cairo, waiting to meet the president. The dog was being awarded the citation, too. When Obama walked in, he smiled. "So this is Cairo?" Obama said.

"Yes, sir," Chesney replied.

Obama said kind words about the creature, whom he called an "integral part of the mission." Both Obama and Biden patted Cairo, and Chesney thought, at that moment, if Cairo could smile, he would have. Chesney could sense the dog was having a good time—but he'd muzzled Cairo, just in case.

The unit had a gift for Obama as well. Not every SEAL had supported Obama in 2008. Politically, some still weren't Obama fans. But almost all of them gave the president high marks for having the courage to approve the mission. The president had trusted them to pull off an impossible operation, and they had rewarded his faith. So now, in the front of the room, they handed him a framed U.S. flag, one they had carried with them on the raid. They had each signed the back of the frame, using their call signs instead of their names. Obama was genuinely touched by the gesture.

After the meeting, Obama moved on to address the thousands of soldiers at Fort Campbell. Speaking under a giant American flag to the troops of the 101st Airborne Division, Obama drew the connection between the troops there and the commandos he called "America's quiet professionals."

"Like all of us, they could have chosen a life of ease. But like you, they volunteered," he said.

Describing the SEAL commandos as "battle hardened" and tirelessly trained, Obama said: "When I gave the order, they were ready. And in recent days, the world has learned just how ready they were."

The president also linked the killing of bin Laden to the broader war, saying it showed the progress that the United States had made in disrupting and dismantling Al Qaeda. The soldiers of the 101st Airborne were pushing back insurgents and allowing Afghans to reclaim their towns.

"The bottom line is this: Our strategy is working. And there is no greater evidence of that than justice finally being delivered to Osama bin Laden."

The crowd erupted in cheers.

That day, at Fort Campbell, O'Neill and Chesney didn't know what was changing in Afghanistan or America. They didn't know what their own futures would hold.

Today, that didn't matter. They had taken part in a dangerous mission—the kind they had only dreamed about after 9/11. It was the way a kid playing a backyard football game dreams of throwing the winning touchdown pass in the Super Bowl. The future would come. They'd deal with it then. For now, they just enjoyed their moment of glory.

EPILOGUE

For all of its might—the reach of the military, the sophistication of the intelligence, the wizardry of the technology—the U.S. government didn't know whether Osama bin Laden was inside the Abbottabad compound until Rob O'Neill walked into that dark bedroom on the third floor of the main house.

It was only then—in the middle of the night of May 1, 2011—that they knew for sure where bin Laden had been hiding.

But the government moved fast to exploit the tens of thousands of papers, the audio and video files, and bin Laden's 228-page personal journal to solve the mystery of where the world's most wanted terrorist had been and what he had been doing in the decade since Tora Bora.

The biggest surprise was how long he had been living in Abbottabad—since 2005. The first rule of operational security for any terrorist on the run is to keep moving—to sleep in a different location every night and never let anyone follow a trail to where you are. Not only did bin Laden stop moving, he set up a sprawling household in the compound. Two of his first four wives lived on the second floor. Then there was Amal, who at twenty-nine was a quarter century younger than her husband. She shared his bed on the third floor. There were also twelve children in the house, the youngest just age two.

John Brennan, Obama's counterterrorism advisor in the White House, told me: "He never should have been in that compound that long. I think he got a little bit too comfortable and confident that he was not going to be found out."

Bin Laden boasted about how long he had been able to avoid detection. In an undated letter, apparently composed in the final year of his life, he wrote, "Here we are in the tenth year of the war, and America and its allies are still chasing a mirage, lost at sea without a beach."

The second surprise was what bin Laden was doing in the compound. CIA Deputy Director Michael Morell said, "Our pre-raid understanding of bin Laden's role in the organization had been wrong. We'd thought that bin Laden's deputy, Ayman al-Zawahiri, was running the organization on a day-to-day basis, essentially the CEO of Al Qaeda, while bin Laden was the group's ideological leader, its chairman of the board. . . . Bin Laden himself had not only been managing the organization from Abbottabad. He had been micromanaging it."

How much of a micromanager was he? The SEALs recovered a spreadsheet of expenses for the terror organization from April to December 2009. In 2010, bin Laden advised a deputy not to give advances to members of Al Qaeda on their monthly salaries. And there was an application recruits had to fill out. One of the questions: "Do you wish to execute a suicide operation?" along with space for contact information for the next of kin.

Through his courier—Abu Ahmed al-Kuwaiti—he also tried to set strategy and maintain discipline inside Al Qaeda. Al-Kuwaiti carried letters and thumb drives that ended up with Atiyah Abd al-Rahman, a Libyan who acted as bin Laden's chief of staff. The communications reflected his changing concerns over the years.

In 2005 to 2006, bin Laden worried about the role of Abu Musab al-Zarqawi, leader of Al Qaeda in Iraq, in the civil war there. Al Qaeda (AQI) was slaughtering other Muslims, both Shia and Sunni. Bin Laden directed them to stop the attacks, which he feared were bad for the brand and would turn "the street" against Al Qaeda—shifting the focus away from the real enemy in the United States. Al-Zarqawi didn't listen.

By 2011, bin Laden's attention had turned to the Arab Spring sweeping across the Middle East. This wasn't a "top down" global jihadist organization following orders. No, this was an organic, spontaneous movement that toppled autocratic regimes in Tunisia and Egypt, and threatened other dictators. Bin Laden hoped the Arab Spring would force the U.S. to withdraw from the region. But he feared the worst thing that could happen to a charismatic leader—becoming irrelevant.

Bin Laden did what he could to hold on to his platform. In 2007, he issued a half-hour-long video message, his first in three years. Concerned about his appearance, he dyed his hair and beard black. And he issued an average of five audiotapes a year.

One thing never changed: his obsession with striking the United States again. In 2011, coming up on the tenth anniversary of 9/11, he called for Al Qaeda affiliates to hit major American cities like New York and Washington, Los Angeles and Chicago, inflicting as many casualties as possible. He talked about assassinating President Obama as well as General David Petraeus, who had turned the tide in Iraq against al-Zarqawi and AQI. He continued to discuss attacking commercial airlines. He even suggested putting trees on railroad tracks to derail trains. But his lieutenants responded that Al Qaeda no longer had the finances or organization to carry out such attacks.

There was something else that came out of the Abbottabad raid—evidence of how bin Laden spent his time during his years in the compound. The SEALs found a stack of books ranging from the *9/11 Commission Report* to Bob Woodward's *Obama's Wars*. But there were also fringe conspiracy tracts, like *Bloodlines of the Illuminati* and *The Secrets of the Federal Reserve* by a Holocaust denier.

He had tapes of Hollywood movies, kids' cartoons (a favorite was *Tom and Jerry*), and an extensive collection of pornographic videos. Most memorable and devastating was a videotape of bin Laden watching clips of himself on television, hunched over, huddled in a blanket, wearing a knit cap, his beard gone gray, holding a TV remote control.

On April 26, 2011, bin Laden wrote a ten-page letter. He tried to latch on to the Arab Spring, writing, "What we are witnessing these days of consecutive revolutions is a great and glorious event." He called for a media campaign to incite "the people who have not revolted yet, and encouraging them to rebel against the rulers." He discussed whether and when to kill French hostages in Libya. And he issued guidance on operational security, stating, "It is proven the American technology and its modern systems cannot arrest a mujahid [a Muslim engaged in holy war] if he does not commit a security error that leads them to him." Five days later, bin Laden would be shot dead inside his own compound.

So what did the U.S. military and intelligence do with what they described as the "single largest collection of senior terrorist materials ever"? They engaged in a process known as F3EA—or Find, Fix, Finish, Exploit, and Analyze. Within weeks, the Obama administration launched a new wave of attacks against senior Al Qaeda leadership. Three top operatives were taken out in the summer of 2011, along with three more in 2012 to 2013. One of the casualties was al-Rahman, the man who'd received bin Laden's communications and served as his chief of staff.

The task force that reviewed the records issued more than four hundred intelligence reports over six weeks. They warned of Al Qaeda plots against U.S. targets, including trains. And the documents were used in the prosecution of Abid Naseer, who was found guilty in New York City of providing material support to Al Qaeda and conspiracy to use a destructive device.

But the most serious impact on Al Qaeda from the raid was something more subtle. Michael Morell said it forced the terror organization to focus on defense, not offense. "The decapitation strategy degrades a terrorist organization. And that happens for two reasons. One is you remove a senior leader. That person gets replaced by somebody, but it takes time for that person to learn his job. And so there is a period of time in which you have weakened the group.

"More important, the decapitation strategy forces a terrorist group to take extraordinary measures to protect themselves. It forces them to put security at the front of their mind. And when you force them to think about their own security, you don't give them the opportunity to think about attacking you."

In the years since Abbottabad, Al Qaeda has suffered a dramatic loss of reach and influence. There are still offshoots. Al Qaeda in the Arabian Peninsula (AQAP) continues to wage civil war in Yemen. In Somalia, the terror group Al Shabaab has close ties to Al Qaeda. There are branches in Northern and Central Africa, Syria and Pakistan and India. But what used to be known as Al Qaeda Central—a sprawling terror network directed from Afghanistan, and later Pakistan—has been rolled up.

There are several reasons for this. First, Ayman al-Zawahiri, Al Qaeda's leader since Abbottabad, is no bin Laden and never was. He's been dismissed as "pedantic" and lacking in charisma. Holed up somewhere in the mountainous tribal area in Pakistan, along the border with Afghanistan, he has failed to inspire jihadists and new recruits.

Al Qaeda hasn't given up. In December 2019, a military trainee inspired by AQAP shot and killed three U.S. sailors and wounded eight others at the naval air station in Pensacola, Florida. And in September 2014, Al Qaeda militants tried to hijack a Pakistani frigate at a naval base in Karachi and use it to attack and sink a U.S. Navy ship, sparking an international incident. The jihadists were stopped in an intense firefight.

But there are bigger factors in Al Qaeda's decline. After President Obama pulled U.S. troops out of Iraq, a rival terror group emerged—the Islamic State of Iraq and Syria, or ISIS. At its height in 2015, ISIS held about a third of Syria and 40 percent of Iraq, seizing the imagination of terrorists and jihadist wannabes across the Muslim world, and focusing the fears of the West. ISIS leader Abu Bakr al-Baghdadi, not al-Zawahiri, became the true successor to bin Laden.

And Al Qaeda not only lost its base in Iraq but also its original home in Afghanistan. That was where bin Laden and the mujahideen had fought the Soviet occupation in the 1980s. It was where Al Qaeda planned the bombing of two U.S. embassies in East Africa in 1998 that killed 224 people. In 2000, Al Qaeda carried out a suicide bombing of the USS *Cole* in Yemen, killing seventeen American servicemen. And it was in Afghanistan where bin Laden planned and ordered the attacks of 9/11 that killed 2,977 people in New York City and the Pentagon and Shanksville, Pennsylvania.

But Afghanistan has not been a safe haven for Al Qaeda since the U.S. launched its War on Terror in 2001. And now it may never be again. Since 2018, the Taliban has engaged in peace talks with the United States. In an agreement signed in February of 2020, the Taliban promised to sever ties with all terrorist organizations, including Al Qaeda. Whether the Taliban will keep that promise is a question for the future.

In 2021, the United Nations released a counterterrorism analysis that amounted to a report on the State of Al Qaeda. It concluded, "Al-Qaida faces a new and pressing challenge concerning its leadership and strategic direction, following an exceptional period of attrition of its senior leaders in various locations."

It noted the assassination of Abu Muhammad al-Masri along with his daughter, who was the widow of one of bin Laden's sons. They were driving through the streets of Tehran when two gunmen on a motorcycle raced up to their car and took them out. The assassins were reportedly Israeli agents, acting on behalf of the U.S. Two things stood out. First, al-Masri was al-Zawahiri's top deputy, and a mastermind of the 1998 bombing of the U.S. embassies in Africa. Second, al-Masri was killed on August 7, 2020, the twenty-second anniversary of the embassy bombings.

The UN analysis also noted unconfirmed reports that al-Zawahiri died in October 2020. But the U.S. State Department website still offers a $25 million reward for information leading to his arrest or conviction. The department notes that Al Qaeda's "cohesiveness the past few years has diminished because of leadership losses from counterterrorism pressure in Afghanistan and Pakistan and the rise of other organizations such as ISIS that serve as an alternative for some disaffected extremists."

In September 2020, on the nineteenth anniversary of 9/11, Al Qaeda released a long video recorded by al-Zawahiri. He attacked the late head of ISIS, al-Baghdadi, for breaking with Al Qaeda. He criticized the Arab television network Al Jazeera for broadcasting a report he said undermined the mujahideen. And he was especially angry that Al Qaeda "has been unjustly accused" of acting as an agent "of America, Israel, Iran, Saudi Arabia . . . and so on." It was a long way from the charismatic message of the man the United States worked so long and hard to bring to justice.

In that same month of September 2020, Christopher Miller, who was then director of the National Counterterrorism Center, wrote an article for the *Washington Post*. "My assessment now is that Al Qaeda is in crisis," he concluded. "The group's leadership has been severely diminished by U.S. attacks. . . . Al Qaeda's forces are similarly in disarray and focused simply on survival. They are on the verge of collapse."

And yet it is premature to say the threat is gone. Michael Morell responded to Miller's analysis, saying that while it's true that core Al Qaeda is in crisis, "the jihadist extremist movement is now much bigger. . . . It now stretches from West Africa all the way to Southeast Asia," and includes followers of ISIS. "So the number of jihadist extremists who are willing to use violence is magnitudes greater today than it was on September 10, 2001. . . . This threat remains significant."

On April 14, 2021, President Joe Biden announced that he would pull all U.S. forces from Afghanistan by 9/11 of that year, the twentieth anniversary of the attack—ending America's longest military engagement. In his speech, the president noted, "We delivered justice to bin Laden a decade ago, and we've stayed in Afghanistan for a decade since."

Biden explained that the terror threat in 2021 had changed dramatically from the threat of 2001. He said it "has become more dispersed, metastasizing around the globe. . . . With the terror threat now in many places, keeping thousands of troops grounded and concentrated in just one country at a cost of billions each year makes little sense to me and to our leaders."

The president concluded by talking about the raid on the compound. "Bin Laden is dead, and Al Qaeda is degraded in Iraq, in Afghanistan. And it's time to end the forever war."

It is testament to bin Laden's terrible legacy that twenty years after 9/11—ten years after the daring mission that took him down—President Biden's announcement still set off a fierce debate whether it was safe to withdraw from the country that served as his base of operations.

In the course of writing this book, I was fortunate to speak with most of the key players—political, intelligence, and military—in the effort to find and take out Osama bin Laden. At the end of interviews that went on for hours, sometimes over several days, I asked each one what they thought the biggest takeaways were from the effort.

Tom Donilon, Obama's national security advisor, had been determined to conduct a rigorous policy review of how to respond to the Abbottabad lead, despite the fact that security was so tight and the discussions were so closely held, without normal staffing. "I'm a big believer in the old Dwight Eisenhower phrase that good process doesn't guarantee you a good outcome. But bad process almost always guarantees a bad outcome. And indeed if you look at the biggest mistakes, if you look at the biggest strategic errors in national security this country has had in the last half century, many of them can be attributed to failed, undisciplined process."

John Brennan, Obama's chief counterterrorism advisor in the White House, who later became CIA director, said, "This type of work was the result of a decade of effort. The intelligence business is very tedious work that requires long-term focus. It just takes time. And there wasn't one particular bit of intelligence that resulted in this. It was painstaking work over the course of many years.

"It wasn't the sort of normal interagency process. But it was a process that was rigorous, was detailed and thorough. And there was a constant effort to try to get as much information and insight as possible, and with a very honest review of the options."

Nick Rasmussen, NSC senior director for counterterrorism, said, "It sounds like I'm an Obama fanboy when I say it this way, but in effect he made up for whatever shortcomings the process had because of his ability to make a kind of reasoned judgment about the intelligence. I read him as not being troubled by the 40 percent versus 70 percent [likelihood bin Laden was in the compound] nearly as much as anybody else was, because he'd already made a judgment that it was either/or. It was probable enough that he had to consider the consequences of not acting, if it were true. And he had to consider the prospect and consequence of acting and having it not be true. So in a sense he was the smartest intelligence consumer. He didn't get twisted around 40/70 nearly as much as others."

Donilon said, "It really did underscore the capabilities that the U.S. has both in terms of intelligence, and also in terms of operational ability. It was a demonstration of a unique set of assets that the United States has. Hardly any other country has the ability to go anywhere in the world and protect our interests."

Hillary Clinton, secretary of state, said, "The SEALs took the time to take the women and children from the house. They wouldn't be injured by shrapnel. There wouldn't be other damage done to the compound that could have injured or killed. When I thought about that, I was so touched that American warriors took the time to put themselves in continuing danger to save the lives of America's enemies. And honestly, I thought that action by the SEALs spoke volumes about America's values."

Gary, the head of the CIA's Pakistan-Afghanistan Department, was typically analytical, making three points. "You brought it to America. And America brought it back to you. We talk about 'Where's the battlefield?' And when they move the battlefield to the United States, we're not going to stop until it's back there. He brought it to our homes and families, and we brought it to his home and family.

"Two, you remove the strategic head of Al Qaeda. He was the strategic leader, and we took that away from Al Qaeda. They can't get it back, and I've read Zawahiri's job evaluation. It's not great.

"Finally, you close a book that opened on 9/11, dismantling the top leadership of the network that organized those attacks. Bin Laden played a unique and persistent role in directing the threat against the homeland. It was time to remove this threat. And the sooner you could do that, the better."

Robert Gates, secretary of defense, who had serious doubts about going ahead with the raid, said, "There's a narrative out there that government can't do anything right, that it stumbles all over itself, that it makes mistakes, that people are venal. People are focused on burnishing their own reputations, and their own turf fights. And I think that this raid is a wonderful example of government performing as Americans would hope it would perform. I think it's an example of the way government ought to cooperate, and the way people subordinated their own egos and pulled together, and something that really worked well. I've seen it in a few instances. But it's all too rare."

Finally, Leon Panetta, director of the Central Intelligence Agency, and later Obama's secretary of defense, said, "There are a lot of moments these days where you question whether or not the pillars of our democracy are going to be there—whether or not we're going to be able to protect our democracy and our Constitution and our way of life. And then I think back on what happened here, where you had the dedication of people who have given their lives to protect this country, and that they did everything they could.

"We're not going to give up. We are not going to give up on our ability to find somebody who attacked our country. That spirit of not giving up, of persisting, of continuing to fight until we got this guy, that spirit is what I think will ultimately save our country, not only today, but in the future."

POSTSCRIPT

The celebrations faded, the flags were folded and tucked away. Life went on. The United States pulled its troops out of Iraq and reduced its numbers in Afghanistan. Al Qaeda's influence diminished after bin Laden's death.

At home, Obama was reelected to a second term in 2012. His campaign coined the perfect bumper sticker: "GM is Alive and Osama bin Laden is dead." (Obama had bailed out General Motors during his first months in office.) Obama's successor was Donald J. Trump, the real estate developer and reality-television star whom Obama had roasted at the White House Correspondents' Dinner the night before the raid. Trump beat Hillary Clinton, the secretary of state who was in the Situation Room that day in May 2011 when the SEALs killed bin Laden.

And another person in the room, Joe Biden, would in turn defeat Trump in November 2020, in a bitter and contentious election that took place in the middle of a deadly global pandemic. Trump refused to concede, falsely claiming election fraud. Two months after Election Day, a group of Trump supporters stormed the Capitol to try to stop Congress from certifying the election results. They failed. Biden was sworn in as the 46th President of the United States on January 20, 2021.

Almost twenty years after 9/11, the Middle East is still unstable.

America is torn by political divisions and racial unrest. For some, the days after the bin Laden raid were the last time the nation felt unified. For those who took part in the hunt for Osama bin Laden, that day is forever seared into their memory.

THE CIA
Leon Panetta

Minutes before the president addressed the nation about the bin Laden operation, Ted Balestreri's dinner was interrupted by a call from Panetta's wife. Sylvia said, "Ted, get the wine opener ready." When he asked why, she said, "Go turn on CNN. The president is going to make an announcement." When he saw the news bulletin, Balestreri smiled and said, "The son of a bitch set me up."

A few months after the raid, Panetta was finally able to enjoy that rare $10,000 bottle of Bordeaux. Balestreri kept the promise he'd made on New Year's Eve—that if Panetta caught or killed bin Laden, he'd open the Château Lafite Rothschild 1870.

In typical Panetta style, he shared the bottle with more than a dozen friends, poured out into CIA souvenir shot glasses. The wine was good, Panetta said, but "it wasn't worth that kind of money."

Panetta made a seamless transition from the CIA to the Defense Department. He served as secretary of defense until 2013, when he retired. He was in his midseventies. It was time to go home to his wife and spend some quality time at the Panetta Institute for Public Policy, encouraging young people to get involved in government.

After the raid, Panetta was given a brick from bin Laden's compound, which he donated to the institute. In a way, it symbolizes what can happen when government agencies work together for the public good.

And that's one of the institute's goals: building strong leaders on both sides of the aisle who can tackle problems facing the nation. It does that by expanding the students' knowledge of public policy—how to get things done on the local, state, and federal levels.

Panetta chafes at the notion that the nation is too divided to do anything meaningful, adding that it's fashionable to say the United States has never been more split. That thinking is "historically ludicrous," he says, noting that the nation fought a civil war to end slavery. He says it's insulting to "our history to pretend that today's divisions are comparable to those."

The country is more united on what's needed to "secure their families and give their children a better life." It's the responsibility of leaders to push America in that direction—"not to score points or win reelection." So, on any given day, Panetta is there, at the institute, fighting the good fight, promoting those principles that can make America a better place.

Michael Morell

When the excitement died down, Morell went back to his old job as deputy director, the second in command at the spy agency. Morell had a new boss, General David Petraeus. But then scandal struck, and Petraeus resigned for engaging in an extramarital affair with his biographer and sharing classified information with the woman. Obama accepted his resignation. Morell was named acting director.

This was the opportunity Morell had been waiting for. Although he was the deputy director at the time of an attack on the U.S. consulate in Benghazi, Libya, in September 2012, it would come back to haunt him. The attack led to the death of Ambassador Chris Stevens and three other Americans. As acting director, Morell and the agency, as well as the Obama administration, faced criticism from the right regarding their handling of the attack and how the news was shared with the world.

Morell denied any cover-up or political influence in messaging. But he was the face of the CIA and had to take the heat. Morell told Obama that he wanted "acting" taken off his title, that he wanted to be named director. But in the end, Obama appointed John Brennan, a member of the president's national security team.

Obama called Morell to his office in January 2013 to tell him the news.

Morell had recommended Brennan for the post. And to Morell's surprise, Brennan had recommended him.

"Have you ever heard of something like that?" Morell asked Obama.

"Not in this town, pal," Obama said.

The president asked Morell what other job he'd be interested in, and Morell responded quickly: "I want to be chairman of the Federal Reserve Board."

They both laughed.

Morell was disappointed. He retired a few months later, after thirty-three years with the CIA. He became senior counselor at Beacon Global Strategies, a national security consulting firm in D.C.

Gary

Gary didn't lose his job that day in May. Quite the contrary. The War on Terror wasn't over, but he knew every terrorist under bin Laden was probably scared. The agency needed to stay diligent, so they didn't "wake up to another 9/11." He promised himself that he wasn't going to "ease off the gas pedal." It wasn't until a month after bin Laden's death that he began to breathe a little easier.

That's when he really began thinking about the significance of the operation. It showed Al Qaeda leaders that "we're going to get you. We're going to bring you to justice, no matter how long it takes."

After the raid, Gary took a step back to reflect on his life and career. Some of his fellow analysts had decided to leave the agency, believing they'd never again work on a case as big as bin Laden's.

But Gary stayed on. He was a lifer, and now he wanted to pay it forward. Several good agents had mentored him at the beginning of his career, and it made him a better operations officer. Now he set out to do the same.

The raid gave him a new perspective. He would still be relentless, but he was going to "hit the pause button" to spend more time with his family. He would help the people around him at the CIA "increase their capabilities."

Gary knew his success was built on the shoulders of brilliant men and women who took a "young eager guy and said, 'Hey, try this way,' or 'No, don't do that. This is the methodology, and this is the theory behind it.' " In the end, Gary would find peace as a mentor, and as a husband and father.

THE VICTIM
Jessica Ferenczy

In the years following the terrorist attacks, Officer Jessica Ferenczy tried to move on with her life. It helped that bin Laden was dead. By 2013, she knew she could no longer work for the police department. After twenty years in uniform, it was time to retire.

She now lives in that house in the Adirondacks and spends her days outdoors. She helps care for her aging father, who lives nearby.

She still writes messages on Jerome's Legacy Page every year on those three special dates.

Ferenczy never married. She never will, she says.

Osama bin Laden was responsible for much sadness in her life, but she finds some solace working outdoors on her land. There she's able to find some peace and some hope. She believes she will meet Jerome again some-day, that they will find each other, no matter how long it takes.

THE SPY
Shakil Afridi

Hours after news broke in Pakistan about the raid, Dr. Shakil Afridi packed up his family and fled from Abbottabad. He was on the run for weeks, but was arrested on May 23, 2011, near the Afghan border.

Afridi was never charged in connection with the bin Laden operation.

Instead, he was accused of aiding—both medically and financially—Lashkar-e-Islam militants in the nearby Khyber tribal region.

His family denied the charges. They said the government was making him a scapegoat for helping the United States in an operation that embarrassed Pakistani officials.

Afridi was sentenced to thirty-three years in prison by a tribal court, later reduced to twenty-three years on appeal. His older brother, Jamil Afridi, said the doctor was being held in "deplorable" conditions and had become extremely weak and frail.

Meanwhile, Afridi has been hailed as a hero in the United States. A year after the raid, Leon Panetta expressed anger that the doctor had been jailed and expressed concern for his safety. "For them to take this kind of action against somebody who was helping to go after terrorism, I just think is a real mistake on their part," he said.

But ten years later, Afridi was still in a Pakistani prison. His family continues to fight an uphill battle for his release.

THE SEALS

Robert O'Neill, the man who killed Osama bin Laden, returned home a hero, but the public didn't know that. They only knew the SEALs took out the terrorist leader.

The military kept the secret, and concealed the SEALs' identities for their protection. The anonymity added to the mystique of SEAL Team 6—the most badass soldiers in the world. Hollywood made movies about them. A television series called *SEAL Team* followed the fictional romances and exploits of a squadron of trigger-happy grunts.

For O'Neill, that drama hit too close to home.

He didn't brag about the mission. He adhered to the SEAL code of silence. But he noticed that some of his buddies—guys he had been friends with for years—were treating him differently. They were jealous. Rumors circulated that he'd signed a book deal.

By 2011, he had been a SEAL for fifteen years. He'd wanted to stay in for at least twenty, and take a full retirement, but now he reconsidered.

O'Neill contemplated life outside the military cocoon. Aside from a paycheck, the military provided him with structure, friendships, and respect. What would he do with himself, once all that was gone? What kind of work could he do? He'd never graduated college and he didn't have a lot of skills that translated to civilian life.

All the deployments had taken a toll on his marriage. He was living with his wife, Amber, but they slept in separate rooms. Finally, he decided to take another deployment. Maybe in Afghanistan, he could get away from the bullshit.

Tragedy struck just before he left. On August 6, 2011, insurgents shot down a Chinook transport helicopter in Afghanistan, killing all thirty-eight people on board. Fifteen Navy SEALs from Team 6's gold squadron and a military dog died in the crash. It was the worst loss in SEAL history.

It was devastating to Team 6, and to O'Neill. In an instant he lost friends of many years, brothers in arms, guys he'd fought alongside.

O'Neill's deployment didn't go as planned. The Afghan winter was fiercely cold. His forward operating base was hit by mortars every day. In the old days, they'd go after the bad guys, but it didn't seem like they were doing that so much now.

And there was one more thing: Being a SEAL was physically difficult. At age thirty-four, O'Neill had started feeling the pain.

Then, on a dangerous mission, he found himself explaining basic tactics to a newly arrived officer. He was frustrated. At that point, O'Neill was "so used to war, none of it was a big deal." He knew that "when you got complacent, you got sloppy. And sloppy kills." That turned out to be his last deployment.

O'Neill had completed four hundred combat missions over sixteen and a half years. He was awarded two Silver Stars and all sorts of other medals. As he prepared to leave the navy, he realized he also "had a mortgage, no pension, no college degree, and no job."

And all that talk about O'Neill writing a book? That faded away when another SEAL on the bin Laden mission wrote *No Easy Day: The Firsthand Account of the Mission That Killed Osama Bin Laden*, which was published in the summer of 2012. It was the autobiography of a SEAL who took part in the mission.

O'Neill thought about setting up a consulting company with some other former SEALs, but that didn't get off the ground. He ended up getting a job as a motivational speaker, where he shared stories of his missions. Over the years, he became a highly sought-after speaker, billed as "the quiet professional," the "man on the ground we have never heard of, but we know exists."

He finally divorced, but is still on good terms with his former wife. He's there for his daughters, trying to make up for all the birthdays and holidays that he missed. And in 2017, O'Neill got remarried.

He met his second wife, Jessica, at one of his speaking engagements. The wedding ceremony in Cape Cod, Massachusetts, was flanked by high security. He knows that for the rest of his life he could be a target for terrorists trying to avenge bin Laden's death.

Meanwhile, O'Neill has created a charity, Your Grateful Nation, which helps veterans transition from the military to everyday life. And O'Neill says he's gone to counseling to help him deal with all the years of combat stress. And he finally wrote a book, *The Operator*, about his life and missions.

At one point he wondered whether being the guy who killed bin Laden was the best or worst thing in his life. Now he's not wrestling with that so much. He just takes one day at a time.

Will Chesney

After the bin Laden mission, Chesney continued his career as a SEAL—but without Cairo. He stopped by the kennel when he could to see the dog. Cairo always recognized him. Chesney knew he'd try like hell to adopt him when Cairo was finally retired, but he wasn't optimistic that would happen anytime soon. Chesney deployed to Afghanistan in 2012, but with a different dog.

One day in the middle of a firefight in an Afghan compound, an insurgent tossed a grenade through a window. Shrapnel riddled Chesney's body.

He was treated at the base, then at an American hospital in Germany, and later at Walter Reed National Medical Center in Maryland. His father flew in to help him recover. Months after Chesney got home, the migraines started. It felt like his head was in a vise. He couldn't think straight.

He tried to return to work, but he couldn't go into the field. He became a SEAL training instructor.

But the debilitating headaches took over his life, triggering a cycle of pain and depression.

Chesney, a happy-go-lucky guy who never let things bother him, slowly changed. He lost his temper easily. He had no patience. He was losing his memory. When he found out his best friend was killed in Afghanistan, it was another blow. He had already lost several friends when the Chinook was shot out of the sky.

By the spring of 2013, he was in rough shape. Only one thing seemed to help him: Cairo was in that kennel in Virginia Beach. Chesney spent more and more time there, playing with the dog. Cairo was eight years old by then. While he had clearly lost a step or two, he was still being used for training.

No one at the kennel said anything about Chesney's frequent visits, which were clearly therapeutic. Back at home, Chesney drank to excess. He sat on his couch, clutching his temples, and looked at photos of his buddies. He wept for all he had lost.

Then, in the fall of 2013, he met a girl named Natalie Kelly in the local coffee shop. They hit it off. Life improved.

Chesney heard that Cairo was set to retire, but that others also wanted to adopt the dog. Chesney fought with the military for months to get him. It was Chesney who had carried a wounded Cairo in his arms as he was bleeding on the battlefield, right? For the first time in a long while, Chesney devoted himself to achieving something, just like he had when he got through BUD/S, or selection for SEAL Team 6.

And in April 2014, almost three years after the bin Laden raid, he took Cairo home. Chesney quickly discovered that Cairo suffered from PTSD, just like he did. The dog didn't like to be alone. He'd follow Chesney everywhere. He hated thunderstorms and sudden loud noises.

Meanwhile, it was clear Chesney had to make some changes in his life. For Natalie, for the friends who stuck by him, and for Cairo. He went to a drug treatment program and got a handle on the drinking.

He got his act together, but then the dog's health began to fail. The vet said he didn't have long to live. Heartbroken, Chesney and Natalie took Cairo on one last road trip, to New York City, to visit the 9/11 Memorial.

Once home, Chesney knew Cairo was suffering. It was time to say goodbye.

The dog's last night in the house was March 31, 2015, Chesney's thirty-first birthday. Cairo slept in his favorite bed. Chesney slept on the floor beside him.

The next day, they went to the vet and picked up the euthanasia drugs. Chesney carried Cairo into the apartment in his arms, just like he had when the dog was wounded, just like he had inside bin Laden's house, so he wouldn't hurt his feet on broken glass. He gently placed him in his dog bed. Fighting back tears, Chesney injected the dog with Tramadol to make him feel more comfortable. And when he was relaxed, Chesney injected the drug that would kill his best friend. Cairo closed his eyes. Chesney lay there on the floor with him, whispering, "Everything is OK, buddy. I love you."

A few minutes later, it was over. Chesney and Natalie took Cairo's body to a small crematorium. A few days later, they picked up his remains. The attendant gave them two urns with Cairo's paw prints on the side. One held his ashes; the other, the hardware that had been inserted in his body to save his life years before.

As he drove home, Chesney got to thinking. Cairo never knew how many human lives he had saved, or how he'd saved Chesney—how he'd helped him recover. Cairo knew how to make people happy.

Chesney wrote a book about his time with Cairo: *No Ordinary Dog: My Partner from the SEAL Teams to the Bin Laden Raid*. It's helped him deal with the emotional and physical pain. He knows he still has a rough road ahead. But whenever things get tough, he thinks of Cairo. And that's helped him deal with all the challenges in his life.

Admiral William McRaven

After the raid, Bill McRaven's legend continued to grow. After thirty-seven years in the military, he knew it was time to retire. He left the navy in 2015 and became the chancellor of the University of Texas. Two years later, he resigned that post, citing health concerns.

Along the way, McRaven wrote several books and gave lectures on leadership, the quality he admired most in Leon Panetta and Barack Obama. They were leaders who built the team that gave McRaven "the latitude to do my job."

"Obama was the consummate team player. . . . He was the smartest man in the room every time we had one of these meetings," McRaven said, adding that Obama made an "incredibly bold decision to do the mission."

In May 2020, McRaven gave a virtual commencement address at the Massachusetts Institute of Technology, where he recalled his time in the SEALs and as a commander of the elite squad. But that day, McRaven really wanted to focus on the future—the big problems facing the world and how they could help solve them.

As a boy in Texas, he'd always wanted to be Superman, "with his powers to fly, with his invulnerability, with his super strength. A hero who saved the world every day from some catastrophe."

But when he grew up and joined the military, he saw more than his share of war, death, and destruction. And that's when he came to the hard truth: Superman and Captain America were not coming to the rescue.

"If we are going to save the world from pandemics, war, climate change, poverty, racism, extremism, intolerance—then you, the brilliant minds of MIT—you are going to have to save the world. But, as remarkable as you are, your intellect and talent alone will not be sufficient," McRaven said.

No, to save the world, they and others like them would need courage, integrity, and compassion. McRaven might not have saved the world that day in May 2011, but his hard work, leadership skills, and grace under pressure paid off in a way the entire nation could appreciate.

It was something understood by the men and officers who had served with him over the years. They showed how much they cared for him.

On a wall leading to his second-floor office in Bagram, McRaven kept a poster tacked up with the words "Wanted: Dead or Alive" above bin Laden's face. It had been there since before McRaven arrived in 2004, and it had served as a reminder to everybody in the building that getting bin Laden was the reason they were there.

When McRaven walked into his office right after the raid, he noticed the poster was gone. He was pissed off. He thought, You've got to be kidding me. Somebody has already decided they're going to steal the poster?

He asked his officers Erik Kurilla and Tony Thomas what had happened to the poster. They smiled and lifted it from behind McRaven's desk. They had framed it for him. McRaven had to hold back tears.

The story didn't end there. A few years later, in May 2016, McRaven put the poster up for auction to benefit the Texas Children's Cancer Center in Houston, Texas. At the fund-raising event for the cancer center, that framed poster fetched $100,000.

After the auction, the couple who bought the poster approached McRaven. The woman tried to talk to him, but he couldn't understand what she was saying because of all the background noise. Looking at her face, he could tell she had been crying.

McRaven said he'd talk to her after the event. So after the three thousand people filed out, McRaven found the couple. Now, in the quiet of the banquet hall, the woman told him why she had placed the bid.

On the morning of 9/11, she had been in one of the towers at the World Trade Center. She was nine months pregnant and left to go to a doctor's appointment.

"If I hadn't gone to my ob-gyn appointment, I would have been in the building when the planes hit," she said. "Who knows where it would have ended up?"

She said they had a little girl. "So we named our child, Grace, by the grace of God."

McRaven was touched by their story. And he felt bad she had paid so much at the auction. "I would have given you the poster for nothing," McRaven said.

He knew the poster probably would have ended up in his garage. "But the fact that it meant so much to these people was just really important to me," he said.

The couple ended up donating the poster to the 9/11 Memorial and Museum in New York City, built on the site of Ground Zero. It's a place where people can learn about what happened on that horrific day all those years ago.

ACKNOWLEDGMENTS

There was only one way I was going to write another Countdown book. And that was if I could get the band back together. Fortunately, they all said yes. I hope you have enjoyed the result of a true team effort.

I thought this was the perfect time to drill down into the bin Laden mission, and not just because this was the twentieth anniversary of that devastating day in September 2001. Of course, that was certainly part of it. But at a time when our nation is so divided—when we can't agree about basic facts, about the truth of what happened—I thought it would be good to remind us all of this country at its best.

And that's what the bin Laden mission was—our nation's leaders pulling together, putting aside partisan division and ego and turf—to bring the mastermind of 9/11 to justice. Our intelligence community refused to give up, and after nine long years of leads that went nowhere, finally followed a dead-end street in Abbottabad to a "fortress."

Our political leaders carefully considered all the evidence and then all the options and took a deeply-considered gamble on what was at best a fifty-fifty proposition.

And then there was our great military that put together a meticulously planned mission that didn't go as rehearsed and still achieved its objective.

There was one problem in telling this story. The operation was so closely held—the principals were so focused on all they had to do—that no one kept a detailed record of exactly what happened. When I started my first interview with Bill McRaven, he made exactly that point. "If there is any disagreement about when something happened, take the other person's version over mine. I was too busy doing my job."

That presented a challenge in trying to write this story. But in hours of interviews, and still more time going over documents that are now declassified, we tried to get the timeline and details correct. And when we weren't sure, we would go back to the key players and check with them again.

In thanking people for making this book possible, I want to start with those public servants who played such a big role in the bin Laden mission and who were so generous to participate in long, detailed interviews. Some of them asked not to be acknowledged. So I will single out one: Gary, the dedicated CIA case officer who ran the Pakistan-Afghanistan Department. He has never told his story before and understood that by talking with us, he was putting himself in danger. We have done everything we could think of to protect his identity. But he was taking a risk, and I thank him for trusting us.

Then there is the band that got back together: my esteemed cowriter Mitch Weiss and our treasured researcher Lori Crim. Mitch is a Pulitzer Prize–winning investigative reporter for the Associated Press. I was honored once again to share a historical foxhole with him. And there's Lori, who has been my researcher on *Fox News Sunday* for more than a decade. I trust her to get the facts straight and keep me honest. And she always comes through.

Then there are my two consiglieres in navigating the challenge of writing a book. My longtime manager Larry Kramer introduced me to Claudia Cross, of Folio Literary Management, before *Countdown 1945*. They took care of everything on the business side—took care of it beautifully—so we could focus on telling this story.

And that brings me to our great publisher. Once again, we partnered with Avid Reader Press, led by editor and publisher Jofie Ferrari-Adler, and his boss, Jonathan Karp of Simon & Schuster. Every step of the way, we had the benefit of their wisdom, experience and support. And we had the backing of the great team they have assembled. I want to thank Ben Loehnen, Meredith Vilarello, Jordan Rodman, Alison Forner, Amanda Mulholland, Jessica Chin, Jonathan Evans, Ruth Lee-Mui, Brigid Black, Richard Ljoenes, Math Monahan, Julianna Haubner, Morgan Hoit, Carolyn Kelly, Elizabeth Hubbard, Gil Cruz, and Amy Guay.

As hard as I worked on this book, I never forgot I had a day job. I thank the executives at Fox News who understood when I went missing for a day or two researching this book. I want to express my gratitude to Fox News Chief Executive Officer Suzanne Scott, President Jay Wallace, Senior Executive Vice President of Corporate Communications Irena Briganti, and Vice President Carly Shanahan, and my team at *Fox News Sunday* that occasionally had to pick up the slack, especially executive producer Jessica Loker and producer Andrea DeVito.

Finally, Mitch and I again thank our families for their understanding while we spent so much time on this book, in addition to his work at AP and mine at Fox News. But after more than a year of sheltering at home during COVID, I suspect our families may have been grateful for some time without us.

Once again, I want to conclude by expressing my gratitude to two members of my family. My daughter Catherine Wallace spent more than a decade in publishing before deciding to change careers. She has been so valuable in guiding me on what seems to be turning into a Countdown series.

And then, there is my beloved wife, Lorraine. You put up with everything, including the day a lightning strike fried my computer. I love you and thank you more than I can express.

NOTES

COUNTDOWN: 247 DAYS

2 "We need to see you alone": Michael Morell, interview with author, October 29, 2020.

2 "Can we go small?": Gary, interview with author, February 9, 2021.

2 "Why don't we go back to my office": Leon Panetta, interview with author, November 23, 2020.

3 "We've found this guy named Abu Ahmed al-Kuwaiti": Morell, interview with author, October 29, 2020.

4 from an unlikely source: Gary, interview with author, February 4, 2021.

5 interrogators waterboarded him 183 times: Morell, interview with author, March 17, 2021.

5 there was a chance he would lead them to bin Laden: Gary, interview with author, February 4, 2021.

6 That's when they intercepted a telephone conversation: Morell, interview with author, October 29, 2020.

6 they placed people at key positions along the roads leading out of Peshawar: Ibid.

7 "May Allah be with you": Bowden, *The Finish*, p. 66.

7 "It's a fortress": Gary, interview with author, February 4, 2021.

8 Of all the things in the surveillance photos: Panetta, interview with author, November 17, 2020.

9 "precise information": Panetta, ABC News, *This Week*, June 27, 2010.

9 "He is, as is obvious, in very deep hiding": Ibid.

9 "We need to know more": Panetta, interview with author, November 17, 2020.

COUNTDOWN: 236 DAYS

10 O'Neill was a details guy: Robert O'Neill, interview with author, December 5, 2020.

11 When he enlisted back: Ibid.

15 when he led a small team on a dangerous mission: Ibid.

16 "Mom, stop worrying": O'Neill, interview with author, January 5, 2021.

COUNTDOWN: 233 DAYS

19 "talk a little bit about our continuing efforts": Barack Obama, obamawhite house.archives.gov, September 10, 2010.

19 "But you still haven't captured him": Reporter, obamawhitehouse.archives.gov, September 10, 2010.

19 "wouldn't solve all our problems": Obama, obamawhitehouse.archives.gov, September 10, 2010.

19 "I don't oppose all wars": Obama, National Public Radio, October 2, 2002.

20 "If we have Osama bin Laden in our sights": Obama, CNN, October 7, 2008.

21 "I want bin Laden to come to the front": Panetta, interview with author, November 17, 2020.

21 "Are we any closer?": Ibid.

22 "If that's the case, we're hopeful": Ibid.

23 "Mr. President, it's very preliminary": Ibid.

23 Tony Blinken, Vice President Joe Biden's national security advisor, was skeptical: Bergen, *Manhunt*, p. 125.

23 "quite careful": Thomas Donilon, interview with author, January 19, 2021.

23 "Number one, Leon, Michael": Panetta, interview with author, November 17, 2020.

COUNTDOWN: 232 DAYS

28 "Hmmm . . . Is this my Christmas present?": Jessica Ferenczy, interview with author, December 5, 2020.

29 Frank suddenly fell into a seizure: Frank Dominguez, interview with author, December 10, 2020.

34 "Today I always try to think": Ferenczy, Legacy.com, September 11, 2010.

COUNTDOWN: 205 DAYS

39 Morell grew up in: Morell, interview with author, October 30, 2020.

39 "It's not good enough": Morell, *The Great War of Our Time*, p. 346.

39 "near perfect birdhouse": Ibid., p. 346.

39 "Economics is one of": Ibid., p. 3.

40 "Come to work here": Ibid., p. 4.

40 "That's interesting. . . . But I'm a little busy": Ibid., p. 6.

42 "Calm down": Ibid., p. 19.

43 "You will really need": Ibid., p. 29.

43 "This is interesting": Ibid., p. 31.

43 "I want you to look": Ibid., p. 41.

45 "Michael, who did this?": Ibid., p. 55.

COUNTDOWN: 198 DAYS

48 "Cairo! Come on, buddy!": Will Chesney, interview with author, September 15, 2020.

48 "Hang in there, boy": Ibid.

53 "Hey, buddy, how you been?": Ibid.

COUNTDOWN: 192 DAYS

55 "If you want a friend": Panetta, interview with author, November 23, 2020.

55 "humanity in the world": Ibid.

58 "We're silent warriors": Ibid.

59 "Who here is in charge": Panetta, interview with author, November 17, 2020.

COUNTDOWN: 182 DAYS

61 The Wolstein Center: *Cleveland Plain Dealer*, October 31, 2010.

63 After only nine months: Obama, obamawhitehouse.archives.gov, December 10, 2010.

64 "I know there is nothing weak": Ibid.

COUNTDOWN: 181 DAYS

65 He filled a bowl: Gary, interview with author, February 9, 2021.

67 "repeat offender": Ibid.

69 "Get ready": Ibid.

COUNTDOWN: 179 DAYS

72 Afridi didn't know it: *New York Times*, January 28, 2012.

COUNTDOWN: 177 DAYS

74 "We're the CIA": Panetta, interview with author, November 23, 2020.

75 "This is the top priority": Ibid.

76 "Do whatever the": Ibid.

76 "You know, I've seen": Ibid.

76 "Can we tap into": Jeremy Bash, interview with author, November 10, 2020.

77 "Have you people used": Panetta, interview with author, November 23, 2020.

77 frustrated in part by Panetta's: Gary, interview with author, February 11, 2021.

78 "I don't think Gary": Bash, interview with author, November 10, 2020.

78 "Suggest anything": Ibid.
78 "Don't worry about whether": Ibid.

COUNTDOWN: 138 DAYS

81 "a band of deluded": Obama, *A Promised Land*, p. 677.
83 "We think he could be": Ibid., p. 679.
83 "What's your judgment?": Ibid.
83 "There's a good chance": Ibid.

COUNTDOWN: 133 DAYS

86 "The alarm went off": Ferenczy, interview with author, December 28, 2020.
87 "You get onto the highway": Ibid.
89 "Baby, Baby Happy Anniversary": Ferenczy, Legacy.com, December 19, 2010.

COUNTDOWN: 121 DAYS

92 In Washington, Panetta rented: Panetta, interview with author, March 19, 2021.
95 "a certain glint in his eye": Ibid.
95 "You're on": Ibid.

COUNTDOWN: 120 DAYS

96 So much had changed: O'Neill, interview with author, December 5, 2020.
98 "Where's bin Laden?": Ibid.

COUNTDOWN: 107 DAYS

102 Meanwhile, Panetta continued quietly: Panetta, interview with author, November 23, 2020.
102 "You shouldn't try to spin": Ibid.

COUNTDOWN: 93 DAYS

105 "We believe The Pacer": Morell, interview with author, October 30, 2020.
105 "Congratulations to you all": Admiral William McRaven, interview with author, November 30, 2020.
109 "can-do guy": Obama, *A Promised Land*, p. 681.
109 "What do you think": McRaven, *Sea Stories*, p. 271.
109 "Sir, it's a compound": Ibid.
110 "How many men": Ibid.
110 "OK, Bill. I don't": Ibid., p. 272.
110 "you can't tell anyone": Ibid.

COUNTDOWN: 75 DAYS

113   Panetta called his counterpart: Panetta, *Worthy Fights*, p. 305.

113   "nitty-gritty work": Nicholas Rasmussen, interview with author, December 3, 2020.

COUNTDOWN: 70 DAYS

116   "What's up, buddy?": Chesney, *No Ordinary Dog*, p. 160.

116   "practically swimming in a puddle": Ibid.

116   "Let's do a little": Ibid., p. 161.

COUNTDOWN: 65 DAYS

120   "talk about what": Panetta, interview with author, November 23, 2020.

122   "If we determine": Ibid.

124   "I think we've": Ibid.

COUNTDOWN: 58 DAYS

126   Afridi had started the vaccination project: *Guardian*, July 16, 2011.

129   "I already told them": Panetta, interview with author, November 23, 2020.

130   "We're still evaluating intelligence": Donilon, interview with author, January 19, 2021.

130   "What the fuck did you expect": John Brennan, interview with author, November 18, 2020.

130   "I need to keep the intelligence": Ibid.

130   "I have to do this": Ibid.

130   "super experienced, super deep": Gary, interview with author, February 11, 2021.

COUNTDOWN: 48 DAYS

132   "Bill, how are you": McRaven, *Sea Stories*, p. 285.

133   "lot going on in the world": Ibid.

133   "Is it Libya?": Ibid.

133   "Make sure the meeting": Hillary Rodham Clinton, interview with author, December 17, 2020.

133   "completely off the books": Ibid.

135   "We could miss our best": Panetta, interview with author, November 23, 2010.

135   "leave a large smoking": McRaven, *Sea Stories*, p. 282.

136   "ISI must know": Ibid., p. 283.

136   "I think the only real option": Panetta, interview with author, November 23, 2020.

137   "Mr. President, Bill is": McRaven, *Sea Stories*, p. 288.

137   "Sir, it's possible": Ibid.

137   "How many do you": Ibid.

137 "At a minimum?": Ibid.

138 "sketched out a concept": Obama, *A Promised Land*, p. 682.

138 "What I can tell you": Ibid.

138 "Let's do the homework": Ibid.

COUNTDOWN: 35 DAYS

140 "extremely experienced in combat": McRaven, *Sea Stories*, p. 290.

141 "Gentlemen, in less than two weeks": Ibid., p. 291.

142 "OK. You know what": Ibid., p. 292.

COUNTDOWN: 33 DAYS

144 "Nothing," one of the flyboys: Bash, interview with author, November 10, 2020.

144 "Would we be able to": Ibid.

145 "It's a bad plan": Brennan, interview with author, November 18, 2020.

147 "Can you get by the air": McRaven, *Sea Stories*, p. 294.

147 "At that point, the sound": Ibid.

147 "What about the women": Ibid.

148 "This is a challenge": Ibid.

148 "If they have a suicide": Ibid., p. 295.

149 "Fight your way out": McRaven, interview with author, November 30, 2020.

149 "Can you do the mission": McRaven, *Sea Stories*, p. 295.

COUNTDOWN: 26 DAYS

152 "Man, I sure wish": O'Neill, *The Operator*, p. 246.

152 "Hey, buddy, pay for": Ibid.

153 "This shit's ending one": Ibid., p. 251.

153 "I know. We didn't": Ibid.

154 "flick of an index finger": Ibid., p. 253.

156 "Pack your gear": Chesney, *No Ordinary Dog*, p. 205.

COUNTDOWN: 25 DAYS

158 Everything was shifting into: Gary, interview with author, March 16, 2021.

158 "What would fourteen days": Ibid.

COUNTDOWN: 24 DAYS

163 "What I'm about to": O'Neill, *The Operator*, p. 274.

163 "What kind of air": Ibid., p. 275.

163 "There will be no": Ibid.

165 "We have reason to believe": Gary, interview with author, March 16, 2021.

165 "holy shit": Bash, interview with author, November 10, 2020.

166 "opportunity of a lifetime": Chesney, interview with author, September 15, 2020.

166 "to keep the world out": O'Neill, interview with author, December 5, 2020.

166 "who went to work on a Tuesday morning": O'Neill, interview with author, November 29, 2020.

167 "measure of revenge": Chesney, interview with author, September 15, 2020.

169 "careful hurry": Bash, interview with author, November 10, 2020.

COUNTDOWN: 20 DAYS

170 "Can you swing by?": John Thompson, interview with author, January 19, 2021.

170 "Not a problem, sir": Ibid.

171 "You want a beer?": Ibid.

171 "You need to keep": Ibid.

172 "Ours is a world beset": Thompson's father's letter to his son. Courtesy of JT Thompson collection.

175 "six or seven decisions": McRaven, interview with author, January 12, 2021.

175 "prepare for the worst, hope for the best": Thompson, interview with author, January 19, 2021.

COUNTDOWN: 18 DAYS

177 They followed the plans: O'Neill, interview with author, December 5, 2020.

178 "read and react": Chesney, interview with author, September 15, 2020.

180 "We're doing it for": O'Neill, interview with author, December 5, 2020.

COUNTDOWN: 16 DAYS

183 "I need all of you": Panetta, interview with author, November 23, 2020.

183 "Sam, what do you": Ibid.

183 "What do you think": Ibid.

183 "Ninety-five percent": Ibid.

COUNTDOWN: 13 DAYS

187 "I assume you guys have": McRaven, Sea Stories, p. 301.

187 "Let's make sure the": Ibid.

187 "We've already taken that": Ibid.

187 "We'll be fine, JT": Ibid.

190 Mullen paid close attention: Admiral Michael Mullen, interview with author, November 17, 2020.

190 "I see that you added": McRaven, Sea Stories, p. 303.

191 "It might not be necessary": Ibid.

COUNTDOWN: 12 DAYS

193 He pushed the president: Panetta, interview with author, November 23, 2020.

193 "the law of diminishing returns": Ibid.

194 "get to the target": McRaven, interview with author, November 30, 2020.

COUNTDOWN: 7 DAYS

195 That's why this call: Chesney, interview with author, September 15, 2020.

196 "I just wanted to let": Ibid.

196 "There's something important": Ibid.

198 Moments after they got home: O'Neill, interview with author, December 30, 2020.

COUNTDOWN: 6 DAYS

199 Jerome would have been: Ferenczy, interview with author, January 5, 2021.

COUNTDOWN: 4 DAYS

202 "But we're not going to": Obama, obamawhitehouse.archives.gov, April 27, 2011.

202 "we do not have time": Ibid.

202 "We're better than this": Ibid.

203 With them at the base: O'Neill, interview with author, January 5, 2021.

COUNTDOWN: 3 DAYS

206 "I need you, and": Panetta, interview with author, November 23, 2020.

207 "I've worked closely": Obama, obamawhitehouse.archives.gov, April 28, 2011.

208 "history was in the room": Donilon, interview with author, January 19, 2021.

209 "from A to Z": Mullen, interview with author, November 17, 2020.

209 "adequately pressure-tested its work": Obama, *A Promised Land*, p. 685.

210 "Even at the low end": Michael Leiter, interview with author, March 18, 2021.

210 "Mr. President, I believe": Morell, interview with author, October 30, 2020.

210 "So, Michael, if you're": Ibid.

211 "There's a formula I've used since I was in": Panetta, *Worthy Fights*, p. 318.

212 "rare opportunity": Clinton, interview with author, December 17, 2020.

212 "I know we're trying": Obama, *A Promised Land*, p. 685.

213 "I'll let you know": Ibid., p. 686.

COUNTDOWN: 2 DAYS

215 And last night, he'd: Obama, *A Promised Land*, p. 688.

215 "ratty old sandals": Ibid., p. 687.

216 It was hard to: Donilon, interview with author, February 5, 2021.

217 "Cartwright mentioned something": McRaven, *Sea Stories*, p. 307.

217 "Well, it's a little": Ibid.

217 "We're just waiting for": Ibid., p. 308.

218 "It's a go": Donilon, interview with author, January 19, 2021.

219 "I'm praying for you": McRaven, interview with author, November 30, 2020.

219 "Get in, get bin Laden": Ibid.

220 "Our forces can do this": Mullen, interview with author, November 17, 2020.

221 "What's going on here?": Ibid.

222 "Fuck the Correspondents' Dinner": Morell, interview with author, October 30, 2020.

222 "Oh, sorry, you can't": Clinton, interview with author, December 17, 2020.

223 "drew the short end of the straw": Brennan, interview with author, November 18, 2020.

223 "Way to go": Ibid.

COUNTDOWN: 1 DAY

224 "The president authorized you": O'Neill, *The Operator*, p. 295.

225 "I do this every night": Ibid., p. 296.

227 "We're all set": McRaven, *Sea Stories*, p. 309.

228 "Well, don't push": Ibid.

228 "If he is there": Ibid.

228 "quietly balanced on a mental high wire": Obama, *A Promised Land*, p. 694.

229 "My fellow Americans": Obama, obamawhitehouse.archives.gov, April 30, 2011.

229 "I know he's taken": Ibid.

COUNTDOWN: 10 HOURS

231 Gary had laid out his clothes: Gary, interview with author, March 16, 2021.

235 What did we miss?: Brennan, interview with author, November 18, 2020.

235 "Isn't that your": Leiter, interview with author, March 18, 2021.

235 "When you find out": Ibid.

236 "Didn't you just get": Ibid.

237 "Look, here's the deal": McRaven, interview with author, January 12, 2021.

237 "Don't try to fly": McRaven, *Sea Stories*, p. 311.

238 "At one point, the": Ibid., p. 312.

239 "The court in the": Ibid.

240 "Michael, what do you": Morell, interview with author, October 29, 2020.

240 "I won't be": Ibid.

241 "It will just take": Morell, *The Great War of Our Time*, p. 167.

241 "It's about time": McRaven, *Sea Stories*, p. 313.

242 "Tonight, we are daring": Ibid., p. 314.

242 "Gentlemen, since 9/11": Ibid.

243 "I wish I was": O'Neill, interview with author, January 5, 2021.

243 "Hey, Dad. I just wanted": Ibid.

243 "I've got to go to work": Ibid.

244 "Launch the assault force": McRaven, *Sea Stories*, p. 315.

247 "One, two, three": O'Neill, interview with author, January 5, 2021.

248 "spectators, not participants": Morell, *The Great War of Our Time*, ebook.

248 "General Petraeus is on": McRaven, *Sea Stories*, p. 316.

249 "Freedom itself was attacked": O'Neill, interview with author, January 5, 2021.

250 "so many people jammed in there": Leiter, interview with author, March 18, 2021.

252 "an electric kind of fear": Obama, *A Promised Land*, p. 694.

252 "Oh, Lord, Murphy turned up": Denis McDonough, interview with author, December 7, 2020.

254 "It's down. Can't use": Morell, interview with author, October 30, 2020.

254 "Bill, what the hell": Panetta, *Worthy Fights*, p. 322.

255 "The SEALs are continuing": McRaven, *Sea Stories*, p. 318.

258 "really intense, stressful experience": Clinton, interview with author, December 17, 2020.

259 "I didn't mean to": O'Neill, interview with author, January 5, 2021.

261 "Khalid, come here": Ibid.

COUNTDOWN: GERONIMO

265 "For God and country": McRaven, interview with author, November 30, 2020.

266 "Shut the fuck up!": McRaven, *Sea Stories*, p. 320.

267 "We got him": Obama, *A Promised Land*, p. 695.

267 "Mr. Vice President, I've": Mullen, interview with author, March 19, 2021.

268 "Dude, I think I just shot": Chesney, interview with author, September 15, 2020.

268 "They found a whole": McRaven, *Sea Stories*, p. 321.

270 "Here's your guy": O'Neill, *The Operator*, p. 312.

272 "Congratulations, Boss": Obama, *A Promised Land*, p. 695.

272 "We still have a long": McRaven, *Sea Stories*, p. 323.

273 "Refueling done yet?": Ibid.

274 "You've got to give her": O'Neill, *The Operator*, p. 316.

274 "I think I can find": Ibid.

274 "Well, I guess I'm out": Ibid., p. 317.

274 "How tall are you?": McRaven, *Sea Stories*, p. 325.

275 "OK, Bill, let me": Ibid., p. 326.

275 "Thank you, sir.": Ibid.

276 "Great job": Panetta, *Worthy Fights*, p. 326.

277 "Today, anything you say": Ibid.

277 "Let's have a draft": Ibid., p. 327.

278 "It's a good thing you": Mullen, interview with author, November 17, 2020.

279 "I guess Hillary told you": Clinton, interview with author, December 17, 2020.

279 "Did something terrible": Morell, *The Great War of Our Time*, p. 167.

281 "a terrorist who's responsible": Obama, obamawhitehouse.archives.gov, May 1, 2011.

COUNTDOWN: AFTERMATH

287 "Osama bin Laden found": *New York Times*, May 2, 2011.

288 "I love you Baby": Ferenczy, Legacy.com, May 1, 2011.

288 "This is a day": United Nations Secretary-General Ban Ki-moon, press release, May 2, 2011.

288 "a resounding victory": Israeli Prime Minister Benjamin Netanyahu, press release, May 2, 2011.

288 "I hope the death": Afghan President Hamid Karzai, press release, May 2, 2011.

290 "offered a catharsis of sorts": Obama, *A Promised Land*, p. 698.

291 "Famously cool under pressure": Ibid., p. 681.

291 "all those around the world": McRaven, interview with author, November 30, 2020.

292 The president wanted to: McRaven, interview with author, January 12, 2021.

293 "What the hell are": Panetta, *Worthy Fights*, p. 329.

296 "You know, Laura and": Morell, *The Great War of Our Time*, p. 174.

297 "a fucking hero": O'Neill, *The Operator*, p. 314.

298 "So this is Cairo?": Chesney, *No Ordinary Dog*, p. 237.

298 "Like all of us": Obama, obamawhitehouse.archives.gov, May 6, 2011.

COUNTDOWN: EPILOGUE

300 quarter century younger: Bowden, *The Finish*. Ebook.

301 "He never should": John Brennan, interview with author, November 18, 2020.

301 "Here we are in": Bin Laden letter, undated.

301 "Our pre-raid understanding": Morell, *The Great War of Our Time*.

301 "Do you wish to": *New York Times*, May, 20, 2015.

302 He even suggested putting trees: Bergen, *Manhunt*. Ebook.

303 "What we are witnessing": *Letter from Usama bin Laden to Atiyatullah al-Libi*, CTC at West Point, www.ctc.usma.edu/wp-content/uploads/2013/10/Letter-from-UBL-to-Atiyatullah-Al-Libi-2-Translation.pdf, April 26, 2011.

303 They engaged in a process: *Letters from Abbottabad: Bin Laden Sidelined?*, CTC at West Point, ctc.usma.edu/letters-from-abbottabad-bin-ladin-sidelined, May 3, 2012.

303 The task force that reviewed: *Washington Post*, July 1, 2011.

303 "The decapitation strategy": Morell, September 11, 2020.

305 "Al-Qaida faces a new and pressing challenge": United Nations Security Council, February 3, 2021.

305 "cohesiveness the past few years": U.S. Department of State, Rewards for Justice, Ayman al-Zawahiri.

306 Al Qaeda "has been unjustly accused": FDD's Long War Journal, September 11, 2020.

306 "My assessment now": Miller, *Washington Post*, September 9, 2020.

306 "the jihadist extremist movement is": Morell, September 11, 2020.

306 "We delivered justice": Biden, April 14, 2021.

307 "I'm a big believer": Donilon, interview with author, January 19, 2021.

307 "This type of work": Brennan, interview with author, November 18, 2020.

308 "It sounds like I'm": Rasmussen, interview with author, December 3, 2020.

308 "The SEALs took the time to take": Clinton, interview with author, December 17, 2020.

308 "You brought it to America": Robert Gary, interview with author, February 11, 2021.

309 "There's a narrative out there": Gates, interview with author, December 1, 2020.

309 "There are a lot of moments": Panetta, interview with author, November 23, 2020.

COUNTDOWN: POSTSCRIPT

311 "Ted, get the wine": Panetta, interview with author, November 23, 2020.

313 "Have you ever heard": Morell, *The Great War of Our Time*, p. 150.

313 "we're going to get you": Gary, interview with author, March 16, 2021.

320 "Obama was the consummate": McRaven, interview with author, November 30, 2020.

321 You've got to be kidding: McRaven, interview with author, January 12, 2021.

322 "If I hadn't gone": Ibid.

BIBLIOGRAPHY

BOOKS

Aid, Matthew. *Intel Wars: The Secret History of the Fight Against Terror.* New York: Bloomsbury, 2012.

Bergen, Peter. *Holy War, Inc. Inside the Secret World of Osama bin Laden.* New York: Simon & Schuster, 2001.

———. *The Longest War: The Enduring Conflict between America and Al-Qaeda.* New York: Free Press, 2011.

———. *Manhunt: The Ten-Year Search for Bin Laden from 9/11 to Abbottabad.* New York: Broadway Books, 2012.

Bowden, Mark. *The Finish: The Killing of Osama bin Laden.* New York: Grove Atlantic, 2013.

Brennan, John. *Undaunted: My Fight Against America's Enemies, at Home and Abroad.* New York: Celadon Books, 2020.

Briscoe, Charles, Richard Kiper, James Schroder, and Kalev Sepp. *U.S. Army Special Operations in Afghanistan.* Boulder, CO: Paladin Press, 2006.

Burke, Jason. *The 9/11 Wars.* New York: Penguin, 2011.

Bush, George W. *Decision Points.* New York: Crown, 2010.

Cheney, Dick. *In My Time: A Personal and Political Memoir.* New York: Simon & Schuster, 2011.

Chesney, Will, and Joe Layden. *No Ordinary Dog. My Partner from the SEAL Teams to the Bin Laden Raid.* New York: St. Martin's Press, 2020.

Clinton, Hillary Rodham. *Hard Choices.* New York: Simon & Schuster, 2014.

Coll, Steve. *The Bin Ladens: An Arabian Family in the American Century.* New York: Penguin, 2008.

———. *Ghost Wars: The Secret History of the CIA, Afghanistan, and bin Laden, from the Soviet Invasion to September 10, 2001.* New York: Penguin, 2004.

Fawaz, Gerges. *The Rise and Fall of Al-Qaeda*. Oxford, UK: Oxford University Press, 2011.

Feith, Douglas. *War and Decision: Inside the Pentagon at the Dawn on the War on Terrorism*. New York: Harper Perennial, 2009.

Frederick, Jim. *Special Ops: The Hidden World of America's Toughest Warriors*. New York: Time, 2011.

Fury, Dalton. *Kill Bin Laden: A Delta Force Commander's Account of the Hunt for the World's Most Wanted Man*. New York: St. Martin's Press, 2008.

Gates, Robert M. *Duty: Memoirs of a Secretary at War*. New York: Alfred A. Knopf, 2014.

Greitens, Eric. *The Heart and the Fist: The Education of a Humanitarian, the Making of a Navy SEAL*. Boston: Houghton Mifflin Harcourt, 2011.

Hastings, Michael. *The Operators: The Wild and Terrifying Inside Story of America's War in Afghanistan*. New York: Blue Rider Press, 2012.

Jones, Seth: *Hunting in the Shadows: The Pursuit of Al Qa'ida since 9/11*. New York: W. W. Norton & Company, 2012.

Kessler, Ronald: *The CIA at War: Inside the Secret Campaign Against Terror*. New York: St. Martin's Press, 2003.

Lawrence, Bruce, ed. *Messages to the World: The Statements of Osama Bin Laden*. New York: Verso, 2005.

McDermott, Terry, and Josh Meyer: *The Hunt for KSM: Inside the Pursuit and Takedown of the Real 9/11 Mastermind, Khalid Sheikh Mohammed*. New York: Little, Brown and Company, 2012.

McRaven, Admiral William H. *Sea Stories: My Life in Special Operations*. New York: Grand Central Publishing, 2019.

———. *Spec Ops: Case Studies in Special Operations Warfare: Theory and Practice*. New York: Random House, 1996.

Morell, Michael, and Bill Harlow. *The Great War of Our Time: The CIA's Fight Against Terrorism—from al Qa'ida to ISIS*. New York: Twelve, 2015.

Obama, Barack. *A Promised Land*. New York: Crown, 2020.

O'Neill, Robert: *The Operator: Firing the Shots That Killed Osama Bin Laden and My Years as a SEAL Team Warrior*. New York: Scribner, 2017.

Owen, Mark, and Kevin Maurer. *No Easy Day: The Firsthand Account of the Mission That Killed Osama Bin Laden*. New York: Penguin Group, 2012.

Panetta, Leon, and Jim Newton. *Worthy Fights: A Memoir of Leadership in War and Peace*. New York: Penguin, 2014.

Runkle, Benjamin. *Wanted Dead or Alive: Manhunts from Geronimo to Bin Laden*. London: Palgrave Macmillan, 2011.

Tenet, George. *At the Center of the Storm: My Years at the CIA*. New York: HarperCollins, 2007.

Woodward, Bob. *Bush at War*. New York: Simon & Schuster, 2002.

———. *Obama's Wars*. New York: Simon & Schuster, 2010.

Wright, Lawrence. *The Looming Tower: Al-Qaeda and the Road to 9/11*. New York: Vintage, 2007.

INTERVIEWS

Bash, Jeremy. November 6, 2020. November 10, 2020.

Brennan, John. November 18, 2020.

Chesney, Will. September 15, 2020.

Clinton, Hillary Rodham. December 17, 2020.

Dominguez, Frank. December 10, 2020.

Donilon, Thomas. January 19, 2021. February 5, 2021.

Ferenczy, Jessica. November 15, 2020. December 5, 2020. December 28, 2020. January 5, 2021.

"Gary." February 4, 2021. February 9, 2021. February 11, 2021. March 16, 2021.

Gates, Robert. December 1, 2020.

Leiter, Michael. March 18, 2021.

McDonough, Denis. December 7, 2020.

McRaven, Admiral William. November 30, 2020. January 12, 2021.

Morell, Michael. October 29, 2020. October 30, 2020. March 17, 2021.

Mullen, Admiral Michael. November 17, 2020. March 19, 2021.

O'Neill, Robert. November 29, 2020. December 5, 2020. December 30, 2020. January 5, 2021.

Panetta, Leon. November 17, 2020. November 23, 2020. March 19, 2021.

Rasmussen, Nicholas. December 3, 2020. March 16, 2021.

Thompson, John. January 19, 2021.

Vickers, Michael. December 11, 2020.

NEWSPAPERS AND TELEVISION REPORTS

BBC News. "UK bomb plot suspect Abid Naseer found guilty." March 4, 2015.

New York Times. "In Osama bin Laden Library: Illuminati and Bob Woodward." May 20, 2015.

New York Times. "Al Qaeda's No. 2, Accused in U.S. Embassy Attacks, Was Killed in Iran." November 13, 2020.

Michael Morell. "The Road to Abbottabad: Ten Years After." September 11, 2020. www.youtube.com/watch?v=d7LbMfyZOZg.

Washington Post. "Bin Laden document trove reveals strain on al-Qaeda." July 1, 2011.

Washington Post. "This 9/11 anniversary arrives with the end of the war on al-Qaeda well in sight." September 10, 2020.

DOCUMENTS AND JOURNALS

Letters from Abbottabad: Bin Ladin Sidelined? May 3, 2012. Combatting Terrorism Center at West Point.

Letter from Usama bin Laden to Atiyatullah al-Libi, April 26, 2011. Combatting Terrorism Center at West Point.

Office of the Director of National Intelligence. Abbottabad Compound Materials. This archive contains more than 470,000 files from Osama bin Laden's private computer, including his personal journal, as well as other materials seized during the Navy SEALs raid.

Rahman, Umer. "Identity, Nationalism and Ethnic Divide: A Case Study on Dr. Shakil Afridi's Reputation." Florida International University. 2013.

Twenty-seventh report of the Analytical Support and Sanctions Monitoring Team concerning Islamic State in Iraq and the Levant (Da'esh), Al-Qaida and associated individuals, groups, undertakings and entities. United Nations Security Council. February 3, 2021.

United States Senate, Committee on Foreign Relations. *Tora Bora Revisited: How We Failed to Get Bin Laden and Why It Matters Today.* November 30, 2009.

United States Senate, Intelligence Committee. *Study on Central Intelligence Agency Detention and Interrogation Program.* December 9, 2014.

Joscelyn, Thomas. "Zawahiri asserts al Qaeda's independence in new message." Foundation for Defense of Democracies' Long War Journal, September 11, 2020.

MAGAZINES

Aikins, Matthieu. "The Doctor, the CIA, and the Blood of Bin Laden." *GQ*, December 19, 2012.

Filkins, Dexter. "Khalid Sheikh Mohammed and the C.I.A." *New Yorker*, December 31, 2014.

Hudson, John. "The Crooked Case Against Pakistan's CIA-Assisting Doctor." *Atlantic*, May 30, 2012.

SPEECHES

Joseph R. Biden. "Remarks by President Biden on the Way Forward in Afghanistan." Washington, D.C., April 14, 2021.

Barack Obama. "Remarks by the President in Address to the nation on the Way Forward in Afghanistan and Pakistan." Washington, D.C., December 1, 2009.

Barack Obama. "Remarks by the President at the Acceptance of the Nobel Peace Prize." Oslo, Norway, December 10, 2009.

Barack Obama. "Economic Recovery." Washington, D.C., September 10, 2010.

Barack Obama. "President Obama on Death of Osama bin Laden." Washington, D.C., May 1, 2011.

Barack Obama. Opposition to Iraq War. Chicago, Illinois, October 2, 2002.

GOVERNMENT WEBSITES

United States Department of State. Rewards for Justice. Wanted: Ayman al-Zawahiri. rewardsforjustice.net/english/ayman_zawahiri.html.

INDEX

Page numbers in *italics* refer to images.

ABOUT THE AUTHORS

CHRIS WALLACE anchors a wide-ranging nightly interview program for CNN+. Prior to CNN, Wallace was the anchor of *Fox News Sunday* for eighteen years where he covered every major political event. Throughout his five decades in broadcasting, he has interviewed numerous U.S. and world leaders, including seven American presidents, and won every major broadcast news award for his reporting, including three Emmy Awards, the duPont-Columbia Silver Baton, and the Peabody Award. He is the *New York Times* bestselling author of *Countdown 1945: The Extraordinary Story of the Atomic Bomb and the 116 Days That Changed the World*.

MITCH WEISS is a Pulitzer Prize–winning investigative journalist for the Associated Press, covering subjects ranging from military misconduct, government corruption, and white-collar crimes to the housing meltdown and unsafe medical devices. He is also the critically acclaimed author or coauthor of nine books.

IMAGE CREDITS